Ready, Set, Read

Best Books to
Prepare Preschoolers

by
Ellen Mahoney and Leah Wilcox

The Scarecrow Press, Inc.
Metuchen, N.J., & London 1985

For permission to reprint poetry excerpts and quotes, thanks to:

Bertha Klausner International Literary Agency, Inc. for Dorothy Baruch's "Merry-Go-Round" from I Like Machinery, copyright © 1933.

E. P. Dutton for A. A. Milne's "Sneezles," reprinted by permission of the publisher from Now We Are Six, copyright © 1927 by E. P. Dutton & Co. Inc., copyright renewal © 1955 by A. A. Milne; and "Halfway Down," reprinted by permission of the publisher from When We Were Very Young, copyright © 1924 by E. P. Dutton, copyright renewal © 1952 by A. A. Milne.

Harper & Row for excerpt from Sylvia Plath's The Bed Book, text copyright © 1976 by Ted Hughes; excerpt from Maurice Sendak's Where the Wild Things Are, copyright © 1963 by Maurice Sendak; excerpt from John Steptoe's Stevie, copyright © 1969 by John L. Steptoe; Marie Louise Allen's "The Mitten Song" from A Pocketful of Poems, text copyright © 1957 by Marie Allen Howarth; and specified text facing Title Page in Eric Carle's I See A Song (Thomas Y. Crowell), copyright © 1973 by Eric Carle. All reprinted by permission of Harper & Row Publishers, Inc.

Little, Brown and Company for David McCord's "Song of the Train" from Far and Few, copyright © 1952 by David McCord; and Ed Emberley's poem from The Wing On a Flea: A Book About Shapes, copyright © 1961 by Edward Emberley.

Macmillan Publishing Co., Inc. for Maud and Miska Petersham's verse from The Rooster Crows: A Book of American Rhymes and Jingles, copyright © 1945 by Maud and Miska Petersham, renewed © 1973 by Miska F. Petersham; and for Sara Teasdale's "Night" from Stars Tonight, copyright © 1930 by Sara Teasdale Filsinger, renewed © 1958 by Guaranty Trust Company of New York, Executor.

Putnam Publishing Group for Dorothy Aldis' "Blum," "Going to Sleep," and "Hiding," reprinted by Permission of Putnam Publishing Group from All Together, copyright © 1952 by Dorothy Aldis. Copyright renewed © 1980 by Roy E. Porter; and text refrain from Wanda Gág's Millions of Cats, reprinted by permission of Putnam Publishing Group, copyright © 1928 by Coward-McCann Inc.

Marian Reiner for Myra Cohn Livingston's "Just Watch," "I Know a Place," "Cooking," and "Discovery" from Whispers and Other Poems, copyright © 1958 by Myra Cohn Livingston.

Library of Congress Cataloging in Publication Data

Mahoney, Ellen, 1918-
   Ready, set, read.

   Includes index.
   1. Children--Books and reading. 2. Reading (Preschool)
3. Bibliography--Best books--Children's literature.
4. Children's literature--Bibliography. I. Wilcox,
Leah. II. Title.
Z1037.M2234 1985   011'.62   83-27087
ISBN 0-8108-1684-9

CONTENTS

ACKNOWLEDGMENTS

We wish to express our sincere thanks to the many children who shared their enthusiasm for fine literature with us and inspired the writing of this book on the importance of reading with preschoolers. Often throughout the book we have included the experiences of these children although occasionally names of the youngsters have been changed.

We are also indebted to colleagues, friends, and family members for support and helpful advice. Dr. Robin Carr, Dr. Carmen Richardson, Dr. Taimi Ranta, Miss Carol Johnson, and Mr. Samuel Rogal, all of the English Department, Illinois State University, and Dr. Lucy Klausser, Education Department, Illinois Wesleyan University, gave us needed encouragement along with very practical help in the reviewing of the text. Illinois State University graduate assistants Camille Brown, Kathy Kaul, Sharon Russell, and Debbie Durso provided real assistance in the search for books and materials.

Mae Durham Roger, Department of Library Science, University of California at Berkeley, has for many years shared her enthusiasm for excellence in literature for young children with us.

It would be impossible to complete a book of this type without the help of many competent librarians. We were indeed fortunate to have the privilege of working with Laura Gowdy, Glenn Gritzmacher, Willard Moonan, and Joan Winters from the staff of Milner Library, Illinois State University, and Vivian Carter, Eleanor Shulman, and Lois White at the Normal, Illinois Public Library. Also we are grateful for the help of Versa Cullen and the support of the entire staff at the Excelsior Branch of the San Francisco Public Library.

We wish to thank our photographer, Martha Wilcox, and typist, Deanna Bilyeu, as well as Edward Barry for his good counsel and Mark, Steven, and Michael Mahoney for their patience and help.

To the memory of
Ellen Grimes Powelson and
James E. McWilliams

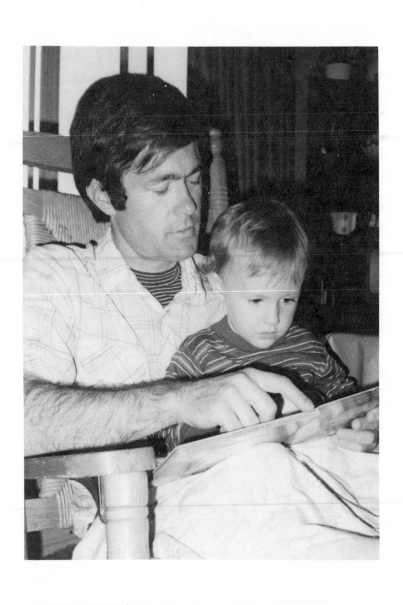

INTRODUCTION

"Readers are made, not born. No one comes into the world already disposed for or against words in print."[1] However, long before boys and girls enter kindergarten they should have developed a positive attitude toward reading, for such an attitude will determine to a great extent their success or failure in the academic world. Parents are their children's first and by far their most important teachers. They must provide the experiences that nurture a love for reading and promote the development of reading readiness skills. It is the encounters that children have with books in their very early and impressionable years that cause them to perceive the pleasure to be found in reading and start them toward successful school experiences. Fortunate children who have had a fine exposure to books in their preschool years will be ready to read and eager for the experience. Some will even start to read before they enter school.

Kindergarten and first-grade teachers will almost invariably say that they know as soon as a child enters school what his or her foundation in reading has been. If a child comes from a reading family where books are a shared source of pleasure, he or she will have an understanding of the language of the literary world and respond to the use of books in a classroom as a natural expansion of pleasant home experiences. Also, this child will know the values of reading and be interested in learning the process, difficult as it may be at times.

Studies of nursery school children show that those who have had the advantage of many language experiences by way of stories and songs have language skills far in advance of those who were deprived of such experiences. Certainly such results are not surprising when we review the conclusions that Benjamin Bloom reached after he synthesized the research that deals with the growth and development of children. In writing about the longitudinal intelligence studies he says, "These results also reveal the changing rate at which intelligence develops, since as much of the development takes place in the first 4 years of life as in the next 13 years."2 How tragic it is that many, many children pass through the most fertile period of growth in their entire lives with little intellectual stimulation!

Busy parents may feel that laying a foundation for a love of books and "setting the stage" for reading is an overwhelming responsibility, but in reality the experiences involved can be some of the most delightful that a family has together. The pleasures found in good stories and good art in picture books provide a mutual enjoyment to be found in very few pursuits. With a good book, who is concerned about generation gaps or levels of appreciation? And the close relationship that develops when a child curls up on a parent's lap and shares a story hour is a treasure to last a lifetime. These experiences far surpass the impersonal observation of canned entertainment from television or even story hours in institutions. This quiet sharing of a concerned adult and one or more children can help fill emotional needs, build security through the very special attention of those who are most dear, and, at the same time, lead to a love of reading.

The most important reason for reading aloud to children is to give them pleasure. This may sound hedonistic, but actually it is the pleasure that children experience through books that causes them to love literature and to develop the interest in reading that is basic to academic success. Of course there are many wonderful by-products of the pleasurable sharing of books. A great deal of information is acquired. Linguistic development proceeds at a rapid pace. This is of great importance since it is through language that the child thinks and communicates. Language in print differs from that of conversation. Hearing books read aloud develops a child's range of comprehension and builds vocabulary. Children become acquainted with many genres of literature, and if parents help guide the selection of the books that will be read, the youngsters will hear some of the best of literature for young children. This is their heritage, and the experience may very well develop the foundation for an appreciation of the world's great literature that will continue throughout life.

Careful investigation of fine picture books develops muchneeded listening skills and "looking skills." The excellent books that are available intensify children's perception and help them enjoy different art styles. The pictures motivate children to read. Children's participation in the reading process is of utmost importance. They soon learn to join in and recite interesting rhymes and rhythms with the reader, to pick up and enumerate the items in a cumulative plot, or to quote short verses and nursery rhymes. Simple stories give them material for dramatic play and help stretch and develop imaginations by providing the basis for art activities and stories of their own. Sometimes stories small children hear help them understand themselves better and build empathy for others or set the beginnings of moral development. In fact, such books can even give adults cues as to how children feel and why they act as they do.

Concerned parents will want to make an important contribution to their children's success by involving them with reading at a very early developmental stage, and they will enjoy the pleasure of shared communication with their youngsters through literature. Throughout the chapters of this book there are quick reviews of some of the many research studies that indicate the positive effects of reading aloud to children upon their subsequent success in school. These studies leave little doubt as to the importance of sharing books with children when they are in the preschool years.

Often a problem arises as to how to select literature that will fit children's needs and interests as they go through the various developmental stages. Sometimes parents are overwhelmed by the plentitude of books. They may easily miss the best of them unless they have made a careful study of literature for early childhood. Parents are busy people! They do not have the time to sift through thousands of books to find the best, yet in education it is the quality, not the quantity, of the experience that counts.

This book has been written to give parents and other concerned adults help in selecting the best of literature and art to share with children and to help them discover ways of involving children in the reading experience. We have attempted to suggest to parents the best materials from which they may want to select what they feel are the most appropriate for the interests of their children. The book has been divided into progressive stages of child growth and development. Literature to fit the interests and needs of youngsters in the various stages has been presented. Stories, poetry, songs, language activities, games, and ideas for generating children's interest in books and starting them to read have been included.

We have presented the classics for young children along
with the best books of the twentieth century. Hundreds of
these books have been annotated. Selected bibliographies
have been placed at the conclusion of each chapter. They
should give parents lists of possibilities from which to draw
for every type of literature for young children. Of the
thousands of books on the market, only those that we consider the best or the most useful at a given developmental
stage could be included; however, we have suggested criteria
for the evaluation of various types of books that parents and
children will encounter in their search for good reading.

In dealing with each age group special emphasis has been
placed on activities that bring children into the reading process. Educators often tell us that we need to act on and participate in an academic adventure to make it a part of our
understanding. Certainly this is true with literature for preschool children. In each chapter of the book attention is
drawn to activities that will help bring children into a love
of books and eventually start them reading on their own.

Many suggestions are given for developing the art and
technique of reading aloud to children. Also there are ideas
for promoting listening skills, art appreciation, and the desire to participate in the reading process. Emphasis is
placed on the development of language skills, and consideration is given to some of the basic concepts that are needed
as children approach the mechanics of reading for themselves. Books that can help satisfy needs and interests of
youngsters are discussed, and many suggestions for presenting books in interesting ways are given.

At the end of each chapter there are lists of books that
will help the child progress during a given stage of learning.
There is no "average child" and certainly we would not want
to categorize needs and interests in literature, but this divi-
sion puts developmental stages into chronological order. It
should help parents find literature that will be appropriate to
the individuality of their children and eventually lead their
youngsters into beginning reading. A listing of helpful references for adult reading is included at the end of Chapter I.

The enthusiasm of parents is of prime importance in the
process of bringing children and books together in a happy
relationship. It is our conviction that this enthusiasm,
coupled with selections from the best of books, can make
children so involved in literature that they cannot wait to

learn to read for themselves. Such an attitude builds up over a long period of time and with much help from interested adults.

Leland Jacobs, an outstanding educator, says, "Literature does not just happen in a child's life. It is in his days because an adult who really cares about children and books gets them together under the best conditions."[3] Concerned parents do care! We hope that this book will be a guide for such parents and for other interested adults to the best of literature for preschool children and the best conditions for the enjoyment of such literature so that children will be well on their way to reading on their own by the time they enter school.

Notes

[1]Aidan Chambers, Introducing Books to Children (London: Heineman Educational Books, 1973), p. 16.

[2]Benjamin S. Bloom, Stability and Change in Human Characteristics (New York: John Wiley and Sons, 1964), p. 88.

[3]Leland B. Jacobs, "Enjoying Literature with Young Children," in Using Literature with Young Children, ed. Leland B. Jacobs (New York: Teachers College Press, 1965), p. 1.

CHAPTER I

LET'S START AT THE VERY BEGINNING
--The Infant Stage--

Introducing the Language

Once upon a time, according to many of the old folktales,
certain fortunate parents were granted three or more wishes
for the future success and happiness of their newborn baby.
If this were to happen today, surely high on the list of most
parents' dreams for their children would be academic success. However, we must accept the fact that the fulfillment
of most of our dreams comes about through our own efforts.
If success in school experiences is to be a basic goal for
our children, we must start early to build the foundation for
such achievement by preparing them for success in reading.
Of course we would not try to push youngsters into the mechanics of reading at a very early age. Instead, our first
accomplishment must be to make them want to read through
an exposure to the joy that is to be found in books. Our
goal should be to make them care enough about reading for
themselves that they will demand that privilege just as soon
as they are capable of acquiring the ability.

Language development is our first concern as we begin to
help the child build a basic foundation for reading. A knowledge of the developmental stages through which a baby progresses in acquiring the needed skills for verbalizing can
help parents to enrich the language environment in ways that
will aid the infant with beginning language facility and at the
same time provide fun for both the baby and caring adults as
they enjoy each particular developmental period. Specialists
in the field of early childhood have discovered that all children go through the same stages in their development.

First there is the listening stage with varied degrees of
attention, then the beginning of vocalization, followed by babbling in a conventional manner with others or perhaps as

1

subjective monologues when the child is alone. Next comes
the lallation stage in which children start imitating the sounds
they hear. The youngsters pick up sound patterns from
"conversations" with adults and from lullabies and rhymes of
spoken language. They begin to try varied tones, intensities,
and pitches as their babbling increases to short sentence
lengths. Later most children go through the jargon stage
when they begin to adopt the inflections and lilt of adult
speech, and even though they are babbling, their speech
takes on emphasis, intonation, and rhythm as if they were
carrying on a real conversation. Babies' sounds start to
follow a phonetic direction that will let them begin to build
words. At this point the child ceases being a "universal
baby" making random sounds that may or may not be used
within the speech of his or her culture and starts being a
native speaker and listener. Even though most of the utter-
ances still belong to the infant's own special language, he or
she is moving toward the purpose of oral language--to give
and receive meaning through sound. Later the youngster will
learn to attach this meaning to the abstract symbols we use
in reading.

Authorities tell us that very small children should be enveloped in language long before they understand the meaning
of the words. In this way they are building their foundation
for speech and reading. However, early conversations with
babies are limited, to say the least. Just chatting on about
nothing can be a bit boring, but here is where the old folk
literature can be very helpful. The rhymes and jingles along
with the simplest baby games can make time spent with babies anything but dull.

During the first year of a child's life folklore will no
doubt provide most literary experiences. A great deal of
this first literature will not be given to the baby through
books but in the old oral tradition that conveyed our literature for hundreds of years before there were printing press-
es, or, in some cases, before there were even written languages. For hundreds of years mothers have sung soothing
lullabies or chanted little ditties to please their children.
These little verses and songs have become, as Andrew Lang
says, like "smooth stones from the brook of time, worn
smooth by constant friction of tongues long dead."[1] Yet,
there they are waiting to fascinate your child, to bring your
baby fun and the joy of language, and to give the very foundation for a love of poetry and an introduction to the pleasures to be found later in literature.

In his discussion of the English and their nursery rhymes the great French scholar Paul Hazard says:

> The English nursery rhymes are often only music, singing vowels, repetitions of sound, simple cadences stressed, full and sonorous rhymes. They [the English people] are not unconscious of the fact that by placing rhythm at the beginning of life they are conforming to the general order of the universe. They have a harmony all their own that is strange, mocking, and tender. The sense is of less importance than the sound. [2]

If you plan to "start at the very beginning," share the soothing effects of lullabies and old ditties or the rhythmical jingle of verses and nursery rhymes as a way of becoming acquainted with your baby while you are still in the hospital. Gentle talk and lullabies provide the infant with the security of love expressed in quiet ways in the strange new world that must often seem frightening to a newborn baby.

The old lullabies are love songs that provide a first intimate language between parent and child. For years psychologists have realized the importance of early communication with a tiny baby, but now the need for such communication is receiving notice in the medical field. Dr. John Lind of Sweden and Professor Carol Hardgrove of the Department of Family Care Nursing, University of California, San Francisco, say:

> Today's increased focus on newborns and yet-to-be-borns, and on parental-infant attachment, helps us understand better why lullabies are so comforting. We know more now about the important function they serve in the bonding process, the development of the brain and the fostering of enjoyment in a healthy parent-infant relationship.... As one of many measures to promote parent-infant bonding, a hospital in Sweden has tried music therapy in the maternity wards.... The philosophy behind the introduction of such non-medical activities on the maternity floor is that singing, rocking, and playing with a baby increase the parent's pleasure in that baby. This pleasure, in truth, causes the parent to observe the baby more closely. The songs and play foster the baby's development as he or she attends to the sounds and rhythms. Such attention is important for later speech development. [3]

It is interesting to note that a newborn baby can distinguish the voice of its mother from all others within two or three days following birth. Fortunately, it matters little whether the mother has a beautiful voice. Her baby will be the least critical listener she will ever have. To the infant it is not the beauty of the rendition of an old song or lullaby that is of importance but rather the bit of soothing rhythm of the song that goes along with the cuddling and caring of the adult.

Don't be concerned if someone tries to tell you that you are spoiling your child by singing to it and rocking it to sleep. Children need just such expressions of love to start them toward the growth of a healthy, happy, self-confident attitude toward life.

If you play a musical instrument ever so little, you may find that your baby will enjoy the accompaniment immensely. One mother tells about holding her daughter in one arm and playing a very simple piano accompaniment to "Brahms' Lullaby" with her free hand while singing to her. The effect on the child was sometimes almost hypnotic. Even though the daughter is now an adult, both she and her mother still find this lovely old song charming and restful. What an excellent way to start an appreciation of music and an enjoyment of the beauty of our language, and to build a bit of personal heritage that can be shared only in one's family!

Of course anything you care to sing to your tiny baby is acceptable. Lullabies can be gay or quiet in mood, but of all our folksongs they are probably the simplest with their very basic appeal.

If you feel that you should refresh your memory or perhaps add some new songs to your repertoire of lullabies and children's songs, there are several books containing collections of such songs that can be of help. One that you might find especially interesting is Lullabies and Night Songs, edited by William Engvick. This is a good collection that includes nursery rhymes along with traditional songs and is illustrated in a whimsical, somewhat humorous way by Maurice Sendak. Included in the book are some poems set to music for the first time, along with many traditional lullabies like "All Through the Night," "Rock-a-Bye, Baby," "All the Pretty Horses," and "Sleep, Baby, Sleep." This book would be a good investment for future musical experiences as the child grows.

The Fireside Book of Children's Songs, edited by Marie Winn and Allan Miller and illustrated by John Alcorn, is a fine collection of many kinds of songs for youngsters. The first part is given to "Good Morning" and "Good Night" songs and has some lovely lullabies.

The Baby's Song Book, compiled by Elizabeth Porter, illustrated by William Stobbs, is made up basically of nursery rhymes, many of which can be used as soothing lullabies. It contains more than eighty selections and is illustrated with bright, exciting pictures.

Gwendolyn Reed is editor of the book Songs the Sandman Sings, which is illustrated by Peggy Skillen. It includes nighttime poems as well as lullabies. Even a tiny baby is not too young to listen to the melodic sound of poetry along with songs.

Dorothy Berliner Commins has given us a book entitled Lullabies of the World that will probably fascinate you as a parent. The songs are taken from many different countries including our own. With each selection she has given interesting background material as to the source and development of the song. Some of these selections might recall lullabies from your own heritage that may have been a part of your early childhood and part of your individual culture that you will want to pass on to your children. The U.S. Committee for UNICEF has published a paperback book entitled Rockabye Baby: Lullabies from Many Nations and Peoples, compiled by Carl Miller, which could also provide a way of sharing a variety of songs.

As you are enjoying songs and conversations with your tiny baby, naturally you realize that it will be some time before you are concerned with such reading readiness skills as left-to-right progression across a page or shapes of words. Nevertheless, when a mother talks and sings to an infant as she bathes, dresses, and feeds it, she is starting the child toward language development and helping him or her lay the very foundation for later success in reading.

Language facility is the basis for reading comprehension, and the rate at which children acquire such facility depends greatly upon the encouragement they receive from caring adults at a very young age. Exposure to language is of utmost importance to even the youngest child. Babies must first be encouraged to develop the motor skills needed for speaking and to enjoy the imitation of sounds. Such experiences come long before they attempt to learn the words that constitute our means of both spoken and written communication.

As the baby grows and becomes more active, parents should continue talking with the child in quiet tones. The naming of objects should begin very early, and the child's name should often be included in conversations and in verses. In an amazingly short time little poems and rhymes, bits of fun, and old traditional verses like "This Little Pig Went to Market," "Baa, Baa, Black Sheep," "Pease Porridge Hot," and "Pat-a-cake, Pat-a-cake," will begin to call forth a rhythmical response from the child. Such early bits of literature should be repeated often so that they can become a part of the family's shared fun.

Nursery rhymes are the best introduction to poetry and we cannot begin too early to share them with small children. As one writer has said, "If you want your child to love Homer, give him Mother Goose."[4] For tiny babies the meaning of the words is not of great importance. It is their rhythm, alliteration, and onomatopoeia that may arrest the infant's attention.

Books of nursery rhymes make an ideal starting point for building your child's own library. You will want to have some sturdy books for the baby to hold just as soon as he or she has developed enough dexterity to do so. Of course these cannot be large or cumbersome, but will need to be small enough to "fit the child's hands." Simplicity is the key for first books. One picture and verse to a page is sufficient. For first looking, pictures should be brightly colored and very realistic with little detail.

As you look for Mother Goose books that your child can enjoy either with an adult or alone, you may want to consider some of these:

The Tall Book of Mother Goose, illustrated by Feodor Rojankovsky, is a favorite that is appropriate for very tiny children. One reason for the continued popularity of this book is the format. It lives up to its name. It is tall, but its unique quality is that it is less than five inches wide. This size affords different advantages. A small child can handle the book quite easily. Also, the format gave the

illustrator the opportunity to present the rhymes separately,
each with one or more illustrations, so that the youngster is
sure of seeing the appropriate pictures for a given rhyme.
This is an especially important feature in books for very
young children. The illustrations are bright, often humorous, and very expressive. The children shown have definite
human qualities; some are almost homely, some are funny,
all are very real. The animal pictures have such a sense
of texture in the feathers or fur that children often want to
touch them.

A more recent interpretation of many of the old rhymes
is to be found in Anne Rockwell's Gray Goose and Gander &
Other Mother Goose Rhymes. Her pictures are uncomplicated,
yet show movement and motion throughout and could be quite
relevant to a young child's experiences.

The White Land: A Picture Book of Traditional Rhymes
and Verses by Raymond Briggs is arranged well for small
children with a close relationship between verses and pictures. There is a bit of humor in the illustrations, but they
are not the slapstick comedy that seems out of place with
traditional rhymes.

Often nursery rhymes for very young children are presented in board books. Such books are composed of several
pages of sturdy cardboard, bound together in book form.
For example, Baby's Mother Goose with pictures by Alice
Schlesinger is a book of this type. It has a format similar
to that of The Tall Book of Mother Goose. The pictures are
realistic and there is a close relationship between rhymes and
illustrations. This is a book that will endure much rough
treatment.

A very small board book, Mother Goose by Gyo Fujikawa,
could be an infant's treasure. The illustrator has selected
just a few of the most appealing rhymes for tiny children.
They are illustrated in bright colors with a charm and vitality in the pictures that probably will appeal to both adults
and babies.

Keep in mind that nursery rhymes will constitute a very
important part of your child's literature for several years.
For babies they provide sound enjoyment, repetition, rhyme,
rhythm, and later, familiar objects to recall; however, their
charm does not end with infancy. They are favorite reading,
singing, and play material well into the lower elementary
grades of school.

Perhaps while your baby is still small, you will want to purchase some beautiful editions of large collections of standard rhymes that can be enjoyed for years to come. These won't be the baby's playthings but special books that are kept for sharing with a caring adult. Such books of real quality and beauty can become family heirlooms.

When you shop for very special nursery rhyme books, you will want to look for a variety of verses that appeal to children. Look for those with worthwhile illustrations, ones that will give your child an early start toward art appreciation. Money spent on books can be a wise investment in your child's future if you take care in choosing the best of literature and the best of illustrations.

You will enjoy your search for just the right books for you and your child because there is a great wealth of beautifully illustrated books of rhymes, and every year more collections are published. These books will provide some excellent conversation pieces, even when your child is just an infant.

There is no right or wrong Mother Goose collection. Whatever your artistic tastes may be, you will find them reflected in some of the nursery rhyme collections. As your child grows, you will find that the great variety of illustrations available will give you an opportunity to introduce him or her to different art styles. For very tiny children more realistic pictures are needed.

Here are a few fine collections that you may want to consider for sharing and enjoying while your child is still very young:

Ever since its first publication in 1916 The Real Mother Goose by Blanche Fisher Wright has been a favorite collection. The flat, brightly colored, old-fashioned pictures do seem very real in their depiction of the verses. They lack humor but give a traditional interpretation of the rhymes with colored pictures on each page. The book includes over 300 verses and is a good introduction to the world of Mother Goose.

Lavender's Blue by Kathleen Lines, pictures by Harold Jones, is also a traditional presentation showing an English setting for the rhymes. The book should not be confusing to a small child because of the individual presentation of rhymes and corresponding pictures. There are fingerplays and nursery games included in the collection. Some of the illustrations are done in rather quiet, muted colors; others are in black and white.

The Baby's Lap Book by Kay Chorao is well named. As the title indicates, this is a book for sharing. It is too large for a baby to hold, but an ideal first book of rhymes to enjoy with the help of caring adults. Illustrations are large and done in soft colors.

For droll humor and just plain fun, do not miss Leslie Brooke's Ring O' Roses. It is a book that may bring as much enjoyment to the adult reader as to the young listener. Take time to savor "To Market, To Market" to appreciate Brooke's ability to add rich humor with his illustrations that extend the simple text of the verse. Of course, he is famous for his illustrations of pigs and these are some of his best. It has been said that you will never again think of a pig as just another animal after you have met Leslie Brooke's pigs. The book is full of illustrations, some full-page in color, others black-and-white drawings, but all provide very imaginative interpretations of the verses. Ring O' Roses is a book to grow on. At first, very young children will be fascinated by the bright colors of the pictures, but as time goes by, they will see more and more fun in Brooke's storytelling illustrations.

The Book of Nursery and Mother Goose Rhymes by Marguerite de Angeli is an aesthetic experience for a child who will enjoy the beautiful pictures done in soft, quiet watercolors. This large collection of rhymes is held together by lovely designs and detailed pictures of the English countryside. Again, this is a book to share, not one for baby's play, but the kind of literature that becomes a part of a family's heritage and tradition.

Start the reading habit very early with your youngster. As you hold the tiny baby on your lap, turn through a brightly colored nursery rhyme book and read the verses. The child will probably begin to attend rather closely to the pictures when visual acuity is attained around five months of age and true focusing of eyes is possible.

One mother said that she felt rather foolish reading verses when she knew her tiny girl had no idea of the meaning of the words. What she did not realize was that the baby was able to distinguish the sound patterns. Little songs with their varied pitch and tone qualities and the lilt of short verses and conversations will fascinate a very young baby. Watch an infant in a one-on-one encounter with a parent and you will often note real intensity of concentration for short intervals. In addition to the acquisition of visual ability, the child is hearing the linguistic flow of the literature and beginning the development of listening skills.

Begin early to lay the groundwork for your child's enjoyment of literature. A grandmother started singing and reciting nursery rhymes to one infant, Becky, when the child was one week old. By the time she was three months old, she became exhilarated with the same rhymes--kicking, waving her arms, gurgling, and cooing when they were said or sung. She would even stare at length at the pictures in a Mother Goose book. The little girl's parents became interested in sharing books of verse and little stories with her so that by the time she was two years old, she was pretending to read, and in her third year she began to recognize a few words in her books, not because she was urged to do so but because literature had become such an important part of her life.

The Language Participant

Babies are social beings. At two months of age they will respond with a smile to a human face and often will make an heroic attempt to emit a vocal response to adults who talk to them. These first non-crying sounds are a production often accompanied by squirming, kicking, and great facial contortions followed by a kind of strangled noise that may be little more than a squeal. But this is the beginning, and is soon followed by gurgles and coos that come spontaneously or in response to others. Language development is accelerated by individual attention and reinforcement given to the child's efforts to communicate; and if this attention comes from persons of prime importance to the baby and is given in a happy, responsive way, the development moves at a rapid pace.

The results of many research studies that have involved early language development lead one to believe that emotion, as well as intellect and the development of motor skills, plays a major role in the learning of the language. Such studies have shown the language development of institutionalized babies to be far below that of infants in a normal environment. Babies respond when familiar adults talk to them. One study has shown a close correlation between the vocalization of infants and that of their mothers, and also between the child's vocalization and the mother's warmth toward the infant. There is even a study that analyzed the relationship between maternal responsiveness and infants' crying. In this study Bell and Ainsworth found that the more responsive the mother was to a baby, the less it cried and that babies with responsive mothers were more likely to communicate in different ways other than crying. [5] It would seem that talking, singing, and playing little games with your baby would be worthwhile to the child's emotional development alone. In fact, there are very sad reports by psychologists about the slow withdrawal of babies whose parents treat them in a cold manner. Studies have also demonstrated a correlation between different types of disturbed parent-child relationships and defective articulation, slowness in beginning to talk, and stuttering.

The young baby's early communication includes babbling, smiling, and reaching. Babbling has been described as "a series of repetitive sounds, uttered in a state of contentment and relaxation."[6] It seems to be a way that babies play with sounds, and it is interesting to note that for the first three months of life all babies make the same sounds. This preverbal communication in the form of babbling helps develop the muscle and brain connections necessary for speech. By talking with babies, playing their little games, and encouraging their babbling and cooing, we are accelerating their physical and cognitive development, helping build a sense of emotional stability, and also promoting a happy feeling of shared enjoyment for both the baby and those who live with it. These experiences give the child advantages that will be apparent later in his or her school activities. And what an easy way to help your child to grow! The youngster is already beginning to enjoy rhythm and cadence--some of the beauty of the language. Your little songs and games help him or her develop auditory discrimination and listening skills that are necessary for learning the language, and the shared fun is setting a positive attitude toward interaction with others in a social situation.

When parents are attempting to expose their children to language experiences, it is extremely important that the youngsters be given a chance to respond and be a part of the conversations. Like most of us, babies soon lose interest in a conversation if they have no opportunity to be a part of it. Children (and adults) learn by doing. They begin with their own jargon and finally move into the language of adults.

Perhaps no other type of learning is as dependent on imitation as the development of language skills. It is very important to give babies time to respond in their own ways to questions, answers, songs, rhymes, games, and to enjoy language participation. Also, babies need a reward for accomplishments--a smile or some quiet, positive reinforcement.

Authorities do not agree as to whether adults should repeat the babbling sounds babies make. Some feel that repetition of such sounds is reinforcing to the infants, giving them a fine feeling of accomplishment. After all, this special baby language is the beginning of phonetic sounds, some of which will later be incorporated into speech. These sounds represent the child's effort to communicate and should be appreciated and perhaps parroted back. Other authorities point out that most of the sounds that very young babies make do not appear in adult speech. They say that the child should be encouraged, but with acceptable language. In this way we are inviting the infant into our language. Apparently it is up to the parents to decide whether or not they will repeat the phonetic sounds babies make in their preverbal attempts. Such exchanges should be fun experiences for both the baby and the parents. Certainly we can accept the idea that we should never indulge in a patronizing "baby talk" when a child is beginning to experience the language. This could have detrimental effects on language development.

At the babbling stage youngsters are already building a foundation for reading. Research tends to show that the more children babble, the better they will speak. 7 Usually the child who talks and thinks well is the one who becomes a good reader.

At approximately six months of age children's spontaneous vocalization will include all the vowel sounds. The funny little egotists will often crow and squeal with delight in their accomplishments as they try their powers of speech, and well they should because these sounds are prerequisite to the comprehension of words that will follow in a few months.

A game that infants enjoy is the repetition of sounds. Holding the child in a face-to-face position, the parent may imitate a vowel sound the child is making and then begin adding a consonant sound to the baby's vowel and repeat the combination, praising the infant when he or she tries making the new sound. Little verses like "Baa, Baa, Black Sheep,"

"Bye, Baby Bunting," or "Peter Piper Picked a Peck of Pickled Peppers," bubble over with their repeated sounds. They can add to the fun, for even small babies often appreciate the alliteration in such rhymes.

Spontaneous conversations as well as nursery rhymes and jingles begin to take on new importance when the baby is about six months old and beginning to learn more about distinguishing between sounds. The repetition and jingly rhymes from Mother Goose "tickle the ear" with repeated sounds and give the child a very significant start toward phonetic development and listening skills.

In reaffirming the child's efforts in a warm, responsive manner, the wise parent is careful not to anticipate the baby's every need and in this way deny chances of expression. Communication must be a two-way street, even at this age. Adults must avoid the overly caring attitude in which all needs and desires are satisfied almost before they are felt. Children should be motivated to try to express themselves. Even in this early stage of language development a child can begin to feel the power of language when he or she is able to have real desires fulfilled by a concentrated effort of using preverbal skills.

All this is not to say that children must be stimulated during all their waking hours. They need time to try their newfound talents and practice their vocalization or just to stare off into nothingness. In fact, the modern child can be so enveloped in family noises and television racket that he or she learns to ignore what is going on. Perhaps this is the beginning of the tuning-out process that goes with so many children to school. Babies need the stimulation that comes from the individual attention of caring people in order to develop their language skills and they also need quiet times in which to assimilate their acquired knowledge.

At about nine months of age they will begin to produce a few real words although they probably won't understand that the words have meanings. At the same time they may comprehend the meaning of some words they hear, especially if the words are accompanied with gestures. The baby will react to his or her name and may comprehend "No!" Eventually he or she will suit actions to words or requests like, "Show me the bottle," or, "Where are your feet?"

The simplest little rhymes are helpful during this period

of learning. Start with the baby's own body. "This Little
Pig Went to Market" has been a favorite for generations.
The touching experience, articulation of each toe, and running the fingers up the baby's leg to tickle the tummy on
"wee, wee all the way home" have amused literally millions
of babies. Many nursery rhymes about parts of the body
can be found. In This Little Pig Went to Market, Norah
Montgomerie has compiled a great variety of such rhymes
under the headings of "Toe and Finger Counting," "Tickling,"
"Foot Patting," "Rocking," "Leg Wagging," and "Face Patting."

Two "toe counting" rhymes from This Little Pig Went to
Market are:

> Wee Wiggie,
> Poke Piggie,
> Tom Whistle,
> John Gristle,
> And old BIG GOBBLE,
>   gobble,
>   gobble.

* * *

> This little cow eats grass,
> This little cow eats hay,
> This little cow looks over the hedge,
> This little cow runs away.
> And this BIG cow does nothing at all,
> But lie in the fields all day!
> We'll chase her,
>   And chase her,
>   And chase her. 8

Some touching games that your baby may like to start
with are:

> Touch your nose,
> Touch your chin;
> That's the way this game begins.
> Touch your eyes,
> Touch your knees;
> Now pretend you're going to sneeze.
> Touch your hair,
> Touch one ear;
> Touch your two red lips right here.

Touch your elbows,
Where they bend;
That's the way this touch game ends.

* * *

This is the circle that is your head.
This is your mouth with which words are said.
These are your eyes with which you see.
This is your nose; mine's part of me.
This is the hair that grows on your head.
This is your hat, all pretty and red.

* * *

Five fingers on this hand,
Five fingers on that;
A dear little nose,
A mouth like a rose,
Two cheeks so tiny and fat.
Two eyes, two ears,
And ten little toes;
That's the way the baby grows.

You might like to try some face tapping verses like these:

Eye winker,
Tom Tinker,
Nose smeller,
Mouth eater.
Chin chopper,
Chin chopper, chin chopper,
Chin chopper, chin.
Brow bender,
Eye peeper,
Nose dreeper,
Mouth eater,
Chin chopper,
Knock at the door,
Ring the bell,
Lift up the latch,
Walk in ...
Take a chair,
And sit down there,
How do you do,
And how do you do,
And how do you do again?

> (The knocking is done on the forehead, the latch
> is the nose, and the verse ends with tapping on
> the chin and tickling down to the tummy.)

Parents often help babies exercise. Little verses like
these that Norah Montgomerie calls "leg wagging types" can
be a help. You can set the exercises as you see fit to the
rhythm of little verses which make the experience more fun
for both the parents and the child.

> Leg over leg,
> As the dog goes to Dover,
> When he comes to a wall,
> Jump! He goes over!

> * * *

> See-saw, sacradown,
> Which is the way to London Town?
> One foot up and one foot down,
> That is the way to London Town.

> * * *

> Up and down the market,
> Selling penny buns,
> One a penny, two a penny,
> Three a penny buns![9]

Of course any little nursery rhymes or verses that you
and your baby enjoy are appropriate whenever the youngster
is in the mood to play. The verses simply provide the music, you and the baby provide the fun.

Many rhymes have the possibility of including a child's
name. With just a bit of improvising you can change the
names of nursery rhyme characters to that of your own
child, and in this way cause the small listener to be really
involved in what is being said. After all, we all tend to
listen with care when our own name is spoken.

Other rhymes and games that provide fun at this time
are ones that have some sudden excitement. Even if a
child does not understand the words, he or she will respond to changes in rhythm and varied voice inflections.
Perhaps the old favorite, "Pop Goes the Weasel," with its
explosive sound will be a youngster's first experience of a

climax in story form. This is exciting literature that prepares the baby for the future joys of reading.

Repetition is important. Going over the same songs and
verses builds a sense of security and enjoyment. Baby
games must be repeated many times before the real fun
comes across and the child knows to watch for the punch
line or the happy hug or bit of a tickle at the end of a
certain rhyme. Repetition also helps children learn the
lilt of the language and even some words or phrases, for
occasionally a word will sink in and be repeated. Encourage joining in with the words even if the child's contribution
sounds like nothing but jargon. Notice that his or her special talk will have the rhythm of the phrases of the verses.

"Peek-a-Boo, I See You" has had a place near the top of
best-liked verses for infants for countless generations. Piaget, psychology's foremost expert in the field of cognitive
growth, helped us to see why this verse and the actions involved hold such interest for eight- to twelve-month-old children. An understanding of object constancy and person permanence begins to develop at this time. Children begin to
realize that things exist independently of themselves, and
even though someone cannot be seen at the moment, that
person is still in existence. For this reason the game of
disappearance and reappearance is meaningful for children
of this age.[10]

Ira Gordon says that we may guess that an understanding
of person and object permanence is a prerequisite to what
could be called a comprehension of word permanence and a
beginning of the understanding of the consistency of language.[11]

"Peek-a-Boo" will remain a favorite for months with your
baby. When children start crawling, they enjoy finding a
partially hidden adult, or a little later will enjoy hiding themselves. Watching a child go through the more advanced
stages of the "peek-a-boo" game could remind one of the
delightful poem by Dorothy Aldis, "Hiding," which starts:

> I'm hiding, I'm hiding,
> And no one knows where;
> For all they can see is my
> Toes and my hair.[12]

One of the best ways to promote involvement and interest

in literary experiences for tiny children is through the use
of simple little fingerplays. They provide great fun and
wonderful opportunities for imitation which is basic to language learning. Youngsters imitate the actions first and
then gradually begin to repeat words and phrases of the little verses. Most children can clap their hands, wave good-
bye, pound their feet, and make a fist by the time they are
eleven or twelve months old. Using such actions in fingerplays helps a child give expression to the rhythm of the
words as they are said or sung. At first the baby is only
beginning to learn control of hands, but watching the parent
and receiving help and encouragement can promote some
skill in coordination. In the beginning the parent will have
to guide motions, but soon baby drama takes over and youngsters will get involved even to the extent of responding to
rhymes with their entire bodies.

We usually think of "Pat-a-Cake" as being one of the first
fingerplays or little games that babies can play. This is one
in which you substitute the child's own name, of course. You
might try it with your youngster at any time, but if the child
doesn't respond as yet, wait until a later period. Baby
games must be fun to be worthwhile.

Some other simple little games are:

Clap your hands 1, 2, 3.
Clap you hands just like me.
Roll your hands 1, 2, 3.
Roll your hands just like me.

* * *

Open, shut them.
Open, shut them.
Open, shut them.
Give a little clap.
Open, shut them.
Open, shut them.
Open, shut them.
Put them in your lap.

* * *

Here is a ball for baby,
Big and soft and round,
Here is baby's hammer,
See how he can pound.

* * *

Two little blackbirds sitting on a hill,
One named Jack, one named Jill.
Fly away, Jack; fly away, Jill.
Come back, Jack; come back, Jill.
(With this verse a closed fist with the thumb up
represents each bird. They "fly away," possibly
behind the reciter's back, and then return.)

* * *

Here is a little beehive.
Where are the bees?
Hidden away where nobody sees.
Soon they come creeping out of the hive.
One, two, three, four, five.
(The hive is the right hand with the fingers curled
under; on the last line you should raise the thumb
and fingers one at a time.)

* * *

Fee, fie, fo, fum,
See my finger,
See my thumb.
Fee, fie, fo, fum,
Fingers gone,
So is thumb.
(For this one, point to the little finger on "fee,"
then to the rest of the fingers, and then the
thumb. At the last, hide the fingers and the
thumb in the hand.)

Several of these verses are too difficult for the baby to
do, but he or she will appreciate an adult's performance,
and later will be able to imitate the actions.

Often the games and fingerplays that babies enjoy the most
are the ones that the infant and the parents have created together. These may become a part of an individual family's
own folklore. Some families are blessed with special relatives who always play certain games and tell stories that become traditional. One very active eighty-eight-year-old aunt
is still making her handkerchief rabbits and reciting the poems that go along with the rabbits' performances. Members
of the family who are now grandparents themselves still enjoy looking over the heads of the children she is entertaining

and watching the fun and remembering this family tradition that developed through their own childhood experiences.

Linguists say rhymes are ideal for learning language. They play on the fun of speech, and parents will want to reinforce that fun with actions that are much appreciated by a baby who is old enough to participate. For instance, try some knee-riding games with a year-old child. You will be rewarded by giggles and squeals of laughter, and the child will be communicating a real desire to repeat the performances long after you are tired.

Here are a few to start the fun:

> Ride a cock-horse to Banbury Cross,
> To see a fine lady upon a white horse;
> Rings on her fingers and bells on her toes,
> And she shall have music wherever she goes.

* * *

> Old Farmer Giles,
> He went seven miles,
> With his faithful dog Old Rover;
> And Old Farmer Giles,
> When he came to the stiles,
> Took a run, and jumped clean over.

* * *

> Ride a cock-horse,
> To Banbury Cross,
> To see what Tommy can buy;
> A penny white loaf,
> A penny white cake,
> And a two-penny apple pie.

* * *

> To market, to market,
> To buy a fat pig,
> Home again, home again,
> Jiggety-jig.
> To market, to market,
> To buy a fat hog,
> Home again, home again,
> Jiggety-jog.

> To market, to market,
> To buy a plum bun,
> Home again, home again,
> Market is done.

If your partner is wanting more action in the rides, you might try:

> This is the way the ladies ride,
> Nim, nim, nim, nim.
> This is the way the gentlemen ride,
> Trim, trim, trim, trim.
> This is the way the farmers ride,
> Trot, trot, trot, trot.
> This is the way the huntsmen ride,
> A-gallop, a-gallop, a-gallop, a-gallop.
> This is the way the ploughboys ride,
> Hobble-dy-gee, hobble-dy-gee.

In case you are becoming rather exhausted, you could try this shorter version:

> This is the way they ride in the city,
> Oh, so nice, and oh, so pretty.
> This is the way they ride in the town,
> Up and down, up and down.
> This is the way they ride in the country,
> Bumpty, bumpty, bumpty, bumpty!

Adults will find that The Oxford Nursery Rhyme Book assembled by Iona and Peter Opie is perhaps the best resource for a great variety of baby games, lullabies, alphabet and number rhymes, and nursery rhymes of many varieties. This book probably would not have a great appeal to infants because the illustrations are small and done in black and white, but it is a fine resource book compiled by real scholars in the field.

Introducing the Book

The child who has encountered books as a part of his or her surroundings from the very beginning of life has a decided advantage over a youngster who has had little such exposure. Adults' attitudes toward books set a pattern for their treatment and may help the baby understand that a book is to be enjoyed, not torn. However, tearing does occur whether purposefully or inadvertently on the part of the child.

It seems that there is a stage that children must go through
when books get destroyed, but try to be patient and keep setting a good example by showing great respect for books.
You are the role model.   If a youngster is scolded or punished for tearing a book, a negative attitude toward books
may result.   One approach to the problem is to give the
child only inexpensive books during this destructive time,
sharing better books with him or her when you have the opportunity to guard them and perhaps make a point of showing the child how to handle them.   Certainly you do not want
to remove all books from the baby's environment even though
it takes time to help a little person learn how to treat them.
In most families some books will be torn and chewed.   Some
toys will also be broken.   Perhaps it will help to keep in
mind that this is just a part of the developmental process,
be it ever so destructive!

Some parents try to avoid unpleasant situations by providing cloth or board books for babies.   Some of these leave
much to be desired.   A cloth book is a flimsy imitation of a
real book and can be difficult for a young child to manipulate.
Illustrations are often poorly done and at best they are toys
rather than books.   Board books are reasonably indestructi-
ble and can be wiped clean of spills.   Until recently many
of these books had crude, garish artwork that was inappro-
priate for small children whose comprehension of pictures is
limited.   Both the content and the illustrations in board books
have been improving.   Here are some that are certainly
worthy of your consideration:

The Baby Board Books Series contains such titles as
Friends, Family, Dressing, and Playing.   Helen Oxenbury
has produced very realistic, simple pictures for these little
books, pictures directly from a baby's world that are not
cute or saccharine sweet, but real.   They are presented in
a manner that could build understanding; for example, an
object is shown on the left-hand page and on the opposite
page is a picture showing its use.   There will be a baby's
bathtub, then a baby taking a bath in the same tub; even a
potty with a child sitting on the potty on the opposite page.
Certainly the illustrator has gotten to the essentials of a
child's world.

Playtime, Bathtime, and Mealtime are among the books
in the Show Baby Series produced by Brimax Books of Cambridge, England, and published in this country by the Borden
Publishing Company.   The pictures in this set of twelve little

books again show the object on one page with some pictured use of the object adjacent to it. The illustrations are brightly colored and again done in the simple, realistic style needed for a baby's comprehension. Some of the later books in the series even show concept contrasts such as big-small, fast-slow.

For very first stories the Max Board Books done by Rosemary Wells would be appealing to infants who are about a year old. Some favorites in this delightful series are Max's Toys, Max's Ride, and Max's New Suit.

Grosset & Dunlap has published a series of board books that are nicely illustrated by Gyo Fujikawa. Let's Eat has just a bit of text but fine clear pictures of food for both people and animals. This is a book about a subject that even a year-old child finds relevant and important. Another in the series is Sleepy Time which shows people and animals relaxing for the night. Babes of the Wild gives fine double-page spreads of animal babies.

Animal Babies and Toys, illustrated by Robert Broomfield, published by Chatto Bodley Jonathan, are some of the best of the board books with their simple, bright pictures to attract infants. Baby's First Toys and Baby Animals are from the Teddy Board Books. They have fine, clear pictures and could serve as first identification books.

The Lady Bird Series, produced by The Ladybird Books, Ltd., in London and published in this country by International Book Centre of Troy, Michigan, includes excellent books for infants.

The pre-toddler group is usually quite interested in household pets. There are several of the long, narrow books showing pets that appear and act very much like the ones that a child may know from his or her own experiences. Both Kittens and Puppies by Jan Pfloog are well illustrated, as are I Am A Kitten and I Am A Puppy by Ole Risom.

Baby Animals by Harry McNaught may help extend a baby's knowledge of different kinds of animals. Of course each animal in this book is shown with its baby, which makes it more interesting.

Board books are taking on a great variety of shapes and forms, perhaps more to attract the adult buyer than to please

the young book connoisseur. Some are interesting, others
seem somewhat dangerous with their sharp points upon which
a child could fall.

We are seeing more "fold books" on the market. These
are made from heavy paper or cardboard which is fastened
together in a long strip that folds in accordion pleats. Such
a format makes it possible to turn through pages as one
would in a regular book or to unfold the entire strip to make
a long picture or frieze. Some of these are well constructed;
however, others start to tear apart even before they can be
sold. Baby Animals, A Grosset Fold Book by June Goldsborough is a sturdy book showing good pictures of baby animals with a minimum of text. A Very Long Tail by Eric
Carle, another fold book, is called "a book of versatile
forms." It can be turned through as a picture book which
shows some mice scampering across the pages until they
find the owner of a very long tail they have been following--
a snake, of course. On the way through the book many animals are shown. First one encounters an animal's tail on
the far right-hand side of the page. Then the reader must
turn to the next page to identify the animal itself. Names
of the animals are on the reverse side for an older child to
study. This book unfolds to make an interesting frieze.

Probably the most popular of all board books for very
tiny children are the touch and feel books or "feelies." Pat
the Bunny by Dorothy Kunhardt has been loved by babies ever
since its first publication in 1940. Books of this kind have
been called toys--really they are, but they can also be a
wonderful way to involve the tiny child in pictures and bits
of text. The texture of the pictures allows the infant to actually pat the soft cotton of the bunny's fur, feel the scratchy
sandpaper used to show daddy's face before he shaves, and
even look into a small mirror, or poke a finger through
mummy's ring. The Telephone Book, also by Dorothy Kunhardt, first published in 1942, allows the child to do many
of the things he or she wants to do, like saying "hello" into
the phone. Because of children's response to these books,
the market has been somewhat flooded with imitations. Some
are not durable and many are simply gimmicks. A parent
surely would want to limit the amount of money budgeted for
books that would be spent on the touch and feel variety, but
a few of the well-done ones will bring real pleasure to an
infant and probably promote an interest in books.

Some parents buy cloth or board books as a safety measure

since almost all year-old babies tend to taste everything, including their reading materials. One pair of proud parents announced that their daughter devoured literature--literally! If you get cloth books in order to keep your baby from swallowing paper, check to be sure that the books are marked "non-toxic." Substituting old magazines for the baby's reading material can be dangerous because traces of lead have been found in some full-color advertisements. There are the plastic-sheeted books which are often put together with plastic spiral bindings. These cause problems, too. The baby can be cut by the plastic, or, worse yet, pieces of the spiral bindings may break off and be swallowed. When considering the alternatives, it seems that except for selected board books, there are not a great many possibilities of good literature for the very young except those found in the usual book form. The best approach is to try to have patience as you continue to educate your child in the proper care of his or her books. Most children learn in a surprisingly short time, especially if they have good role models.

Even six months is not too young an age to start establishing a special reading time. Plan such a time when your baby is ready to settle down for a few minutes. For some babies just before nap time is appropriate. Select books with large, bright pictures, ones that you can discuss with the child. In fact, select books that you, too, will enjoy. This will probably be the only time in the youngster's life when your tastes can be a paramount factor in the selection of books to read aloud.

Of course the baby will not understand most of the words that you read, but a short interval set aside each day to share books can be a very special time. Just the happy assurance of being held and given individual attention can relate a book to security and joy--a good way to promote a love of literature and introduce the model of the reading parent, even though the reading consists of disjointed phrases at first. As you read, point to the pictures and talk about them with the child, reinforcing any response that you may get.

Of course you will rely heavily on nursery rhymes and books about things in the child's immediate world, but a youngster nearing a first birthday may also be ready for a few little story books along with some identification and situation books. In selecting these, remember that your little son or daughter has very little background and experience to

aid in understanding; however, don't hesitate to share any
literature that seems to interest the child. Perhaps it is
only the musical qualities of the language that he or she is
attending to, but such an appreciation is a very important
step in language development and well worth your time to
promote.

It is wise to borrow a variety of books from the library
to find what seems to interest the youngster at this time.
Do not be disappointed if you have bought a book you think
will be thoroughly enjoyed only to have the child display no
interest in it whatsoever. Just put the book aside for a few
weeks, and you may find when you next present it, you have
a favorite that must be read many times.

At the end of the first year of life babies are already at
different developmental stages and have their individual interests and backgrounds of experience. It is difficult to predict what little stories may attract them, but here are some
of the first books that have been especially popular with
children at the "beginning to walk and talk" age:

Margaret Wise Brown's Goodnight Moon has become a
"baby classic." This favorite of pre-toddlers is an account
of a bunny saying good night to all the things in its room.
"Goodnight bears, Goodnight chairs; Goodnight kittens, Goodnight mittens," and on it goes, including the child's world in
rhythmical language. It must seem very real to tiny children.
They want to hear it again and again, and often the reading
of this book becomes a part of the family's goodnight ritual.
Babies identify objects in the pictures. Also, they begin
even this early adding their own text as they say goodnight
to items that may not be included in the book. This little
winner is now in paperback, which may or may not stand up
against the constant use that it will probably get.

Where Is It? can provide a first little mystery story, as
Tana Hoban shows through her fine, clear photographs a
white rabbit involved in a hide-and-seek game, searching for
a prize of hidden carrots. Her One Little Kitten is done in
a similar style.

Garth Williams has a wonderful talent for illustrating books
for babies. His pictures are well defined, simple, and make
for excellent "naming" or identification experiences. Two of
his best for very young children are Baby's First Book and
Baby Farm Animals. The pictures in these books vibrate

with their appeal, yet they are not too sweet or cute as many pictures for babies and toddlers tend to be.

The Great Big Animal Book by Feodor Rojankovsky has fascinating pictures of farm animals with some text to go along with the pictures. For beautiful, bright paintings of wild animals try Grabianski's Wild Animals by Janusz Grabianski.

ABC and counting books often attract babies, not for number or letter concepts but because they usually have large, flat, easily recognized pictures. ABC Bunny by Wanda Gág, published in 1933 and now in paperback, is a classic among alphabet books and can be enjoyed by very tiny children. Its large lithographs provide an excellent artistic experience, and the animals the bunny meets, as he hops from one page and letter to the next, are interesting characters. The short text is set to music and can be sung as you go through the book with your baby.

Helen Oxenbury's ABC of Things can provide exciting identification experiences for little children. ABC An Alphabet Book with photographs by Thomas Matthiesen is a good example of a book developed from clear, simple pictures of things in a child's immediate world.

A book that will attract a small person who is beginning to enjoy the effect of ear-tickling language is You Can't Catch Me by Joan Kahn with pictures by Elizabeth Bridgeman. It has story rhymes often ending with noisy effects like "splash, splash, splash," or "smash, smash, smash." Some one-year-olds respond with hearty laughter to such alliteration and onomatopoeia, especially if the reader is enjoying the language too, and adding dramatic effects. Jay Bird by Marie Hall Ets has similar little verses about animals, with onomatopoeia at the end of the verses providing opportunities to imitate the sounds the animals make.

Babies are often fascinated by surprise formats in books. H. A. Rey's little fold-out book Where's My Baby? has a picture of an animal on each double-page spread. When you pull up the fold on the right-hand side of the picture, you find the animal's baby hidden inside. Bruno Munari is a versatile Italian artist who is interested in functional design. His book Who's There? Open the Door! can fascinate even a very small child. The child reader keeps opening the door as he or she turns the pages and finds yet another surprise

inside. Eric Carle's The Secret Birthday Message is developed on rather a similar format. Its pages are varied
shapes and sizes with peek holes and surprises until the last
page where one finds the birthday surprise--a puppy.

These are only a few of the books that can interest a
year-old child. If you feel that your youngster is ready to
follow some very simple plots, you may want to try some of
the books suggested for toddlers. The important thing is to
find what your child responds to and then to enjoy the books
together. Some children are so fascinated with sharing
books that they seem to be willing to listen to almost anything that is read to them. One young veterinarian read his
professional journals to his small daughter. She would sit
attentively for rather long periods of time, probably simply
enjoying her father's voice and the special attention of this
caring adult. Other youngsters are such dynamos that it is
difficult for them to sit still for even a short time. Don't
be discouraged if this is the case with your youngster, but
keep sharing bits of what may arrest his or her attention
until the child begins to see the enjoyment to be found in
books.

A Word of Caution

Piaget has demonstrated stages through which learning
progresses. A child moves from one stage to the next.
There is no fixed age at which any development takes place,
but we can be alert to provide a happy learning environment
and to reinforce development in a quiet manner. The whole
process of learning should be fun during infancy. The child
must never be made to feel tension, for we cannot force development of language any more than we can force a child to
start reaching or pointing before he or she is ready. You
will want to encourage successes, but remember that matu-
ration rates vary with each child. It is not a question of
how soon, but rather how well a youngster accomplishes a
developmental task and also how intrigued he or she is becoming with new experiences. The wise parent involves
children with situations and experiences that are interesting
from the child's point of view, starting from the child's
level of understanding and experience.

A precocious third-grade student once said to his teacher,
"It seems as if whenever a teacher says, 'We are going to
play a game,' she is getting you into a lot of work!" Actually a baby's play is his or her work, for the tiny child

is continually exploring and learning about the world, even practicing the foundations of language through chatter. The games parents play with children, the songs they sing, and the verses they recite should be fun for all concerned and never thought of as tests or landmarks that must be reached in an infant's development. As soon as we get serious about accomplishment, we have made our games something undesirable. Tiny children should never be forced but rather encouraged into activities. Let them be leaders in their fun. Their attention span is very limited, but real involvement in activities is possible for short periods of time and can promote learning.

A Firm Foundation

At the end of your child's first year, you will probably think of the wonderful development the youngster has made in such a short period of time. If you have been conscientiously exposing the child to literature, you and your baby probably have greatly enjoyed the experience; yet you may ask, "What has all this to do with reading?" So far in the child's life he or she is only beginning the basic preparation for learning to read by acquiring the foundation of language. During the child's first year language has been introduced. As yet, the youngster has little mastery of it, but he or she has been working on the vocal development needed for the special skills of reproducing sounds and has even begun to understand word permanence. The year-old baby exhibits interest in joining in conversations through babbling. By responding to the child's efforts, you are stimulating growth and giving dignity to his or her place in society.

What has been done in this first year to help the child develop a love of language, literature, and reading? The first lullabies and gentle talk have helped build a sense of security and love. Continued conversations along with nursery rhymes and little poems have helped the baby acquire an idea of language patterns and cadence and have encouraged him or her to experiment with linguistic sounds and rhythms. The fun of the simplest verse games and Mother Goose rhymes has involved the child in early literature and encouraged participation in language play and language fun. They have given the introduction to our great literary heritage that has come to us through the oral tradition. Little songs and verses have tickled a sense of rhythm and some may even have started an understanding of basic story structure as the child has waited for the excitement of the climax of rhymes like "Hickory, Dickory, Dock," "Jack and Jill," or "Pop Goes the Weasel." Books have been introduced as objects that bring shared pleasure. Fingerplays have helped with eye-hand coordination and have given the youngster a vehicle through which to express his or her response to rhymes. They have stimulated an enjoyment of rhythm--the basis of a love of poetry. Pleasurable experiences with language have emerged through personal attention from the most important people in the baby's life.

If in this very first year of your child's life you have helped him or her to develop an appreciation of the worth of literature and have stimulated language development, you have begun helping your child toward academic success. It was Plato who said, "the beginning is the most important part of the work."

Notes

[1]Quoted in Anna Curtis, "Mother Goose Bridges the Cultures," Grade Teacher, 73, No. 3, p. 56.

[2]Paul Hazard, Books, Children and Men, trans. Marguerite Mitchell (Boston: The Horn Book, Inc., 1944), p. 81.

[3]John Lind and Carol Hardgrove, "Lullabies," Children Today, 7, No. 4, pp. 7-8.

[4]Quoted in Sister Mary Joan Patricia, S.S.J., "Mother Goose to Homer," Catholic Library World, 23 (December 1951), p. 75.

[5]Mollie Smart and Russell C. Smart, Infants: Development and Relationship (New York: Macmillan Company, 1973), pp. 163-169.

[6]Ibid. p. 165.

[7]Arnold Arnold, Teach Your Child to Learn from Birth to School Age (Englewood Cliffs, NJ: Prentice-Hall, 1971), p. 63.

[8]Norah Montgomerie, This Little Pig Went to Market (New York: Franklin Watts, Inc., 1966), p. 17.

[9]Ibid. p. 39.

[10]Mary Ann Spencer Pulaski, Understanding Piaget: An Introduction to Children's Cognitive Development (New York: Harper & Row, 1971), pp. 18-20.

[11]Ira Gordon, Infant Experience (Columbus, OH: Charles E. Merrill Publishing Co., 1975), p. 74.

[12]Dorothy Aldis, comp., "Hiding," in Everything and Anything (New York: Minton, Balch & Co., 1927), p. 5.

Books Discussed in This Chapter

Baby Animals. New York: Grosset & Dunlap, n.d.
Baby's First Toys. New York: Grosset & Dunlap, n.d.
Bathtime. Alhambra, CA: Borden Publishing Co., 1976.
Briggs, Raymond. The White Land: A Picture Book of
 Traditional Rhymes and Verses. New York: Coward-
 McCann, 1963.
Brooke, Leslie. Ring O' Roses: A Nursery Rhyme Picture
 Book. New York: Frederick Warne & Co., 1977.
Broomfield, Robert. Animal Babies. Lawrence, MA:
 Chatto Bodley Jonathan, 1979.
_____. Toys. Lawrence, MA: Chatto Bodley Jonathan,
 1979.
Brown, Margaret Wise. Goodnight Moon. Illus. by Clement
 Hurd. New York: Harper & Row, 1947. (Paper-
 back. 1977.)
Carle, Eric. A Very Long Tail: A Folding Book. New
 York: Thomas Y. Crowell, 1972.
_____. The Secret Birthday Message. New York: Har-
 per & Row, 1972.
Chorao, Kay. The Baby's Lap Book. New York: E. P.
 Dutton, 1977.
Commins, Dorothy Berliner. Lullabies of the World. New
 York: Random House, 1967.
De Angeli, Marguerite. Book of Nursery and Mother Goose
 Rhymes. Garden City, NY: Doubleday and Company,
 1954.
Engvick, William, ed. Lullabies and Night Songs. Illus. by
 Maurice Sendak. New York: Harper & Row, 1965.
Ets, Marie Hall. Jay Bird. New York: The Viking Press,
 1974.
Fujikawa, Gyo. Babes of the Wild. New York: Grosset &
 Dunlap, 1977.
_____. Let's Eat. New York: Grosset & Dunlap, 1975.
_____. Mother Goose. New York: Grosset & Dunlap,
 1968.
_____. Sleepy Time. New York: Grosset & Dunlap,
 1975.
Gág, Wanda. The ABC Bunny. New York: Coward-
 McCann, 1933. (Paperback. New York: Coward-
 McCann, 1978.)

Goldsborough, June. Baby Animals, A Grosset Fold Book. New York: Grosset & Dunlap, 1981.

Grabianski, Janusz. Grabianski's Wild Animals. New York: Franklin Watts, Inc., 1969.

Hoban, Tana. One Little Kitten. New York: Greenwillow, 1979. (Paperback. New York: Scholastic Book Services, 1981.)

_____. Where Is It? New York: Macmillan Company, 1974. (Paperback. New York: Windmill, 1978.)

Kahn, Joan. You Can't Catch Me. Illus. by Elizabeth Bridgeman. New York: Harper & Row, 1976.

Kunhardt, Dorothy. Pat the Bunny. Racine, WI: Western Publishing Co., 1962.

_____. The Telephone Book. Racine, WI: Western Publishing Co., 1962.

Lines, Kathleen. Lavender's Blue. Illus. by Harold Jones. New York: Franklin Watts, Inc., 1954.

Matthiesen, Thomas. ABC, An Alphabet Book. New York: Grosset & Dunlap, 1981.

McNaught, Harry. Baby Animals. New York: Random House, 1976.

Mealtime. Alhambra, CA: Borden Publishing Co., 1976.

Miller, Carl, comp. Rockabye Baby: Lullabies from Many Nations and Peoples. New York: U.S. Committee for UNICEF, 1975.

Munari, Bruno. Who's There? Open the Door! Cleveland: World Publishing Co., 1957. (Paperback. New York: Philomel Books, 1980.)

Opie, Iona, and Peter Opie. The Oxford Nursery Rhyme Book. Additional illustrations by Joan Hassell. Oxford: Clarendon Press, 1955.

Oxenbury, Helen. Dressing. New York: Simon & Schuster, 1981.

_____. Family. New York: Simon & Schuster, 1981.

_____. Friends. New York: Simon & Schuster, 1981.

_____. Helen Oxenbury's ABC of Things. New York: Franklin Watts, Inc., 1972.

_____. Playing. New York: Simon & Schuster, 1981.

Pfloog, Jan. Kittens. New York: Random House, 1977.

_____. Puppies. New York: Random House, 1979.

Playtime. Alhambra, CA: Borden Publishing Co., 1976.

Porter, Elizabeth, comp. The Baby's Song Book. Illus. by William Stobbs. New York: Thomas Y. Crowell, 1972.

Reed, Gwendolyn, ed. Songs the Sandman Sings. Illus. by Peggy Skillen. New York: Atheneum Publishers, 1969.

Rey, H. A. Where's My Baby? Boston: Houghton Mifflin, 1956. (Paperback. n. d.)

Risom, Ole. I Am a Kitten. Illus. by Jan Pfloog. Racine, WI: Western Publishing Co., 1970.

_____. I Am a Puppy. Racine, WI: Western Publishing Co., 1970.

Rockwell, Anne, comp. Gray Goose and Gander & Other Mother Goose Rhymes. New York: Thomas Y. Crowell, 1980.

Rojankovsky, Feodor. The Great Big Animal Book. Racine, WI: Western Publishing Co., 1976.

_____. The Tall Book of Mother Goose. New York: Harper, 1942.

Schlesinger, Alice. Baby's Mother Goose. New York: Grosset & Dunlap, 1980.

Wells, Rosemary. Max's New Suit. New York: Dial Press, 1979.

_____. Max's Ride. New York: Dial Press, 1979.

_____. Max's Toys: A Counting Book. New York: Dial Press, 1979.

Williams, Garth. Baby Farm Animals. Racine, WI: Western Publishing Co., 1953.

_____. Baby's First Book. Racine, WI: Western Publishing Co., 1955.

Winn, Marie, and Allan Miller, eds. The Fireside Book of Children's Songs. Illus. by John Alcorn. New York: Simon & Schuster, 1966.

Wright, Blanche Fisher. The Real Mother Goose. Chicago: Rand-McNally & Co., 1916.

Further Reading for Parents

Almy, Millie, E. Chittenden, and Paula Miller. Young Children's Thinking: Studies of Some Aspects of Piaget's Theory. New York: Teachers College Press, 1966.

American Library Association. Let's Read Together. 4th ed. Chicago: American Library Association, 1981.

Applebee, Arthur N. The Child's Concept of Story. Chicago: The University of Chicago Press, 1978.

Arbuthnot, May Hill. Children's Reading in the Home. Glenview, IL: Scott, Foresman and Co., 1969.

Bader, Barbara. American Picturebooks from Noah's Ark to the Beast Within. New York: Macmillan Company, 1976.

Baring-Gould, William S., and Ceil Baring-Gould. The Annotated Mother Goose. New York: Charles N. Potter, 1962.
Beadle, Muriel. A Child's Mind: How Children Learn Dur-
ing the Critical Years from Birth to Age Five. Garden City, NY: Doubleday and Company, 1970.
Bettelheim, Bruno. The Uses of Enchantment: The Meaning
and Importance of Fairy Tales. New York: Alfred
A. Knopf, 1976.
_____, and Karen Zelan. On Learning to Read: The
Child's Fascination with Meaning. New York: Alfred
A. Knopf, 1982.
Billington, Elizabeth T., ed. The Randolph Caldecott Treas-
ury. New York: Frederick Warne & Co., 1978.
Butler, Dorothy. Babies Need Books. New York: Atheneum
Publishers, 1980.
_____, and Marie Clay. Reading Begins at Home: Pre-
paring Children for Reading Before They Go to School.
Auckland: Heinemann Educational Books, 1979.
Caplan, Frank, ed. The First Twelve Months of Life. New
York: Grosset & Dunlap, 1971. (Paperback. New
York: Bantam, 1978.)
_____. The Second Twelve Months of Life. New York:
Grosset & Dunlap, 1979. (Paperback. 1979.)
Chambers, Aidan. Introducing Books to Children. London:
Heinemann Educational Books, 1973.
Child Study Association of America. Reading with Your
Child through Age 5. New York: Child Study Asso-
ciation, 1972.
Chukovsky, Kornei. From Two to Five. Trans. and edited
by Mariam Norton. Berkeley: University of Califor-
nia Press, 1963. (Paperback. 1966.)
Cianciolo, Patricia. Illustrations in Children's Books. 2nd
ed. Dubuque, IA: William C. Brown, 1976.
_____. Picture Books for Children. 2nd ed. Chicago:
The American Library Association, 1981.
Coody, Betty. Using Literature with Young Children. 2nd
ed. Dubuque, IA: William C. Brown, 1979.
Cullinan, Bernice, and Carolyn W. Carmichael, eds. Liter-
ature and Young Children. Urbana, IL: National
Council of Teachers of English, 1977.
Duff, Annis. Bequest of Wings: A Family's Pleasures with
Books. New York: The Viking Press, 1944.
Durkin, Dolores. Children Who Read Early. New York:
Teachers College Press, 1966.
Favat, F. Andre. Child and Tale: The Origins of Interest.
Urbana, IL: National Council of Teachers of English,
1977.

Glazer, Joan L. Literature for Young Children. Columbus, OH: Charles E. Merrill Publishing Co., 1981.

Glazer, Susan Mandel. Getting Ready to Read: Creating Readers from Birth through Six. Englewood Cliffs, NJ: Prentice-Hall, 1980.

Gordon, Ira J. Baby Learning through Baby Play: A Parent's Guide for the First Two Years. New York: St. Martin's Press, 1970. (Paperback. 1970.)

_____. Child's Learning through Child's Play: Learning Activities for Two- and Three-Year-Olds. New York: St. Martin's Press, 1972. (Paperback. 1972.)

Haviland, Virginia. Children's Literature: A Guide to Reference Sources. Washington, D.C.: Library of Congress, 1966.

Hazard, Paul. Books, Children and Men. 4th ed. Trans. by Marguerite Mitchell. Boston: Horn Books, 1960.

Hopkins, Lee Bennett. The Best of Book Bonanza. New York: Holt, Rinehart & Winston, 1980.

Huck, Charlotte. Children's Literature in the Elementary Schools. 3rd ed. New York: Harper & Row, 1979.

Hürlimann, Bettina. Picture-Book World. Trans. and edited by Brian Alderson. Chicago: World Book, 1965.

Jacobs, Leland B., ed. Using Literature with Young Children. New York: Teachers College Press, 1965.

Johnson, Ferne, ed. Start Early for an Early Start: You and the Young Child. Chicago: American Library Association, 1976.

Justin, Sue, ed. Opening Doors for Preschool Children and Their Parents. 2nd ed. Chicago: American Library Association, 1981.

Klemin, Diana. The Art of Art for Children's Books. New York: Charles N. Potter, 1966.

Lamme, Linda. Raising Readers: A Guide to Sharing Literature with Young Children. New York: Walker and Company, 1980.

Lanes, Selma G. Down the Rabbit Hole: Adventures and Misadventures in the Realm of Children's Literature. New York: Atheneum Publishers, 1976.

Larrick, Nancy. A Parent's Guide to Children's Reading. 4th ed. Garden City, NY: Doubleday and Company, 1975.

Linder, Leslie L. A History of the Writings of Beatrix Potter. New York: Frederick Warne & Co., 1971.

MacCann, Donnarae, and Olga Richard. The Child's First Books: A Critical Study of Pictures and Text. New York: H. W. Wilson Co., 1973.

McGovern, Edythe M. They're Never Too Young for Books.
Los Angeles: MarVista Publishing, 1980.
Meeker, Alice M. Enjoying Literature with Children. New
York: The Odyssey Press, 1969.
Opie, Iona, and Peter Opie. The Oxford Dictionary of Nur-
sery Rhymes. New York: Oxford University Press,
1951.
_____, comps. The Oxford Nursery Rhyme Book. Illus.
by Joan Hassall. New York: Oxford University Press,
1955.
Pines, Maya. Revolution in Learning: The Years from
Birth to Six. New York: Harper & Row, 1967.
Smith, Lillian H. The Unreluctant Years: A Critical Ap-
proach to Children's Literature. New York: The
Viking Press, 1967. (Paperback. New York: Pen-
guin, 1977.)
Sutherland, Zena, Dianne L. Munson, and May Hill Arbuth-
not. Children and Books. 6th ed. Glenview, IL:
Scott, Foresman and Co., 1981.
Tinker, Miles. Preparing Your Child for Reading. New
York: Holt, Rinehart & Winston, 1971.
Trelease, Jim. The Read-Aloud Handbook. New York:
Penguin, 1982.
White, Dorothy M. Neal. Books Before Five. New York:
Oxford University Press, 1954.
Winn, Marie. The Plug-In Drug: Television, Children and
the Family. New York: The Viking Press, 1977.
Yardley, Alice. Young Children Thinking. Englewood
Cliffs, NJ: Citation Press, 1973.

Other Book Suggestions for This Age Level

Baby Animals. Illus. by T. Izawa and S. Hijikata. New
York: Grosset & Dunlap, 1970.
Baby's First Book. New York: Grosset & Dunlap, n.d.
Baby's Toys. Illus. by Alice Provensen and Martin Proven-
sen. Racine, WI: Western Publishing Co., 1972.
Broomfield, Robert. The Baby Animal ABC. New York:
Penguin, 1968.
Bruna, Dick. Dick Bruna's ABC Frieze. New York:
Methuen, 1976.
_____. Egg. New York: Methuen, 1975.
Cansdale, George. The Ladybird Book of Pets. Lough-
borough, Leicestershire, England: Wills & Hepworth,
1957.

Cellini. ABC. New York: Grosset & Dunlap, 1975.

Crowther, Robert. The Most Amazing Hide and Seek Alphabet Book. New York: The Viking Press, 1978.

Curry, Nancy. An Apple Is Red. Los Angeles: Bowmar Publishers, 1977.

Dunn, Judy. Things. Illus. by Phoebe Dunn and Tris Dunn. Garden City, NY: Doubleday and Company, 1968.

Farm Animals. Illus. by Art Seiden. New York: Grosset & Dunlap, 1962.

Fujikawa, Gyo. Babies. New York: Grosset & Dunlap, 1963.

_____. Gyo Fujikawa's A to Z Picture Book. New York: Grosset & Dunlap, 1974.

_____. Our Best Friends. New York: Grosset & Dunlap, 1977.

_____. Sleepytime. New York: Grosset & Dunlap, n.d.

_____. Surprise, Surprise. New York: Grosset & Dunlap, 1978.

Gagg, M. E. Puppies and Kittens. Illus. by H. Wolley. Pelham, NY: Merry Thoughts, 1966.

_____. The Zoo. Illus. by Barry Driscoll. Pelham, NY: Merry Thoughts, 1960.

Hall, Bill. What Ever Happens to Puppies? Illus. by Virginia Parsons. Racine, WI: Western Publishing Co., 1965.

Izawa, T. My First Book of Numbers. Rappongi Minato-ku, Tokyo: Zokeiska Publications, 1971.

Kittens. Illus. by Art Seiden. New York: Grosset & Dunlap, 1962.

Look at Us. London: Brimax Books, 1975.

Miller, J. P. Farmer John's Animals. New York: Random House, 1979.

Oxenbury, Helen. Beach Day. New York: Dial Press, 1982.

_____. Good Night, Good Morning. New York: Dial Press, 1982.

_____. Monkey See, Monkey Do. New York: Dial Press, 1982.

_____. Mother's Helper. New York: Dial Press, 1982.

Pfloog, Jan. Animals on the Farm. New York: Alfred A. Knopf, 1962.

Puppies. Illus. by Art Seiden. New York: Grosset & Dunlap, 1962.

Risom, Ole. I Am A Bear. Illus. by J. P. Miller. Racine, WI: Western Publishing Co., 1967.

_____. I Am a Bunny. Illus. by Richard Scarry. Racine, WI: Western Publishing Co., 1967.

_____. I Am A Mouse. Illus. by J. P. Miller. Racine, WI: Western Publishing Co., 1967.

Rojankovsky, Feodor. Animals on the Farm. New York: Alfred A. Knopf, 1967.

Scarry, Richard. Richard Scarry's Egg in the Hole Book. Racine, WI: Western Publishing Co., 1964.

_____. What Animals Do. Racine, WI: Western Publishing Co., 1968.

Seeing. London: Brimax Books, 1974.

Show Baby Opposites; Take a Long Look. London: Brimax Books, 1973.

Sukus, Jan, and William Dugan. The Shopping Book. Racine, WI: Western Publishing Co., 1970.

Wingfield, Ethel, and Harry Wingfield. A Ladybird First. Loughborough, Leicestershire, England: Ladybird Books, Ltd., 1970.

_____. A Ladybird Second. Loughborough, Leicestershire, England: Ladybird Books, Ltd., 1970.

Witte, Eve, and Pat Witte. The Touch Me Book. Illus. by Harlow Rockwell. Racine, WI: Western Publishing Co., 1961.

_____. Who Lives Here? Illus. by Aliki. Racine, WI: Western Publishing Co., 1961.

CHAPTER II

MOVING INTO LANGUAGE AND LITERATURE
--The Toddler Age--

Learning to Learn

Infants literally toddle out of babyhood somewhere between the ages of twelve and sixteen months. With hard-learned upright locomotion they free themselves of a great deal of restraint and are ready to explore their world. What an exciting time this is when a child seems

> To see a World in a Grain of Sand
> And a Heaven in a Wild Flower
> Hold Infinity in the palm of your hand
> And Eternity in an hour. [1]

With the ability to walk comes the first real push toward autonomy accompanied by true ambivalent behavior. Youngsters strike out boldly to explore as only they see fit, but the very next moment may find them clinging to parents, seeking reassurance about their security and their small egos. Parents are sometimes amazed at the boundless energy that these little ones possess and their determination to satisfy their curiosity. The world is theirs to explore, and they intend to do just that! They probe, pry, grab, taste, smell, and take apart whatever they can possess, not because of destructive urges, but because of their desire to know. This can be a trying time for both toddlers and their parents, yet it is a very important time, for the youngsters are learning to learn and acquiring the basic knowledge from contacts and experiences that will be the foundation for their developing ability to reason.

Parents, who may be feeling somewhat harassed as they try to learn to cope with this little bundle of energy that has replaced their sweet, cuddly baby often do not realize what a uniquely sensitive developmental stage the child is experiencing at this particular time. Research is showing the great importance of the linguistic, social, and intellectual skill development that takes place and also what harm can be done by thwarting a child's natural curiosity and growing sense of wonder.

We no longer accept the theory that a child has a fixed, inherited intellectual capacity. Modern research has shown that the child's early learning experiences will have a permanent effect on his or her mental abilities. "Bloom, after analysis of major longitudinal studies, concluded that general intelligence develops lawfully; that the greatest impact on IQ from environmental factors would probably take place between 1 and 5 with relatively little impact after age 8."[2] Most of this impact comes from the home and through everyday relationships with persons who provide the youngsters with care, love, and security. Because parents are the major figures in the child's environmental setting, they are the natural teachers at this crucial time. Fortunate is the child who is born into what is sometimes called the "culturally abundant environment," but even more fortunate is the youngster whose parents enjoy helping him or her in the continuing search for knowledge.

In her book How to Raise a Brighter Child, Joan Beck emphasizes the vital importance of the child's home environment during the toddler stage. She discusses the long-term Harvard Preschool Project in which researchers headed by Dr. Burton White are conducting ongoing research which is aimed at obtaining accurate, basic knowledge about the ideal development of young children. Two of the important conclusions that they have reached are these: "The most critical age in the development of superior, competent children is between one and three years. The most crucial requirements for competent growth are freedom to explore in a safe environment and encouragement and help in learning language."[3]

If we seriously consider the findings from the Harvard project or those of many other researchers in the field of early childhood development, we can no longer justify putting the toddler into a playpen to ensure the youngster's safety and our own sanity. To give a child "freedom to explore in a safe environment" we must "child-proof" the house to remove hazards and then let the young investigator explore, adding to and enriching the environment so that it will be stimulating and interesting. By confining a toddler in a small area we are restricting his or her curiosity, dulling interest in learning and in powers of sustained concentration, and teaching the youngster to live with boredom. Certainly this is a poor preparation for academic success.

Of course this does not mean that successful parents hover over their children constantly. Instead, they are available when they are needed and often encourage the youngsters' interest in the environment, but they give children opportunities to make their own discoveries and to think for themselves.

Since help and encouragement in learning the language is a basic consideration for competent growth at this time, providing the child with a rich verbal background is one of the most important contributions that parents can make toward a child's future success. The verbal facility that children acquire in the pre-reading developmental stage will determine to a great extent their comprehension of the printed page when they are ready to read.

According to the eminent child psychologist Bruno Bettelheim, "Recent research has confirmed that a child's academic success or failure (so largely dependent on his reading skills) is closely related to his early experiences with speech at home." Ideally these early experiences with speech begin when the child is a tiny baby with "conversations," rhymes, songs, and shared fun. Gradually the baby learns to contribute in his or her way to the communicative interaction. During the toddler stage, a child begins to feel a real need for learning the language and responds positively to the help and encouragement given by caring adults. "If the child is to realize his potential to talk--and his potential to read-- the necessary skills must be encouraged." Bettelheim says that the best way to teach children to talk is to encourage them to say anything they choose and to reinforce and praise them for their attempts to pronounce a word, be the attempts ever so clumsy. Giving language a deep emotional significance makes the hard work of learning to control sensori-motor actions and refine imitative and listening skills well worthwhile. [4]

Rates of development vary and we should not assume that youngsters will develop a particular motor, social, or language skill at any given time. Children set their own timetables. They seem to have critical growth periods when they will leap forward with new skills, then they may reach a plateau when progress is much slower. Some parents enjoy stimulating the child as long as they can see real development taking place, but then lose interest when gains are not obvious. What is needed is continual interest in the little person's world with reinforcement and encouragement given by the parents whatever the developmental stage may be. Enjoyment of each stage of learning is necessary if we are to stimulate children in a happy, healthful manner. Games, books, songs, and basic language learning should all be fun.

Absorbing and Experiencing the Language

Children usually approach their first birthday with a vocabulary of from three to ten words which perhaps only the parents can understand. For the most part the young toddler's conversations are still conducted in pure jargon. If this is all that is expected of the youngster, there will be slow progress; but if the child finds that attempts to use words are rewarded, vocabulary will grow steadily. The best approach is to surround small children with carefully spoken language. Talk with them a great deal, sing songs, recite nursery rhymes, share books, and explain what is going on in their world. Children will enjoy the jingle of rhymes and the pleasant experiences of communication even though their contributions are mostly jargon. Little by little they will pick up the words, especially if their efforts are appreciated. It is interesting to note how much youngsters who are entering the toddler stage understand speech. They know their names and the names of significant people in their environment. They will often come when called or look for a toy or pet upon request. Listening is a very important part of language development at this time. Children understand many words and even short sentences long before they attempt to use the words. The first months of the second year seem to be a period when children are absorbing and experiencing language in preparation for the time when they will actually be able to use it. It may be that communication is not as fascinating as the new independence that has come with the exploration which is now possible with newly developed skills of locomotion; but very soon a child will see possibilities of controlling his or her environment through language.

Some children become interested in books at a much earlier age than do others. The child who has been surrounded by books and sees parents reading has a decided advantage, but even this may not be enough to entice some very active toddlers who may give a bit of attention to the colors of the pages, but quickly drop a book for something more manipulable if they are not given adult help. The pictures may not make sense to the child who may even be holding the books upside down. Do not think that pictures will explain themselves to a twelve- to eighteen-month-old toddler if he or she has had little experience with books. However, if an adult takes time to show the child that this is a ball, this is a doll, and so on, the results can be exciting.

Early in the second year of life children become interested in labeling both people and objects. Such labeling seems to give them a sense of order in their world. Alert parents can help satisfy this need and of course contribute to vocabulary growth by taking time to help children attach names to whatever interests them.

Pointing also becomes an important communicative device at this time. Children may start this activity when they are as young as nine months, but vocalization along with the pointing usually does not occur until they are about fourteen months old. Pointing helps children express interest in their immediate environment and also in pictures in their books. Usually pointing leads to labeling and subsequent language growth. It also promotes shared interests and is a basis for picture book appreciation.

The transfer from the labeling of things to the naming of objects in pictures is a real step in enjoyment and involvement with books. Such identification can become a great discovery game and is a first step toward reading. This pre-reading skill should begin long before children have the necessary vocabulary and attention span to listen to a simple story.

Sometime in the second year children begin to transfer from a picture in a book back to the object represented. For example, little Amy studied her picture book with great care, pointing to the pictures and listening as her mother helped her label them. She gave each page careful thought. Suddenly her face became quite animated as she looked at a picture of a doll. With an air of great self-assurance she ran and found her doll which she put by the book. Next came a picture of a ball which brought forth the same reaction. Finally she woke up the family's pet dog, a sixty-pound German Shorthair Pointer, and with all the determination that only a toddler can show, she tried to drag him over to sit by the picture of a dog in her book. She was indeed proud of this new association she had made between her book and the real world!

Books used for the identification game of labeling and naming should be sturdy. Board books are still helpful at this time because children want to possess the pictures they are studying. Books for labeling do not need a text. Tiny children supply their own texts just by labeling pictures, and a few months later they may be able to add an action word to the name of an object, making very simple two-word sentences like, "Bus go," or "Doggie run." This is involvement with literature and also language development for a toddler.

In selecting books of this type you will still want to watch for large, colorful, uncluttered pictures of objects in the toddler's own world. Someone has said that pictures for very young children must be as real as their own fingers and toes. Almost any picture book can be used for identification and vocabulary building, but the ones that a child in the early toddler stage will probably find most interesting are simple books that show clear, well-defined pictures. Little rhymes for texts can be captivating, but very young toddlers need little or nothing in the way of plot. For appropriate literature in this "look-say" period you will want to rely on some of the better board books along with very simple picture books. Here are a few promising books that you may want to consider:

Richard Scarry's Early Words is a good early identification book. It tells about Fanny Bunny's house and activities on a toddler's level of interest. The pictures are bright and simple. The book is sturdy enough to withstand a great deal of wear.

Things to See, a Child's World of Familiar Objects with pictures by Thomas Matthiesen has fine color photographs for identification and enjoyment.

I Spy by Lucille Ogle and Tina Thoburn, illustrated by Joe Kaufman, is a tall, narrow book with clear pictures on heavy paper that is durable. There are just two objects to a page. This helps a very young child avoid the confusion that may be caused by several pictures on a page.

Don't miss the Dick Bruna Series of sturdy little board books. They have very simple, flat, bright pictures done

in the primary colors. The line drawings make recognition
of objects and situations easy for tiny children. Some of
this series are actually very simple concept books. Two
fine Dick Bruna books for a young toddler are The Apple
and B Is for Bear. Because of their simplicity and charm
these books may very well become real treasures to your
small child.

Richard Scarry's What Animals Do might help young children start to think in terms of action words along with the
labels they are able to put on the animals in the pictures.
The simplest of the picture dictionaries can also help with
the identification games that toddlers love to play. After
children progress beyond the first labeling stage, the "Adam-
and-Eve stage, " as May Hill Arbuthnot called it, they can
begin the game of finding certain objects pictured on a page.
This, of course, leads easily into expanding and elaborating
upon comments made about pictures.

Much of the charm of reading to your child may be tem-
porarily lost when your son or daughter has reached the early toddler stage. Suddenly the little person becomes involved
with the whole activity in rather a primitive way by grabbing,
holding, and even chewing the books; however, involvement is
what we want, and we have to go along with the process.
For a time books are more toys than they are literature.
One great interest that develops somewhere around the age
of fourteen months is in the manipulative skill of page turning. At first, eye-hand coordination is such that a child
will turn several pages at a time, but eventually this skill
is refined so that a book can be leafed through, page-by-
page. The youngster is quite pleased with this accomplishment; in fact, turning pages seems to become his or her
one great literary pursuit for a time. This can be frustrating when you try to read and are lucky to get just a phrase
completed before the page is flipped. But it is all a part
of the growing process and eventually the contents of a book
again become more interesting than the manipulation of pages.

Toddlers give their books hard use. The supply of special books that resist mutilation is limited and includes only
a small amount of the good literature that we want to share
with youngsters. Also, children need to handle and experience real books. Fortunately they are great imitators and
as they watch adults treat books with care, they usually
learn rather quickly to do the same, especially if they have
learned to associate the reading of books with a warm,

comfortable, special time. However, accidents do happen and very special books still need to be saved for sharing with an adult.

On the other hand, we do not want to expose youngsters to only the least-expensive books with blatant illustrations simply because there would be no great loss if these books were torn. To encourage a sense of wonder and joy in young children we want to surround them with easily accessible, beautifully illustrated literature that will become a part of their lives. If a child has nothing but "dime-store flats," those inexpensive, usually poorly composed books that are readily available in supermarkets, we can hardly expect him or her to develop tastes for the best of art and literature. We have to accept the fact that books may not last forever, at least not in their material form; but shared literature, even for the very young child, often lives on in the listener's mind for a lifetime after the books themselves are gone.

On the Brink of Speech

When a youngster reaches the age of eighteen months, he or she will probably have a vocabulary consisting of some fifteen to twenty-five words; however, the child's verbal comprehension will greatly exceed the speaking vocabulary. Do not hesitate to read any book that your toddler seems to enjoy. A small child's apparent understanding of subjects in which he or she is interested will sometimes amaze you. As you go through the books, you can help expand vocalization by discussing the pictures with your toddler, reading what text he or she wants to hear, and, above all, by enjoying books together. These are experiences that are leading toward reading readiness, and this fine, secure feeling of sharing books is building a positive attitude toward learning.

Around the eighteenth month there is usually a real spurt in linguistic development. The child becomes more adept at vocalizing sounds and more astute in learning the names of things. Up to this point the youngster's thinking has been in images: the word is simply the embodiment of an object or an action. Now words are gradually becoming thought symbols.

In "A Primer of Literacy" Bruno Bettelheim says, "Learning to talk and to understand speech enables the child to communicate his thoughts and feelings to others, and to check the validity of his views against their responses.   Learning to read builds directly on this achievement. "[5]

According to Fred M. Hechinger, Education Editor of the New York Times, "Skill with words and comprehension of ideas that sprout from thoughts behind words are probably the most essential prerequisites for formal learning. "[6]

Communication with children in a way that will establish the very base of their language development might sound like a frightening undertaking if we did not realize that such communication is simply the natural fostering of children's interest in what is around them.   Such communication is not a serious task, but an interesting and rewarding experience for those who care about youngsters' thinking and reasoning powers and are willing to offer children the personal dignity and encouragement that are always needed.

Naturally communication with a small child takes place casually and is never considered a lesson; rather it is a happy sharing time for all participants.   Anytime we become tense about a learning situation with a toddler, we may very well have done far more harm than good for the child.   We should encourage him or her in a positive way, correctly repeating the words that the child is attempting, matching words and extending phrases along with giving reassurance and appreciation of the efforts the child has made. Such feedback should be immediate.   The child's attention span is short at this time and first conversations are not lengthy.

An eighteen-month-old toddler usually uses his or her own name and recognizes the names of members of the family and pets.   This is a fine time to make a small photo album or scrapbook for your son or daughter, putting in pictures of things that are of real importance to the youngster. These can be mounted on cardboard and perhaps covered with plastic to help protect them.   Such a book is inexpensive and can have real meaning to a tiny person.   It gives stature to the child, and think of the verbalization it can generate!

One mother used such pictures very effectively with her twenty-month-old daughter, Megan, when they came from Hawaii to visit grandparents in California.   Megan had a little trouble adjusting to the new situation, but fortunately her mother had brought along her collection of pictures of her

daddy and her home. Whenever Megan seemed upset, her
mother got out the pictures and they discussed them. This
seemed to reassure Megan that her daddy and the things she
loved at home were still in existence.

By now new experiences and the child's ever-expanding
world of interests help bring new meaning to the first literature of jingles and nursery rhymes. The first appeal of these
little rhymes was their musical cadence and rhythm, but now
they are beginning to provide games and activities that toddlers love. Interest in "Pat-a-Cake" is still strong and forms
of "Peek-a-Boo" are becoming more sophisticated. The child
will risk longer periods of hiding to experience the joy of reunion with a loved one. "Ring Around the Rosy, " "I'm a
Little Teapot, " and "The Mulberry Bush" are all fun games
to try with your toddler.

Children who are eighteen months of age may be able to
name three or more parts of their bodies. There are many
rhymes and fingerplays that can help this language development. Examples of such rhymes are to be found in almost
any fingerplay book. Here are a few that you might try with
your toddler to start the activity:

Head and Shoulders

Head and shoulders, knees and toes, knees and toes,
Head and shoulders, knees and toes, knees and toes,
Eyes and ears and mouth and nose,
Head and shoulders, knees and toes, knees and toes.
(This can be said or sung slowly at first; later you
may like to speed up the tempo each time you repeat
the verse.)

* * *

Here Are My Ears

Here are my ears.
Here is my nose.
Here are my fingers.
Here are my toes.
Here are my eyes,
Both open wide.
Here is my mouth,
With white teeth inside.
Here is my tongue,

That helps me speak.
Here is my chin,
And here are my cheeks.
Here are my hands,
That help me play.
Here are my feet,
For walking today.
(Actions suit words.)

* * *

Me

My hands upon my head I place,
On my shoulders, on my face,
On my knees, and at my side,
Then behind me they will hide.
Then I raise them up SO high,
'Till they almost reach the sky.
Swiftly count them--1, 2, 3,
And see how quiet they can be.
(Follow words with actions; at the end bring hands
slowly down to lap.)

* * *

Two Little

Two little feet go tap, tap, tap.
Two little hands go clap, clap, clap.
A quiet little leap up from my chair.
Two little arms reach high in the air.
Two little feet go jump, jump, jump.
Two little fists go thump, thump, thump.
One little body goes round, round, round.
And one little child sits quietly down.
(Actions suit words.)

* * *

Busy Hands

Hands on shoulders, hands on knees,
Put them behind you, if you please.
Raise hands high up in the air,
Down at your sides, now touch your hair.
Hands at side now you may place,

Touch your elbows, now your face.
Raise hands high up as before,
Now you may clap 1, 2, 3, 4.
Now sit down, hands folded once more.
Eyes to the front, feet on the floor.
(Actions go with the words.)

* * *

My Wiggles

I wiggle my fingers,
I wiggle my toes.
I wiggle my shoulders,
I wiggle my nose.
Now the wiggles are out of me,
And I'm just as still as I can be.
(Wiggles go with words.)

Fingerplay books are a good investment at this time.
They can give you and your toddler hours of fun; they will
help the child with eye-hand coordination and also promote
interest in poetry. One of the most inexpensive, yet complete paperback books of fingerplays is Ring a Ring O' Roses,
available from the Flint Public Library, 1026 East Kearsley,
Flint, Michigan 48502. [7]

Here are other books you may enjoy that are available in
book stores or at the library:

Emilie Poulsson's Finger Plays for Nursery and Kindergarten, published late in the last century, is still a favorite
book today. It includes a set of eighteen fingerplays ranging
from "All for Baby" to "Santa Claus." Rhymes are accompanied by elaborate black-and-white drawings that show positions for hands and fingers for the various actions. Complete musical scores are given.

In Finger Plays and Action Rhymes, Frances E. Jacobs
undertook to develop a companion volume to the Poulsson
book with more contemporary topics. Photographs show
finger/hand positions and several rhymes have musical accompaniments.

Marc Brown has included some old standard verses in
Finger Rhymes. A small child will appreciate his illustrations in which he presents one rhyme on a two-page spread.

Some of the fingerplays in Do Your Ears Hang Low ? by Tom Glazer would be enjoyed by your toddler although others in this collection should be used when the child is a bit older. The book is an interesting selection of fifty fingerplays with musical accompaniments.

This would be a good time to purchase some new nursery rhyme books, or at least to borrow a few from the local library. Your child will enjoy some different verses and new pictures. He or she will still need simple, clear pictures. Just one verse to a page along with corresponding illustrations is still a good arrangement for a toddler, who can become confused with several pictures on one page. Remember to watch for rhymes in which the child's name can be substituted in the verse.

Mother Goose; Or the Old Nursery Rhymes by Kate Greenaway is a small, "fit-in-the-child's-hand" book of forty-four rhymes. One rhyme appears on a page with full-color illustrations. Greenaway's Edwardian characters are quaint and stiff. Lovely details in the pictures make this a charming collection.

Brian Wildsmith's Mother Goose: A Collection of Nursery Rhymes is a large book with one rhyme on a page and includes many of the old standard rhymes. The pictures offer a rich, vivid artistic experience but might be confusing to very young children because of their somewhat abstract nature. You might be interested in trying this book to see if your child is ready for Wildsmith's exciting art.

Mother Goose: Seventy-seven Verses with Pictures by Tasha Tudor is a good selection for the younger child. Tudor's watercolor and pen-and-ink illustrations are realistic and exquisitely drawn in soft colors. Again, we have one rhyme with its illustration given on a page. Most of the rhymes are brief with plenty of action in the pictures.

For a change of pace, you and your toddler may enjoy some of the nursery rhyme books that are developed around one particular theme or are single-verse editions. For example, Mother Goose: If Wishes Were Horses and Other Rhymes by Susan Jeffers is a collection of rhymes featuring horses: "If Wishes Were Horses, " "Ride Away! Ride Away!, " "This Is the Way the Ladies Ride, " "Ride a Cock Horse to Banbury Cross, " and many, many more. Jeffers' illustrations of horses and riders show plenty of action and often take up an entire page. One rhyme may continue across a full page and onto the next. Both black and white children appear in the pictures. The drawings of the animals are particularly realistic.

Hush Little Baby: A Folk Lullaby, illustrated by Aliki, has brightly colored double-page spreads showing the story of this old lullaby with the scored melody.

Paul Galdone has developed several verses into separate one-rhyme book form. Your toddler will probably enjoy The History of Simple Simon, The House that Jack Built, Old Mother Hubbard and Her Dog, and Tom, Tom, the Piper's Son. Galdone's large, colorful pictures show a great deal of fun and action, and because of their simplicity they appeal to very young children.

Keep watching for nursery rhyme books that seem to appeal to your youngster, ones that you can enjoy sharing. These books can provide fun for a toddler and at the same time promote vocalization, stretch attention spans, promote awareness of the storybook world, and increase enjoyment of rhythmical responses. Even more important is the interaction they promote between the child and the caring adults who are helping the toddler develop happy attitudes and build a good self-concept. The key to such accomplishments is fun and play for all participants.

At this age youngsters begin to recognize characters in the rhymes. They feel quite important when they can supply the names as an adult reads the rhyme. Supplying a name or a word to a verse as the person reading the rhyme points to the word in the book can be a child's first oral reading experience. This is just the involvement that we want as we begin our attempts to interest children in reading.

Your child may start being somewhat selective and request certain rhymes, bringing the reader back to them and insisting on "Dumpy Dumpy" or "Down the Hill, " for example. Of course, such requests should be honored and the special interest should be appreciated.

Even though language skills are developing at an amazing rate, the eighteen-month-old child still babbles, often mixing his or her personal jargon with understandable words. Often toddlers will go about their play activities talking to themselves in ways that sound as though they are reciting favorite nursery rhymes. However, when one listens closely, very few words are recognizable even though all the rhythm and cadence is very clear. This age is probably the height of complicated intonations in the art of babbling. Many syllables will be strung together and the inflections used are so like that of regular speech that one often feels that the child is carrying on a casual conversation in some incomprehensible language.

Caring adults help toddlers build vocabulary and casually invite them into the language of their culture by supplying the grammatical, phonetic, and semantic feedback that will encourage them to expand their skills. Remember that we do not teach children language, we simply help them to experience it. There are different, simple techniques to be used with picture books that will promote involvement and extend expressive language as a youngster labels objects and attempts to discuss the pictures. Parents should be alert to reinforce children's interests and make them feel that their observations are important so that they will want to continue verbalization. When small children are trying to discuss pictures or everyday experiences, parents should not only echo what the youngsters have said, but they should also expand the ideas using complete sentences. If a youngster is still in the labeling stage and points to a dog in a picture, giving the appropriate name, the mother may say, "Yes, it is a big, brown dog that is running fast," always keeping her conversation on a level close to the child's thinking and matching words the child has used, yet extending the meaning. This gives the youngster new words and continues the language experience with the parent acting as the language model. The toddler age truly is a critical period, yet parents can give their children the advantage of a rich, verbal background in very pleasant ways.

Real Verbalization Begins

Although a one-year-old infant probably has a vocabulary limited to a very few words that can be understood by only the most ardent of admirers, the first half of the second year is marked by great gains in comprehension of the language. It is in the second half of the second year that real verbalization begins to take place. At the age of twenty-one months a child's vocabulary will probably have developed to include about twenty words that can be enunciated clearly, and phonetic production is developing rapidly.

The actual reading that you do with your child at this point may be quite disjointed because the toddler wants to get into the act with you. Do read with enthusiasm, and employ all the tricks you can think of to arrest the child's attention. Substitute the child's name and names of household pets whenever this seems logical in the book texts. Both you and your listener will laugh at the sound effects you will find yourself incorporating into the reading if you relax and really have fun sharing literary sessions with a toddler. Many simple books about animals are available. If the text does not include "animal language," make up your own, encouraging your child to assist. At this time we are not concerned with accuracy of text but vocabulary building and just plain fun that will convince small children that books are a great source of enjoyment.

Martha Alexander's Pigs Say Oink has been called "a first book of sounds." The detailed pictures in this book are done in soft, lovely colors. The animal sounds are printed next to the pictures, but this part of the text will not be needed after your toddler has learned to contribute his or her sound effects. Both you and your child can have a great deal of fun with this selection.

Alvin Tresselt's Wake Up Farm, which is illustrated by Robert Duvoisin, would make a fine "noise book." This is one you will not want to miss. Toddlers appreciate the big pictures done in sunny, bright colors. The text follows along, telling what the farm animals say as they wake up. Last of all, the little farm boy wakes up and joins in the activities.

In Margaret Wise Brown's The Country Noisy Book, illustrated by Leonard Weisgard, a little dog named Muffin goes to the country and hears all the sounds for the first time. Toddlers will enjoy contributing sound effects for the text.

Mischa Richter's book Quack? will provide much fun and participation in reading. Each time the duck says, "Quack?" to an animal, it responds with its characteristic sound. The child will enjoy trying to get the right response to the questioning quack.

Don't limit yourself to only animal books for sound effects. Books like Crash, Bang, Boom and Gobble, Growl, Grunt, both by Peter Spier, will bring forth peals of laughter from your young listener if you can find the stamina to read them with enthusiasm.

Hullabaloo ABC is Beverly Cleary's picture book. It was illustrated by Earl Thollander. In it two children go about the farm listening to machinery songs, animal sounds, and various noises of the activities around them. A toddler will enjoy the active, humorous pictures and the onomatopoeia all combined to make a different ABC book. In another year or two, he or she will appreciate the humor that Cleary and Thollander bring to the book.

In Noisy Book, another book by Margaret Wise Brown, illustrated by Leonard Weisgard, the dog, Muffin, has his eyes bandaged. He hears all the sounds around. In reading this book you can let your listener supply the key words as Muffin hears "tick tock," "buzz buzz," "meow," and other sounds and tries to decide what they are.

The Father of Kindergarten, Friedrich Froebel, said, "What a child imitates he begins to understand." Perhaps noisy books provide ways to build a lot of understanding; at least such books initiate a lot of fun and participation in reading.

Children must go at their own pace with books. A twenty-month-old child's enjoyment of a picture book may amount to simply matching pictures, seeing the same object on consecutive pages. The toddler may still be at the identification stage and not as yet be able to realize that there is a little story unfolding in the subsequent pictures; but this does not mean that the child is not enjoying books on his or her comprehension level.

An early growth of imaginative powers comes when a toddler tries to imitate what is being shown in a picture--eating food, drinking from a cup, or driving a car. All such activities show a development of the use of symbols to stir creativity and stimulate little pretend games.

Books for toddlers come in a variety of forms and shapes, but many people like to give small children very small books that seem to fit their hands. These do save tearing and are easy to hold. Classic examples of these little books are the ones about the Little Family written and illustrated by Lois Lenski. The simple drawings in these books have a great appeal for children. Some of the texts are too difficult for

a toddler, yet it is surprising how they often attract very
young children. Perhaps they are simply information or experience books to the tiny child. Cowboy Small tells what a
cowboy does. The Little Farm gives a picture of a farmer's
life as it might be perceived by a youngster. In The Little
Auto, the man drives his little car, stops at the signal light,
gets gas, and probably does just the things that a toddler
feels he or she would do if it were possible to drive a car.
Whatever the charm of these books, they must seem very
realistic and interesting to children for they have been popular for years.

Little Jessica and her mother traveled on a small plane
between two islands in Hawaii. The pilot was required to do
everything for the passengers of his plane from loading their
luggage to acting as tour guide. Jessica insisted on calling
him "Pilot Small" until finally her mother had to explain that
the Lois Lenski book The Little Airplane was Jessica's favorite reading material.

There is even a song book that goes with the Lenski stories entitled Songs of Mr. Small. Clyde Robert Bulla supplied
the music. These are songs to extend and enrich the books
in the series. Some can be enjoyed by toddlers; others will
appeal more to slightly older children.

"Tiny books for tiny people" seem to be increasing in
popularity. Here is a sampling of some of the better books
and series that your toddler will probably enjoy:

John Burningham has a delightful series of small books
that could become your child's first storybooks. They have
simple, clear pictures and short texts about familiar and immediate life experiences of very young children. The Baby,
The Blanket, The Dog, and The Friend are a few of the
books in this series. Once you introduce these books, you
may find that your little boy or girl will become intrigued
with them. John Burningham is a favorite author/illustrator
in the world of young children.

Appley Dapply's Nursery Rhymes is a lovely introduction
to the Beatrix Potter classics. The tiny pictures illustrate
some of the old favorite rhymes all in the usual nursery
rhyme style. Potter always insisted that her books be published in a diminutive format so that they would fit the hands
of small children. If you feel that your child is ready for
other wonderful little Potter books, you might start with The
Story of a Fierce Bad Rabbit and The Story of Miss Moppet.

You may have already purchased some of the lovely little board books done by Gyo Fujikawa when your youngster was just beginning to want to hold and handle books. Now is the time to buy others in this series. All are illustrated in a quaint, beautiful fashion. Some you might like to consider at this time are Come Out and Play, My Animal Friends, Make-Believe, Fairyland, and Here I Am.

Another book that toddlers often appreciate is Mary Ann's Mud Day by Janice M. Udry, illustrated by Martha Alexander. In it, Mary Ann announces, "This is going to be a mud day," and so it is. She has great experiences and makes many mud creations which please her very much. Her mother has a different reaction.

Freight Train by Donald Crews is larger in size. It is an excellent example of an informational book for toddlers. Freight Train was an Honor Book for the Caldecott Award of 1979. Its big, expressive pictures leave no doubt in a child's mind that they depict a train. Even at this time when children must have representational pictures, Crews adds excitement by using bright, somewhat blurred colors when the train is moving fast; however, very small children have no trouble catching the meaning and the movement of these illustrations.

Another book of similar size and format is Each Peach Pear Plum by Janet and Allan Ahlberg. This is an "I Spy" book that can give small children a feeling of accomplishment when they are able to use their knowledge of nursery rhymes or folk characters to guess the new people that will appear as one turns the pages. The pictures are delightful.

Books of this kind that are on a small child's level of understanding are a wonderful tool for the development of vocabulary and language comprehension. They broaden a youngster's experiences and help satisfy a basic need to understand his or her world.

As you go through a book with a toddler, let the child take whatever time he or she wants to absorb the pictures and the bit of text that goes along with them. The youngster will probably be full of questions. These questions need answers, but not lectures. Use the child's interest and questions to encourage further speech and stimulate the development of ideas that perhaps will lead to further questions.

Almost any reading materials that interest your little girl or boy, even parents' magazines, can provide pictures for discussion. Be alert to use whatever is at hand. Check the library and you will probably be able to find picture books that deal with subjects that are of special interest to your child.

A book that could stimulate a great deal of verbalization is The House by Carol Watson and Colin King. The illustrations in this book are brightly colored and sharply defined. The pages alternate, with one showing different parts of the house and many objects to identify; the following page gives some activity that goes on in that part of the house. There are humorous touches that add to interest in the book. The Town by the same author and illustrator has about four uncluttered pictures to a page. Everything is labeled so that the youngster can have the experience of seeing the word printed by the picture that he or she might label or discuss.

Scarry's On the Farm is a kind of small child's farm encyclopedia. This book includes questions and asks the child to point to different objects.

Eleanor Schick's City in the Summer is one of many books that could be used by city children for identification and discussion of things within their environment. There are large double-page spreads with some text included. City Cat and Country Cat by Marlies Merk Najaka are two little board books showing scenes of the city and country with a bit of text that tells of the cat's experiences.

Richard Scarry's Best Word Book Ever has large, very busy pages showing animal characters having some funny experiences as they learn about colors, numbers, the alphabet, seasons, work, parts of the body, and a whole storehouse of information. This is a book covering many concepts. It is a good identification book for those children who will not be confused by the great number of pictures and activities on a page.

As you talk with toddlers and discuss their books, remember that even though they are usually uninhibited, enthusiastic participants in the language learning process, they can be discouraged with too much correction. Parents need to be subtle in their teaching. Resist the temptation to correct pronunciation continually. Appreciate the youngster's attempts to use new words. If, for example, the child should point to an animal and say, "Oc res," don't deflate him or her with, "Say rhinoceros carefully." Just take a casual approach, saying, "Yes, it is a rhinoceros." In this way you give the child positive reinforcement for trying a difficult word along with the opportunity to hear the word pronounced correctly. Take the same approach when children are first combining words into sentences. Watch that you are not continually correcting sentence structure, but reword what a child says in correct usage, acting as a model, hoping that through imitation the youngster will gradually adopt the correct structure and usage. With such an approach you do not frustrate the child in his or her efforts. Discussion of picture books affords many opportunities for such subtle language development.

ABC and number books, many of which are actually variants of nursery rhymes, are popular with two-year-old children, perhaps because most of them are simple with brightly colored illustrations of objects that are easy to identify. Of course we are not expecting the toddler to start reciting the ABC's or to begin counting at this time, but it is a good idea to start pointing to the letters and even tracing over them with your finger as you share the book just to start your young listener's interest in the shapes of letters. These books have illustrations that are great for labeling and some even have little pint-sized stories. Since toddlers are usually much more intrigued by rhythmical, flowing language than they are by meaning, try reading Edward Lear's jingly alphabet in Nonsense Books, which starts:

> A was once an apple pie,
> > Pidy
> > Widy
> > Tidy
> > Pidy
> > Nice Insidy
> > Apple Pie![8]

It chants itself through the alphabet in a way that has entranced young listeners for many years. The first of Lear's Nonsense Books were published in 1846. They are still being reproduced. See if your child won't think some of the verses are great fun.

For a much more modern text there is Apples to Zippers: An Alphabet Book by Patricia Ruben. This book is illustrated with clear photographs that show objects which can be recognized easily by a very young child.

In Bruno Munari's ABC the alphabet is presented with large, clear pictures for each letter. The very short text ties the pictures together stressing alliteration. A fly buzzes across the pages. Toddlers may find its performance as interesting as the pictures themselves.

John Burningham's ABC shows fine double-page spreads. In every instance both the upper- and lower-case letters are given plus one word that begins with each letter. Opposite the letter page with its word there is either one picture or a collection of pictures of the object named. The bright illustrations will interest very young children.

Garth Williams presents his usual exciting, beautiful pictures in a large book entitled Big Golden Animal ABC. Like most of his books, this one holds special charms for both small children and their parents.

Brian Wildsmith's ABC also has large, exciting colorful pictures that could be just right for your toddler. His Brian Wildsmith's 1, 2, 3's will have a similar appeal.

Susanna Gretz's Teddy Bears ABC and Teddy Bears, One to Ten both probably have real appeal to tiny children because of their fascination with teddy bears; also these bears are interesting and do what toddlers expect them to do.

One, Two, Three to the Zoo by Eric Carle is a book "to grow on." The toddler will enjoy just looking at the animals, but later, the fact that at the bottom of each picture there is an engine pulling cars carrying the animals that have been shown on previous pages will add to the counting experiences. Carle's My Very First Book of Numbers would be a better starting number book because in it number concepts are presented in a simpler manner.

Tana Hoban's excellent illustrations for Count and See make this book a fine counting book for small children with its clear-cut, black-and-white photographs of familiar objects. My Big Golden Counting Book by Lilian Moore will probably be a real favorite with your youngster. There are rhymes for each picture and the illustrations are done in Garth Williams' style.

Children are often exposed to short cumulative plots through number books. In a story like Carle's The Rooster Who Set Out to See the World there are two cats, three frogs, four turtles, etc., following along. Carle even adds an extra counting device at the top of the page showing the numbered animals. As night comes, the animals (and the numbers) begin to drop off from the pictures.

Chicken Little, Count-to-Ten by Margaret Friskey is the story of a small chick who keeps asking groups of animals how to get a drink of water. Each time Chicken Little tries to imitate the way a different group of animals drinks, he is unsuccessful. Finally a drop of water hits him on the head. He tips his head back and catches the next drop. Then he remembers that chickens have to drink by letting water "run downhill."

Toddlers' language development undergoes real advancement when they begin combining two or more words, for then they are beginning to learn to verbalize their thoughts. Adults can encourage progress by asking simple questions like, "What is that?" or "What is he doing?" and by following responses with elaboration that helps the child get the feeling of sentence structure. "Who," "what," "when," and "where" questions can be used at this time, although Piaget found that it is not appropriate to ask "how" and "why" questions of children until they have reached what he termed the "intuitive stage," which is between ages four and seven years.

Be alert to find books that will stretch a child's imagination and help develop powers of creative thinking. One such book is It Does Not Say Meow by Beatrice Schenk de Regniers. This book has exciting illustrations by Paul Galdone and the text is done in poetic form. It might be called a child's first riddle book. See if your toddler is ready to join in on this guessing game.

It Looked Like Spilt Milk by Charles G. Shaw provides more fun as a child tries to imagine what object is being depicted in very simple, yet striking blue-and-white silhouettes. This could be a new and rather exciting experience for a child who has had a rich exposure to picture books.

Whose Eye Am I? by Crosby Bonsall is a challenging book. In it a small boy sees an eye peeking through a hole in the fence. He starts on a search to find what animal this particular eye belongs to. The text of the story is probably far too difficult for a toddler, but you and your little son or daughter can enjoy turning through the pages, enjoying the excellent photographs of animals done by Ylla, and making up your own story for this mystery.

A Tree Is Nice, written by Janice May Udry and illustrated by Marc Simont, is an aesthetic experience for small children. The "joyous pictures" of trees at different seasons of the year could help adults and children alike appreciate the beauty around them. This is the kind of informational book that can help promote a toddler's sense of wonder. It was the winner of the Caldecott Award for the best illustrated children's book of 1956.

Young children are very interested in faces. With excellent photography, George Ancona shows eyes for seeing, ears for hearing, noses for smelling, along with likenesses and differences in Faces. Barbara Brenner has provided a simple, lyrical prose text for this book. Another book that George Ancona has illustrated that could be of interest to toddlers is My Feet Do by Jean Holzenthaler. The pictures in this book would certainly stir the imagination with all the attention they give to the accomplishments of children's feet.

But Where Is the Green Parrot? by Thomas Zacharias, illustrated by Wanda Zacharias, can be a riot of fun when the young child searches through one imaginative picture after another trying to find the green parrot in each. Such a book provides real involvement and participation in early literature.

Toddlers still need help to appreciate picture books. Some parents feel that they have fulfilled their obligation to interest children in books if they simply supply picture books, but a two-year-old child still needs sharing experiences in order to comprehend the wealth of the illustrations. If you have ever observed small children who have not had the advantage of sharing books with adults, you have probably seen them pick up a book, stare at it momentarily, but soon drop it for other interests. Their short attention span does not lead them into an extended effort to enjoy the pictures if they have had no experience in the pleasures of literature.

Even the child who has shared books since babyhood still needs to talk about pictures with adults or older children. As your youngster nears the age of two, he or she will enjoy long periods of such discussion, and what better way is there to extend vocabularies and develop new ideas than through a secure, positive experience of shared enjoyment?

Let toddlers determine how far they will go on with a reading activity. We cannot expect their active minds to be involved for any great length of time. Of course you will never try to fit a young child into a rigid schedule or expect some given responses. The reading you do and the games you play are not tests of any performance level. They are only enjoyable ways of learning geared to the pace that the child sets.

Two-year-old toddlers are starting to develop some understanding of simple concepts like up-down, in-out, big-little, hot-cold, etc. Such understanding must come through direct experience, but gradually they will be able to use picture books to enlarge their knowledge. Looking at books like J. P. Miller's <u>Big and Little,</u> and perhaps, even dramatizing the concepts demonstrated can make new ideas quite meaningful.

One very clever grandmother made a special doll for Krissi, the active toddler in her family. The doll was named Kelly. Next, she made a concept book showing both Krissi and Kelly sitting on the table, then sitting under the table; going into the house, then out of the house; walking up the hill, then down the hill; and having many other such experiences together. This became Krissi's favorite doll and favorite book. Both were very real to her, and in addition to giving her much pleasure, they also helped her develop a real understanding of the concepts depicted in the book, probably because she associated so very closely with the characters and the simple actions.

Concept and identification books should not be given to a toddler to promote an accumulation of facts; rather they should be used to satisfy a child's need to know and understand his or her immediate world and to help the youngster enjoy discoveries about the environment. Books that help satisfy such needs can promote a positive feeling toward reading. We never really know how a child perceives a given book, but our goal should be to help small children feel that literature provides satisfying, happy experiences. Because of the child's very limited experiences and background, first books may be little more than language experiences and identification or participation activities. Just as soon as children are able to follow simple plots, they will have the great world of storybooks opening up to them. It is impossible to say at what age a child will reach this stage; however, you can start reading simple little stories and nursery tales at any time. Let the child enjoy the books on his or her own level of understanding. At first the youngster may only appreciate the pictures and, perhaps, the musical quality of the language, but gradually the stories will take on meaning.

Simple stories and nursery tales that have cumulative plots like "The Gingerbread Man" provide a good starting point for first storybooks. In books with such plots one short episode is given: "I've run away from a little old woman." Then the second event takes place: "I've run away from a little old man." The next picks up the first event, repeats it, and then adds the next episode to it: "I've run away from a little old woman; I've run away from a little old man." Such repetition not only adds to the rhythm of the story, but it keeps reminding the young listener of the happenings in the plot and keeps them in order for the child who is not able to remember a sequence as yet. Paul Galdone has illustrated several of the old nursery tales that are developed through cumulative plots. You might like to consider some of them as first storybooks. His Henny Penny, The Gingerbread Boy, and Old Woman and Her Pig all incorporate a great deal of fun and excitement into the illustrations which may bring real chuckles to your toddler. Marcia Brown gave us a Russian version of "The Gingerbread Boy" in The Bun: A Tale from Russia. One Fine Day by Nonny Hogrogian won the Caldecott Award for its exciting pictures of the fox who gets his tail cut off and has to search long and hard for help in getting his tail back. This is another fine cumulative plot.

Toddlers may be able to enjoy others of the very simplest nursery tales. It is a good idea to look for picture books in which only one story is given because the illustrations are a needed tool to help the tiny child as he or she begins some understanding of plot development. Again, the Paul Galdone books are some of our best resources. He has retold and illustrated The Three Little Pigs, The Three Billy Goats Gruff, Three Bears, and The Little Red Hen. All are good versions of simple nursery tales.

There is a whole array of excellent first storybooks that a child who is almost two years old may be interested in hearing. Here are just a few outstanding selections that your son or daughter may be ready to enjoy:

Mr. Gumpy's Outing is a favorite story in which John

Burningham uses large, expressive, often humorous pictures to tell of Mr. Gumpy's boat trip. Two children, a rabbit, a cat, a dog, a pig, a sheep, chickens, a calf, and a goat all want to go along. Even though they have all been asked to behave, pandemonium breaks out and the boat tips over. However, they all manage to swim ashore, get themselves dried out, and go to tea with Mr. Gumpy.

Ask Mr. Bear by Marjorie Flack is an ideal first storybook for toddlers. Danny goes to several animals and finally to Mr. Bear in his search for just the right birthday present for his mother. There is much repetition, imitation of animal sounds, and finally, a surprise ending when Mr. Bear suggests a bear hug. This is a story that includes the listener, who helps with the animal sounds, eventually learns the repetitive text, and may even reward the reader with a hug.

My Teddy Bear has lovely pictures by one of Japan's leading artists, Chiyoko Nakatani, who says that a picture book is a child's personal art gallery and the illustrations must be works of art. Both the pictures and the simple text show a child's experiences with a favorite stuffed bear.

The Box with Red Wheels by Maud and Miska Petersham tells of a baby who is in a special box outside under a tree. All the curious farm animals come to inspect, but the mother shoos them away only to find that she must invite them back when she sees she has made the baby unhappy. The pictures tell the story in bright, clear colors.

Mirra Ginsburg's The Chick and the Duckling, illustrated by Jose Aruego, is a funny, "me too" book in which the duckling tells of his experiences and for each the chick announces that he has done the same until the duckling decides to go for a swim. This changes the entire situation, of course, for the chick can't swim. The pictures are expressive and enjoyable.

Rosie's Walk by Pat Hutchins is a picture book which shows Rosie, the hen, walking along nonchalantly while the fox who is following her gets into one difficulty after another. Toddlers will not understand some of the humor but they will enjoy following Rosie and the fox across the bright, sunny pages.

On Mother's Lap by Ann Herbert Scott is a lovely Eskimo

story about Michael, who has always had his mother's undivided attention. He brings his toys, puppy, and reindeer blanket all onto his mother's lap, but then the baby wakes up. Michael doesn't want to include the baby, but then he finds that "there's always room on mother's lap" and it feels good to rock together.

Green Eyes by A. Birnbaum is the story of a kitten Green Eyes. It explores the world around its home and experiences the change of seasons. Large expressive pictures are done in bright colors with heavy line drawings to interpret the story to a child.

Do You Want to Be My Friend? by Eric Carle lets the child travel from page to page and animal to animal on the search for a friend for the mouse. The pictures are done in bright collages. In the guessing game that Carle devises for toddlers there is always a clue as to what animal will be encountered next. Its tail appears on the preceding page.

These are just a few of the fine books that await your child. May Hill Arbuthnot, an authority in the field of children's literature, paraphrased the old adage about one man's meat being another man's poison and said that one man's book may be another man's boredom.[9] So it is with children's books. You will enjoy the search for the best for your child, but don't be disappointed if some of your choices are rejected. Usually this indicates that the youngster has not as yet become interested in the subject or has not reached the particular developmental stage to appreciate it. Remember, when you are reading a book to your child, your interest and enjoyment are contagious. In many cases what a child needs in order to become involved with a book is your enthusiasm.

Music and Verse

Rhythm is a part of the young child's very being. He or she responds to it in many ways, from pounding spoons on highchairs to trying to dance to the beat of music and verse. Just saying the old nursery rhymes brings out the ring and rhythm and starts the small body's response. Many rhymes have been set to music for games. As soon as a child has become a reasonably stable walker, he or she can participate in musical games like "Down by the Station," "Looby Loo," or "Reach for the Sky." These and many other games are to be found in an inexpensive paperback, Wee Sing: Chil-

dren's Songs and Fingerplays by Pamela Conn Beall and
Susan Hagen Nipp, illustrated by Nancy Klein.   Directions
for activities along with musical scores are given.   This
little book could add real enjoyment to your sharing time
with your toddler.   The Golden Song Book includes many
favorite songs and games for small children.   These were
collected by Katharine Tyler Wessells.

Several books containing just one singing game or musical experience are available.   The Farmer in the Dell, illustrated by Diane Zuromskis, has quaint, simple pictures that
will interest a child in this game.   Another that can be really fun is Six Little Ducks by Chris Conover.   This is taken
from the rhyming story about "the brave little duck with a
feather on its back."   Music is included.   I Went For a
Walk by Lois Lenski, music by Clyde Robert Bulla, is a
sing-along book that takes one through the town to get involved with people and activities, and then home again to
experience the bustle of the neighborhood.   All is in rhyme,
and with the music provided we follow along with "I went for
a walk and what did I see?"

There are many fine records that encourage children's
response to music and rhyme.   Some favorites that your
child will probably enjoy greatly are: "Put Your Finger in
the Air," done by Woody Guthrie; "Mother Goose," with
Cyril Ritchard, Celeste Holm, and Boris Karloff as readers
and containing music by Hershy Kay; "Golden Treasury of
Mother Goose and Nursery Songs," directed by Mitch Miller;
and perhaps some of the popular Hap Palmer Series, like
"Learning Basic Skills Through Music, Vol. I," which is appropriate for very young children.   "Tom Glazer's Music for
Ones and Twos" with Tom Glazer is ideal for the youngest
listeners.   Nancy Raven's "Wee Songs for Wee People" is a
collection of traditional nursery rhymes set to music.

Don't limit your youngsters to children's records, but
surround them with classical music and folk recordings.
This is the time to introduce the best of music to children.
They will respond.

A few musical toys, like rhythm sticks, a tambourine, or
a small drum may be a good investment at this time, but
often youngsters are just as happy bouncing around to the
rhythms they make with a spoon and an old pan--if parents
can stand the din!   Clapping verses and games can be enjoyed by both the child and parents.   Games like "Hot Cross

Buns" and "Pease Porridge Hot" are favorites at this stage.
Here are some other activities that can involve the toddler
in jingles with clapping:

Clap Your Hands

Clap, clap, clap your hands,
As slowly as you can.
Clap, clap, clap your hands,
As quickly as you can.
(Then try roll your hands, shake your hands, rub
your hands, pound your fists, wiggle your fingers,
or any other activity that your child seems to en-
joy.)

* * *

Handy Pandy

Handy pandy, Jack-a-dandy,
Loves plum cake and sugar candy,
He bought some at the grocer's shop
And out he came, hop, hop, hop!
(Start with clapping, end with hopping.)

* * *

Pop! Goes the Weasel

All around the cobbler's bench,
The monkey chased the weasel.
The monkey thought 'twas all in fun,
Pop! Goes the weasel.
(Sing this one, rolling hands until you come to
"Pop," where you should clap. This can be a
circle game with walking around at first and
falling down on "Pop.")

* * *

Hands

Roll, roll, roll your hands,
As slowly as can be;
Roll, roll, roll your hands,
Do it now with me.
Roll, roll, roll your hands,

As fast, as fast can be;
Roll, roll, roll your hands,
Do it now with me.
(On the next verse, use shake your hands, clap
your hands, and finally, for the last verse, try
tap your feet.)

* * *

Clap, Clap, Clap

Let your hands so loudly clap, clap, clap.
Let your little foot go tap, tap, tap.
Then fold your arms and close your eyes,
And quiet be.
Let us climb the ladder, do not fall.
'Till at last we reach the steeple tall.
Then fold your arms and close your eyes,
And quiet be.
(Follow the words with actions.)

Games of this type help a toddler develop the ability to
imitate and to enjoy rhythmical responses. Such accomplishments bring real pleasure and help build a good self-image.
Soon the child will be trying to say the words of the accompanying verses.

With action rhymes, jingles, and fun you introduce children to the world of poetry in a very pleasant way. Keep
the endearing qualities of nursery rhymes in mind when you
begin selecting first poetry for your toddler. Remember, it
is the rhythm that they first enjoy rather than the word meaning. The poems need to "sing" to warrant their full appreciation. Rebecca's grandmother introduced a first book of poetry to her when the little girl was twenty months old. Her
first reaction to the poems was a somewhat guarded attention
with little enthusiasm until they came to A. A. Milne's
"Christopher Robin went hoppity, hoppity, hop...." Following the reading of this selection grandmother was allowed to
read a poem or two at a time, but invariably she would be
interrupted with, "Where's Hoppy?" They would have to return each time to Christopher Robin because this was poetry
to this little toddler. She added her own response by hopping each time to the rhythm. Rebecca is twelve now and
has been writing her own poetry for several years.

There is a whole world of verse awaiting your child; in

fact, most of the book texts that a toddler enjoys are written in a poetic or rhythmical form. Soon you, as a parent, will be enjoying the search for anthologies of poems for children or special collections that will please your preschool child. As for now, nursery rhymes hold the greatest poetic charms for your toddler, but you may enjoy trying a few simple verses that have real musical qualities like those found in The First Book of Poetry, compiled by Isabel J. Peterson and illustrated by Kathleen Elgin, or in Poems and Verses to Begin On, selected by Donald J. Bissett, or in Poems to Read to the Very Young, selected by Josette Frank.

Reading Readiness Continues

As a parent you have probably had time spent with your child greatly enriched if the two of you have shared bits of our folklore heritage by way of nursery rhymes and tales, folk songs, games, and action rhymes. Also, you have enjoyed many lovely picture books and even very first informational books that have pleased your toddler. You have no doubt come a long way toward fostering a positive attitude toward books if you have given generously of your time in sharing literary experiences with your child. These have been happy, rewarding times when your little one has sat on your lap and received your undivided attention as you enjoyed books together. However, as your toddler reaches a second birthday, you may wonder what progress has been made toward the time when he or she will read alone. What reading readiness skills is the youngster developing and, perhaps, even more important, what is the little person's attitude toward reading?

Think of the different kinds of literature you have introduced to your toddler as you have read and played together! There were simple little books for identification and knowledge on a tiny child's level; then later, concept books that helped the youngster understand more about the world in which we live. Through nursery rhymes, poetry, and fingerplays, you have helped develop auditory discrimination and motor skills. Enjoyment of these verses has promoted concentration and has stimulated the memorization of bits of poems. Your child has begun to appreciate the storytelling qualities of illustrations through fine picture books that you have shared. By introducing very simple little stories, you have helped your toddler begin to learn about plot sequence and the joys that reading will hold for him or her.

Already your child probably knows how one holds a book, right side up, and how one turns the pages from front to back. Even this constitutes a part of pre-reading skills which we assume that children know, but some have had no experience with books when they come to school.

By running your finger along the line of print from left to right, you have helped your future student understand how the text progresses across the page and realize how important the printed words are. (One small child explained to his friend that those marks are what you read if you can't read pictures.)

Of course you have helped with vocabulary building and with an understanding of grammatical structure that is needed to form sentences. By now your child is probably making two-word sentences which you are casually expanding into more meaningful thought patterns as you talk, read, or discuss pictures in the books.

You are already helping your son or daughter develop listening skills that are very important in learning to read. These skills will continue to develop as you help the child respond to phonetic sounds and alliteration in rhymes or very short stories that can hold his or her attention, or when you share little folk songs or games like "Ring Around the Rosey" where the child must listen for the punchline.

The toddler is progressing in visual discrimination skills if adults are helping him or her learn to give careful attention to pictures. He or she is beginning to note likenesses and differences and to observe at least some details in pictures. There is no doubt that pictures play an important part in basic reading texts. Children learn to "read the pictures" which explain and extend the text and give context clues. Even at the age of two, children need the practice of interpreting illustrations in their picture books to expand their understanding of what they hear read.

The child who has been read to is already appreciating the fun that books offer. If a youngster comes from a family that enjoys literature, he or she is probably already pretending to read and often repeating bits and pieces of what has been read aloud. Perhaps the most important understanding you have helped your child to gain is that reading is an enjoyable activity.

The fortunate toddler who has had a rich exposure to literature from very early childhood may very well cling to a book in one hand and drag on mother's or father's clothing with the other, demanding, "Weed now!" Here we have a fine candidate for success as a future reader, even though he or she may be a "happy botheration." This child's parents are probably the type who let the "matters of consequence" that the Little Prince in Antoine de Saint Exupery's excellent fable said adults are concerned about slip by. They have no doubt enjoyed setting their toddler on the road to an appreciation of literature and a desire for reading.

Notes

[1]William Blake, "Auguries of Innocence," in William Blake: The Complete Poems, ed. Alicia Ostriker (New York: Penguin, 1977), p. 506.

[2]S. P. Marland, Jr., Education of the Gifted and Talented, Vol. 1, Report to the Congress of the United States (Washington, D.C.: U.S. Commission of Education, Office of Education, August 1971), p. 31, (ERIC ED 056 243).

[3]Joan Beck, How to Raise a Brighter Child: The Case for Early Learning, rev. ed. (New York: Pocket Books, 1975), pp. 85-86.

[4]Bruno Bettelheim, "A Primer for Literacy," in The Child's Mind, ed. Margot Witty, Harper's Magazine, 256, No. 1535, (April 1978) p. 56.

[5]Ibid. p. 56.

[6]Fred M. Hechinger, "Passport to Equality," in Pre-School Education Today, ed. Fred M. Hechinger (Garden City, NY: Doubleday and Company, 1966), p. 2.

[7]The Flint Public Library, Ring A Ring O' Roses (Flint, MI: The Flint Public Library, 1977).

[8]Edward Lear, Nonsense Books (Boston: Little, Brown, 1943), n. p.

[9]May Hill Arbuthnot et al., Children's Books Too Good to Miss, 6th ed. (Cleveland: The Press of Case Western Reserve University, 1971), p. ix.

Books Discussed in This Chapter

Ahlberg, Janet, and Allan Ahlberg. Each Peach, Pear, Plum.

New York: The Viking Press, 1978. (Paperback. Scholastic Book Services, 1981.)

Alexander, Martha. Pigs Say Oink. New York: Random House, 1981.

Aliki. Hush Little Baby: A Folk Lullaby. Englewood Cliffs, NJ: Prentice-Hall, 1968.

Beall, Pamela Conn, and Susan Hagen Nipp. Wee Sing: Children's Songs and Fingerplays. Illus. by Nancy Klein. Los Angeles: Price, Stern, Sloan Publishers, 1981.

Birnbaum, A. Green Eyes. Racine, WI: Western Publishing Co., 1973.

Bissett, Donald J., ed. Poems and Verses to Begin On. New York: Noble & Noble, 1967.

Bonsall, Crosby N. Whose Eye Am I? Illus. by Ylla. New York: Harper & Row, 1969.

Brenner, Barbara. Faces. Illus. by George Ancona. New York: E. P. Dutton, 1970.

Brown, Marc. Finger Rhymes. New York: E. P. Dutton, 1980.

Brown, Marcia. The Bun: A Tale from Russia. New York: Harcourt Brace Jovanovich, 1972.

Brown, Margaret Wise. The Country Noisy Book. Illus. by Leonard Weisgard. New York: Harper, 1940. (Paperback. 1976.)

Brown, Margaret Wise. Noisy Book. Illus. by Leonard Weisgard. New York: Harper, 1939.

Bruna, Dick. The Apple. New York: Methuen, 1975.
_____. B Is for Bear: An A-B-C. New York: Methuen, 1977.

Burningham, John. The Baby. New York: Thomas Y. Crowell, 1975.
_____. The Blanket. New York: Thomas Y. Crowell, 1976.
_____. The Dog. New York: Thomas Y. Crowell, 1976.
_____. The Friend. New York: Thomas Y. Crowell, 1976.
_____. John Burningham's ABC. Indianapolis, IN: Bobbs-Merrill Co., 1967.
_____. Mr. Gumpy's Outing. New York: Holt, Rinehart & Winston, 1970.

Carle, Eric. Do You Want to Be My Friend? New York: Thomas Y. Crowell, 1971.
_____. My Very First Book of Numbers. New York: Thomas Y. Crowell, 1974.
_____. One, Two, Three to the Zoo. New York: World Publishers, 1968.

_____. The Rooster Who Set Out to See the World. New York: Franklin Watts, Inc., 1972.

Cleary, Beverly. Hullabaloo ABC. Illus. by Earl Thollander. Oakland, CA: Parnassus, 1960.

Conover, Chris. Six Little Ducks. New York: Thomas Y. Crowell, 1976.

Drews, Donald. Freight Train. New York: Greenwillow, 1978.

De Regniers, Beatrice S. It Does Not Say Meow. Illus. by Paul Galdone. New York: Seabury Press, 1972.

Flack, Marjorie. Ask Mr. Bear. New York: Macmillan Company, 1958. (Paperback. 1971.)

Frank, Josette. Poems to Read to the Very Young. Illus. by Eloise Wilken. New York: Random House, 1982.

Friskey, Margaret. Chicken Little, Count-to-Ten. Illus. by Katherine Evans. Chicago: Childrens Press, 1946.

Fujikawa, Gyo. Come Out and Play. New York: Grosset & Dunlap, 1968.

_____. Fairyland. New York: Grosset & Dunlap, 1981.

_____. Here I Am. New York: Grosset & Dunlap, 1981.

_____. Make-Believe. New York: Grosset & Dunlap, 1981.

_____. My Animal Friends. New York: Grosset & Dunlap, 1981.

Galdone, Paul. The Gingerbread Boy. New York: Seabury Press, 1975.

_____. Henny Penny. New York: Seabury Press, 1968.

_____. The History of Simple Simon. New York: McGraw-Hill, 1966.

_____. The House that Jack Built. New York: McGraw-Hill, 1961.

_____. The Little Red Hen. New York: Seabury Press, 1973. (Paperback. New York: Scholastic Book Services, 1975.)

_____. Old Mother Hubbard and Her Dog. New York: McGraw-Hill, 1960.

_____. Old Woman and Her Pig. New York: McGraw-Hill, 1961.

_____. Three Bears. New York: Seabury Press, 1972. (Paperback. New York: Scholastic Book Services, 1973.)

_____. The Three Billy Goats Gruff. New York: Seabury Press, 1973.

_____. The Three Little Pigs. New York: Seabury Press, 1970.

_____ . Tom, Tom, the Piper's Son. New York: McGraw-Hill, 1964.

Greenaway, Kate. Mother Goose; Or the Old Nursery Rhymes. New York: Frederick Warne & Co., 1882.

Gretz, Susanna. Teddy Bears ABC. Chicago: Follett Publishing Co., 1975.

_____ . Teddy Bears, One to Ten. Chicago: Follett Publishing Co., 1968.

Ginsburg, Mirra. The Chick and the Duckling. Illus. by Jose Aruego. New York: Macmillan Company, 1972.

Glazer, Tom. Do Your Ears Hang Low? Illus. by Mila Lazarevich. Garden City, NY: Doubleday and Company, 1980.

Hoban, Tana. Count and See. New York: Macmillan Company, 1972. (Paperback. 1974.)

Hogrogian, Nonny. One Fine Day. New York: Macmillan Company, 1971. (Paperback. 1974.)

Holzenthaler, Jean. My Feet Do. Illus. by George Ancona. New York: E. P. Dutton, 1979.

Hutchins, Pat. Rosie's Walk. New York: Macmillan Company, 1968. (Paperback. 1971.)

Jacobs, Frances E. Finger Plays and Action Rhymes. Photos by Lura Owen and Courtney Owen. New York: Lothrop, Lee & Shepard, 1941.

Jeffers, Susan. Mother Goose: If Wishes Were Horses and Other Rhymes. New York: E. P. Dutton, 1979.

Lenski, Lois. Cowboy Small. New York: Henry Z. Walck, 1949.

_____ . I Went for a Walk. Music by Clyde Robert Bulla. New York: Henry Z. Walck, 1958.

_____ . The Little Airplane. New York: Henry Z. Walck, 1938.

_____ . The Little Auto. New York: Henry Z. Walck, 1934.

_____ . The Little Farm. New York: Henry Z. Walck, 1942.

_____ . Songs of Mr. Small. Music by Clyde Robert Bulla. New York: Henry Z. Walck, 1954.

Matthiesen, Thomas. Things to See: A Child's World of Familiar Objects. New York: Platt & Munk, 1966.

Miller, J. P. Big and Little. New York: Random House, 1975.

Moore, Lilian. My Big Golden Counting Book. Illus. by Garth Williams. Garden City, NY: Western Publishing Co., 1957.

Munari, Bruno. Bruno Munari's ABC. Cleveland: Collins-World, 1960.

Najaka, Marlies Merk. City Cat. New York: McGraw-Hill, 1980.
_____. Country Cat. New York: McGraw-Hill, 1980.
Nakatani, Chiyoko. My Teddy Bear. New York: Thomas Y. Crowell, 1976.
Ogle, Lucille, and Tina Thoburn. I Spy. Illus. by Joe Kaufman. New York: American Heritage Press, 1970.
Petersham, Maud, and Miska Petersham. The Box With Red Wheels. New York: Macmillan Company, 1949. (Paperback. 1973.)
Peterson, Isabel J., comp. The First Book of Poetry. Illus. by Kathleen Elgin. New York: Franklin Watts, Inc., 1954.
Potter, Beatrix. Appley Dapply's Nursery Rhymes. New York: Frederick Warne & Co., 1917.
_____. The Story of a Fierce Bad Rabbit. New York: Frederick Warne & Co., 1906.
_____. The Story of Miss Moppet. New York: Frederick Warne & Co., 1906.
Poulsson, Emilie. Finger Plays for Nursery and Kindergarten. Illus. by L. T. Bridgman. Music by Cornelia C. Roeske. New York: Lothrop, Lee & Shepard, 1893. (Paperback. New York: Lothrop, Lee & Shepard, 1971.)
Richter, Mischa. Quack? New York: Harper & Row, 1978.
Ruben, Patricia. Apples to Zippers: An Alphabet Book. Garden City, NY: Doubleday and Company, 1976.
Scarry, Richard. Early Words. New York: Random House, 1976.
_____. On the Farm. Racine, WI: Western Publishing Co., 1976.
_____. Richard Scarry's Best Word Book Ever. Racine, WI: Western Publishing Co., 1963.
_____. What Animals Do. Racine, WI: Western Publishing Co., 1968.
Schick, Eleanor. City in the Summer. New York: Macmillan Company, 1969. (Paperback. 1974.)
Scott, Ann Herbert. On Mother's Lap. Illus. by Glo Coalson. New York: McGraw-Hill, 1972.
Shaw, Charles G. It Looked Like Spilt Milk. New York: Harper, 1947.
Spier, Peter. Crash, Bang, Boom. Garden City, NY: Doubleday and Company, 1972.
_____. Gobble, Growl, Grunt. Garden City, NY: Doubleday and Company, 1971.

Tresselt, Alvin R. Wake Up Farm. Illus. by Roger Duvoisin. New York: Lothrop, Lee & Shepard, 1955.

Tudor, Tasha. Mother Goose: Seventy-seven Verses with Pictures by Tasha Tudor. New York: Henry Z. Walck, 1944.

Udry, Janice M. Mary Ann's Mud Day. Illus. by Martha Alexander. New York: Harper & Row, 1967.

_____. A Tree is Nice. Illus. by Marc Simont. New York: Harper, 1956.

Watson, Carol, and Colin King. The House. Hueysville, KY: Hayes Books, 1980.

_____. The Town. Hueysville, KY: Hayes Books, 1980.

Wessels, Katharine Tyler. The Golden Song Book. Illus. by Kathy Albert. Racine, WI: Western Publishing Co., 1981.

Wildsmith, Brian. Brian Wildsmith's ABC. New York: Franklin Watts, Inc., 1963.

_____. Brian Wildsmith's Mother Goose: A Collection of Nursery Rhymes. New York: Franklin Watts, Inc., 1965.

_____. Brian Wildsmith's 1, 2, 3's. New York: Franklin Watts, Inc., 1965.

Williams, Garth. Big Golden Animal ABC. Racine, WI: Western Publishing Co., 1957.

Zacharias, Thomas. But Where is the Green Parrot? Illus. by Wanda Zacharias. New York: Delacorte Press, 1968.

Zuromskia, Diane. The Farmer in the Dell. Boston: Little, Brown, 1976.

Some Recordings Young Children Enjoy

Channing, Carol. Carol Channing Reads and Sings. Caedmon TC 1305.

_____. Winnie the Pooh. Caedmon TC 1408. (Cassette: CDL 51408.)

Fun and Games. Peter Pan 8073.

Glazer, Tom. Activities and Game Songs. Vol. 1 and 2. CMS 657-658. (Cassette: X4657, X4653.)

_____. Music for Ones and Twos. CMS 649. (Cassette: 7653.)

Goldilocks and the Three Bears, Hereafter This, and Dick Whittington and His Cat. Spoken Arts 1039.

Grimes, Tammy. Where the Wild Things Are and Other Stories by Maurice Sendak. Caedmon TC 1531.

Guthrie, Woody. Songs to Grow On. Folkways Records FC 7501.

Ives, Burl. Burl Ives Sings Little White Duck and Other Children's Favorites. Harmony HS 14507.

Jenkins, Ella. Early Childhood Songs. Scholastic R 7630.
_____. Jambo and Other Call and Response Songs with Ella Jenkins. Folkways R 7661.
_____. Rhythms of Childhood with Ella Jenkins. Scholastic 7653.
_____. You'll Sing a Song and I'll Sing a Song. Folkways Records FC 7501. (Cassette: Folkways/ Scholastic FC 60105.)

Marching Along Together. Decca DL 74450.

Palmer, Hap. Learning Basic Skills through Music. Vol. 1. Educational Activities ARLP 514. (Cassette: 10-514.)
_____. Simplified Folk Songs. Educational Activities AR 518. (Cassette: 10-518.)

Peter Paul and Mommy. Warner Brothers-Seven Arts Records WS 1785. (Cassette: Warner Brothers/Seven Arts CWY 1785.)

Rainy Day Record. Bowmar 138.

Raven, Nancy. Hop, Skip and Sing. Pacific Cascade LPL 7015.
_____. Wee Songs for Wee People. Pacific Cascade LPL 7012.

Richard, Cyril, et al. Mother Goose. Caedmon TC 1091.

Schwartz, Tony. 1, 2, 3, and a Zing, Zing, Zing. Folkways Records FC 7003.

Sesame Street: Bert and Ernie Sing Along. CRA CTW 22068.

Seeger, Pete. Abiyoyo and Other Sleepy Time Story Songs for Children. Folkways FTS 31500.
_____. Birds, Beasts, Bugs and Bigger Fishes and a Foolish Frog. Folkways FC 7611.
_____. Birds, Beasts, Bugs and Little Fishes. Folkways FTS 31504.

Visit to My Little Friend. Young People's 10005.

Other Book Suggestions for This Age Level

Ahlberg, Janet, and Allan Ahlberg. Peek-A-Boo! New York: The Viking Press, 1981.

Allen, Frances C. Little Hippo. Illus. by Laura J. Allen. New York: G. P. Putnam's Sons, 1971.

Ancona, George. It's a Baby! New York: E. P. Dutton, 1979.

Arno, Ed. The Gingerbread Man. New York: Scholastic Book Services, 1967.

Battaglia, Aurelius. Mother Goose. New York: Random House, 1973.

Brown, Margaret Wise. The Golden Egg Book. Illus. by Leonard Weisgard. Racine, WI: Western Publishing Co., 1976.

_____. The Seashore Noisy Book. Illus. by Leonard Weisgard. New York: Harper, 1941.

Burningham, John. The Cupboard. New York: Thomas Y. Crowell, 1975.

_____. The Dog. New York: Thomas Y. Crowell, 1975.

_____. The Friend. New York: Thomas Y. Crowell, 1975.

_____. Mr. Gumpy's Motor Car. New York: Macmillan Company, 1975. (Paperback. New York: Penguin, 1977.)

_____. The Snow. New York: Thomas Y. Crowell, 1975.

Carle, Eric. The Very Hungry Caterpillar. Cleveland: Collins-World, 1969.

Carroll, Ruth. Where's the Bunny? New York: Oxford University Press, 1950.

Chenery, Janet. 1 Nose 10 Toes. Illus. by Art Seiden. New York: Grosset & Dunlap, 1981.

Coatsworth, Elizabeth. Under the Green Willow. Illus. by Janina Domanska. New York: Macmillan Company, 1971.

Craig, Helen. The Mouse House ABC. New York: Random House, 1979.

Crowther, Robert. The Most Amazing Hide-and-Seek Alphabet Book. New York: The Viking Press, 1978.

Domanska, Janina. The Little Red Hen. New York: Macmillan Company, 1973.

Garten, Jan. The Alphabet Tale. Illus. by Muriel Batherman. New York: Random House, 1964.

Goffstein, M. B. Sleepy People. New York: Farrar, Straus and Giroux, 1979.

Greet, W. Cabell, et al. My Pictionary. New York: Lothrop, Lee & Shepard, 1970.

Hutchins, Pat. Clocks and More Clocks. New York: Macmillan Company, 1970.

Keats, Ezra Jack. Whistle for Willie. New York: The Viking Press, 1964.

Kent, Jack. Jack Kent's Hop, Skip, and Jump Book. New York: Random House, 1974.

Krauss, Ruth. The Happy Day. Illus. by Marc Simont. New York: Harper & Row, 1980.

Lenski, Lois. Papa Small. New York: Oxford University Press, 1951.

————. Policeman Small. New York: Henry Z. Walck, 1962.

Mitchell, Cynthia. Playtime. Illus. by Satomi Ichikaka. Cleveland: Collins-World, 1979.

My House. Racine, WI: Western Publishing Co., 1978.

Nakatani, Chiyoko. My Teddy Bear. New York: Thomas Y. Crowell, 1975.

Palazzo, Tony. Animal Babies. Garden City, NY: Doubleday and Company, 1960.

Pienkowski, Jan. ABC. New York: Harvey House, 1981.

————. Colors. New York: Harvey House, 1975.

————. Numbers. New York: Harvey House, 1975.

————. Shapes. New York: Harvey House, 1975.

Rey, Hans A. Anybody at Home? Boston: Houghton Mifflin, 1956.

————. Feed the Animals. Boston: Houghton Mifflin, 1956.

————. See the Circus. Boston: Houghton Mifflin, 1956.

Rockwell, Harlow. My Kitchen. New York: Greenwillow, 1980.

Rojankovsky, Feodor. Animals in the Zoo. New York: Alfred A. Knopf, 1962.

Scarry, Richard. Is This the House of Mistress Mouse? Racine, WI: Western Publishing Co., 1964.

————. Richard Scarry's Color Book. New York: Random House, 1976.

Seuss, Dr. Mr. Brown Can Moo, Can You? New York: Random House, 1970.

Ten Little Motor Cars. Cambridge, England: Brimax Books, 1978.

Ten Little Ponies. Cambridge, England: Brimax Books, 1976.

Tolstoy, Alexei. The Great Big Enormous Turnip. Illus. Helen Oxenbury. New York: Franklin Watts, Inc., 1968.

Tudor, Tasha. A Is for Annabelle. New York: Henry Z. Walck, 1954.

Virin, Anna. Elsa's Bears. New York: Harvey House, 1978.

Wells, Rosemary. Benjamin and Tulip. New York: Dial Press, 1973.

Williams, Garth. Chicken Book: A Traditional Rhyme. New York: Delacorte Press, 1970.

Wynne, Patricia. The Animal ABC. New York: Random House, 1977.

CHAPTER III

A CRITICAL TIME FOR LEARNING
--Two-to-Three-Year-Olds--

The Troublesome Twos

The two-year-old is sometimes called a "vibrating question mark." The world is very new to this tiny child--a place of wonder and excitement. Parents are often amazed, and even exhausted, by their child's potential to learn and by his or her drive to bring order and understanding out of everyday experiences. It is difficult for adults, who have become oblivious to much of their own surroundings, to comprehend the excitement of ordinary happenings. A walk through the park with a child must be interrupted with long intervals for careful study of whatever is along the way. To the two-year-old, just being able to climb up and down the stairs without help is an accomplishment which must be repeated and savored again and again. Stops must be made at special places for special thought. A. A. Milne, who seemed to understand the thinking of small children very well, explains in "Halfway Down":

> Halfway down the stairs
> Is a stair
> Where I sit.
> There isn't any
> Other stair
> Quite like
> It.
> I'm not at the bottom,
> I'm not at the top;
> So this is the stair
> Where
> I always
> Stop.
> Halfway up the stairs
> Isn't up,

And isn't down.
It isn't in the nursery,
It isn't in the town.
And all sorts of funny thoughts
Run around my head:
"It isn't really
Anywhere!
It's somewhere else
Instead!"[1]

The two-year-old is an active, busy little person who often displays a short attention span and goes hurrying from one interest to another. Yet he or she also has quieter times in the day when simple toys and picture books attract attention. By the time a youngster has reached the age of two, language skills have usually advanced far enough that many needs can be expressed. The ability to communicate helps develop feelings of security so that for a time, at least, the youngster is a rather calm, friendly little person. However, this developmental period may be all too short, for at about two-and-a-half years of age the negative phase usually evolves and the entire household is faced with a trying time because of the youngster's great drive for independence and continual assertion of rights. It does help to know that it is a stage that most youngsters go through and will pass.

A very striking characteristic during this period is a demand for sameness. Perhaps because the world seems confusing to the youngster, a very structured routine gives security. Joan Beck says:

> This is the age when the growing brain of the child is trying to form generalizations from observations, to draw conclusions, to formulate concepts from perceptions. That's why children of this age are so insistent upon routine and ritual. It gives them a sense of order and continuity from which they can draw valid and workable conclusions. [2]

Parents can help their children establish reasonable routines that all can live with, but difficulties will probably arise when changes in the routine must take place.

The two-and-a-half-year-old is demanding and bossy; however, such characteristics do not indicate that the child feels secure in his or her rights. Rather, such actions are an expression of unsure feelings. Unreasonable demands are

the child's way of testing his or her situation. Later, when
the small person has acquired more self-assurance, such demands will not be necessary. The youngster is working
through what Secretary of Education T. H. Bell calls the
"great experience of early childhood," "finding out that you
are someone who counts in a very interesting world.... If
that experience does not come in the years of early development, all later experience is likely to be tinged with a sense
of futility and doubt."[3]

Children need this drive for independence and self-
assertion even though some of their actions can be very trying. One two-year-old, Victoria, upset a friendly visitor in
her home by stiffening her little body to its full height,
clenching her fists, stamping her feet, and screaming, "I
does it myself!" when the visitor tried to help her find a
lost ball. Interestingly enough, the remark of a teacher of
young children who was also visiting in the home was, "Now
there is a good candidate for an early reader. She knows
what she wants and she is going after it!"

According to the Swiss psychologist Jean Piaget, the two-
year-old is probably just entering what he called the preoperational period of intellectual development. During this
period, which may last up to the age of seven, the child
learns to use language as symbols to represent his or her
world.[4] The youngster is beginning to think through problems and to plan ahead. At the age of two, children are
very egocentric in their thinking. To them reality is their
personal world and themselves. It is not that they are nec-
essarily selfish, but their experience does not take them beyond their immediate environment of which they are, of
course, the center. Consequently, books for very young
children must include opportunities for ego involvement.
Concepts or ideas presented in books must be ones to which
the small listener can relate. Imagination is beginning to
develop, but stories must be thoroughly grounded in reality
for very young children before they can move out into new
ideas.

A small child is not bothered by fanciful animal characters if the setting and situation of the story is in accord
with the youngster's experiences of reality. The fact that
the three bears live in a cozy house with its neat furnish-
ings is quite acceptable. Once the child has a comfortable
feeling about the background of the story, then he or she
can move on to enjoy some different happenings or ideas

that may add to the growth of new understandings. The use of good literature can help children move away from egocentricity, where everything centers on themselves, to a gradual acceptance of a broader scope in their thinking.

A Very Important Learning Period

We are faced with the sobering thought that the two- to three-year-old youngster is in a critical learning period. We can get an idea of the importance of this present developmental period by considering Genevieve Painter's review of studies conducted to test the effect of placing retarded children in more intellectually stimulating environments. The studies showed that when such intervention took place at ages one to three, there was a difference between the experimental and the contrast groups of over 50 I. Q. points. If intervention occurred when children were four and five years of age, increases in I. Q. amounted to less than one-half of those that were produced at the earlier age. When intervention did not take place until age six when the children entered school, increases in I. Q. were only one-half of those resulting when intervention had taken place two years earlier. [5]

Stimulating surroundings are clearly desirable during the early stages of intellectual development. Parents are responsible for providing the intellectual and emotional environment that will sustain cognitive growth. A little environmental learner must be free to make observations, draw conclusions, and develop powers of reasoning. At the same time, a child needs supportive adults who provide assistance when it is needed. As Maya Pines says, "In a rich environment the child begins to get 'kicks' out of learning soon after birth. If nothing arouses him, however, or all his attempts at learning are squelched, he will stop seeking this pleasure--to everyone's loss."[6]

One way of providing stimulating surroundings is by supplying books that pertain to children's immediate interests. For example, two- to three-year-old youngsters are fascinated by household items. Just the shapes and colors of common articles that seem mundane to us are a source of great wonder to them. Such articles seem to demand prying, chewing, feeling, and turning. The more something can be made to bang and crash, the more interesting it is. Books that supply verses or stories about fascinating objects are often appreciated because they are based on children's own experiences.

Many nursery rhymes relate to things children encounter in their everyday lives. Old Mother Hubbard's cupboard takes on new meanings when it is compared with cupboards at home. Or Walter de la Mare's poem, "The Cupboard" can add to the interest.

The Cupboard

I know a little cupboard,
With a teeny tiny key,
And there's a jar of Lollipops,
   For me, me, me.
It has a little shelf, my dear,
As dark as dark can be,
And there's a dish of Banbury Cakes,
   For me, me, me.
I have a small fat grandmamma,
With a very slippery knee,
And she's Keeper of the Cupboard,
   With the key, key, key.
And when I'm very good, my dear,
As good as good can be,
There's Banbury Cakes, and Lollipops,
   For me, me, me. [7]

What child doesn't know about lollipops--and that they are usually locked away! Personal possessions are very important to a youngster. Poems like "The Mitten Song" by Marie Louise Allen are real in a child's world, and can even be chanted to distract the youngster from the problems of getting dressed to go outside on cold days.

The Mitten Song

"Thumbs in the thumb-place,
Fingers all together!"
This is the song
We sing in mitten-weather.
When it is cold,
It doesn't matter whether
Mittens are wool,
Or made of finest leather.
This is the song
We sing in mitten-weather:
"Thumbs in the thumb-place,
Fingers all together!" [8]

Any good anthology of poetry for small children will supply a parent with appropriate poems and verses that seem to speak directly to a child. Children are especially interested in poems that deal with something they have experienced. These poems, and also stories that relate closely to a small child's experiences, provide what the educational psychologists might call the "right match" for learning to enjoy books at the two- to three-year-old's developmental level.

Amazing Language Development

In his delightful book From Two to Five, Kornei Chukovsky, the Soviet Union's best-loved author of children's books, says, "It seems to me that, beginning with the age of two, every child becomes for a short time a linguistic genius. Later, beginning with the age of five or six, this talent begins to fade." Chukovsky reminds us, however, that for all the young child's sensitivity to language, the basis for his or her linguistic aptitude is imitation. "The young child acquires his linguistic and thinking habits only through communication with other human beings." The child's "speech giftedness" is determined in part by his or her ability to apply grammatical forms in the right situations:

> If an adult had to master so many grammatical rules within so short a time, his head would surely burst--a mass of rules mastered so lightly and so freely by the two-year-old "linguist." The labor he thus performs at this age is astonishing enough, but even more amazing and unparalleled is the ease with which he does it. [9]

Two-year-old children have been absorbing language all their young lives; now they are ready to learn to talk. They have probably built up a basic vocabulary of some fifty to one hundred words. In six months' time they will double this number, and by the time they are three, they will double the number of words they used at two-and-a-half. In fact, between the ages of two-and-a-half and four-and-a-half they learn around fifty new words each month! By two-and-a-half most children will have mastered the vowel sounds. Some consonant sounds will still give them trouble and cause difficulty with articulation of certain words. Two-and-a-half-year-olds use short sentences usually consisting of two or three words, simple combinations of verbs and nouns.

As children's vocabularies increase, the meaningless

jargon they often used as toddlers is discarded. Usually
these youngsters talk to themselves more than to an adult or
another child. They enjoy using their newfound arts of verbalization in naming things in their environment. Such identification, whether it is done while they are looking through
picture books or in their immediate surroundings, gives them
a feeling of accomplishment, but it also helps them bring order into their world. Dialogue depends on their mood. They
may respond to questions an adult asks, or may go happily
along discussing a picture or a situation alone. Again, books
can help with opportunities for dialogue because each new picture provides fresh stimulation for discussion and for "What's
that?" and "Why?" questions, which are heard more and more
as curious youngsters progress.

In explaining language development at this stage Margaret
Gillespie and John Conner say, "Words begin to stand for
images and adult language is approximated. Words begin to
accompany action and also to describe it. Groupings of words
are random and derived mainly by trial and error."10 As
soon as children begin associating words with objects and actions, they seem to use language as a way of thinking aloud.
Much of the talking they do will be noncommunicative speech.
Children play with words, often just enjoying the rhythmic
sounds which seem to give accompaniment for their play.
They may chant a part of a nursery rhyme in the same way
that an adult might sing a catchy tune while working. They
employ many verbal sound effects in their solitary play,
buzzing toy airplanes through the air, zooming fire trucks,
or dinging play telephone bells in a combination of motor
and verbal activity.

Children give themselves directions as they play or simply talk in a monologue as if they must explain to themselves what each activity is about. Very often they will repeat a word, phrase, or line of a little poem. Perhaps
they don't understand the meaning at all, but just enjoy the
sound.

One of the really delightful characteristics of children's
speech is their ability to make up names for objects or even
acquaintances. Some of these are very creative and can be
expressive to the point of embarrassment.

Two-year-olds understand a surprising amount of language
used in their environment and they are continually gaining
new insights. Mary Lukens Coxon shows how early language
development leads directly into first reading experiences:

As the child is gaining the ability to talk about his experiences and relates the language of others to experience, he moves a step farther and makes another discovery. He learns that one thing can stand for or represent another. His mother points to a picture in a book and says, "That's a puppy." Pictures represent the real things and have the same label or name. He learns that a green light indicates that cars may go and that it represents the word GO. Through experiences of this kind he learns that he can use pictures or other representations to gain information. For example, pictures on cans and boxes tell what is inside.[11]

Assisting Language Development

Robert L. Doan says, "The single most important facet of intellectual growth is probably the development of language skills. It is with language that humans think, communicate, and reason."[12] It goes without saying that a knowledge of language is essential if one is to learn to read. Can you imagine being asked to learn to read in a foreign language?

For small children, home is the ideal place for developing language skills and parents are by far the best teachers. There is time to learn at one's own pace by imitating, labeling, experimenting with new sounds, grouping words, and enjoying language games. There are no academic pressures, nor is there any need to perform on an equal basis with other children in a group.

Parents are in a position to understand their children's needs and to give reinforcement to their learning in ways that cause youngsters to feel happy about their accomplishments. In the book Parent Education Evelyn Pickarts and Jean Fargo say:

How the young child learns to think, use language, feel about himself and others, view the world and his place in it, and unpack the meaning of his experiences is significantly affected by the way in which the parent interacts with him. These learnings are not the result of didactic teaching but are implicit in the content of daily interaction between parent and child.[13]

Be sure to take time to listen to your two-year-old and try to understand your youngster's level of reasoning. Be glad that he or she attempts to ask questions. This is a sign of intelligence as well as a sign of a desire to learn. Don't overburden the little questioner with many facts or long explanations. Just try to answer questions simply at your child's level of understanding. Be genuinely interested in what is important to your son or daughter. You may not be terribly excited about such things as blocks that are being pushed about the floor like imaginary trains, yet if you take the time to appreciate your youngster's developing imagination and growing linguistic powers, just quiet observations of creative play can be intriguing.

As a parent you are in the ideal position to stimulate language growth. When you are talking with your little boy or girl, you will want to teach new words whenever the occasion arises; but do so in a relaxed manner, knowing that if the word is not learned at that particular moment, it will be later. Help your child feel good about trying, not anxious about succeeding with each attempt.

Resist the temptation to compare your youngster's accomplishments with those of siblings or friends. Children learn at varied rates. Keep in mind that it is not the rapidity with which your son or daughter moves through the developmental stages that is important. Rather it is the quality of experience and understanding that your youngster gains and the pleasure that is experienced in the learning process.

Since your child is learning through imitation, the discussion of picture books can be a real help. The books provide activities and interests that may not be readily available in the immediate environment. Choose books with action in the pictures and help your little boy or girl talk about those that seem most interesting. Many of your child's remarks will characteristically be reductions. You may say, "Look at that boy run!" Your child's imitation will probably be, "Boy run!" This is a "telegram sentence" in which your youngster picks up the key words. Remember to expand your child's statement, adding adjectives and adverbs.

Some simple concept books provide good sources for such discussions. Both you and your child will probably enjoy the verses in If You Were an Eel, How Would You Feel? by Mina and Howard Simon, and this book can stimulate a lot of talk about the actions in the very expressive watercolor illustrations.

Look for books that speak to your son or daughter's

special interests, those that show action and perhaps some humor in the illustrations. The text of Tin Lizzie by Peter Spier is probably much too difficult for a two- to three-year-old child, but if your youngster enjoys old vehicles, this book provides a wealth of discussion material in its detailed, often funny pictures. Tana Hoban's Dig-Drill Dump-Fill fascinates many children. Its realistic photographs show numerous large machines that are seen around city streets, demolishing buildings, dumping gravel, and even picking up the trash. This is a wordless book with a picture dictionary in the back to label the various machines. Red Light, Green Light by Golden MacDonald centers around two large signal lights: red for STOP and green for GO. The book follows the travels of both people and animals as they leave in the morning and return at night. It has great possibilities for promoting the first recognition of the two words, stop and go. With the help of the color of the signal lights, your child can feel that he or she is actually participating in the reading of the book by supplying these words.

A Very Special House by Ruth Krauss is another book that should stimulate a lot of good comments about just the house your small child might like. The text is rhythmical, and Maurice Sendak's happy little character plays through the pages doing all the things a child likes to do in a house, without ever once being reprimanded. The satisfaction on his face expresses pure delight as he jumps on beds, writes on walls, sprinkles cookie crumbs about, and has a marvelous time.

To enhance the fun and learning as you are going through such books, ask your child to point out various objects and actions in the pictures. Simple little questions like, "Where is the dog?" or "Show me the ball," help to sharpen visual perception and give your little boy or girl a feeling of involvement in the activity.

Parents, Children, and Books

Studies the past thirty years have clearly shown that home experiences can be more important than school experiences in determining whether or not a child will be successful at reading. [14] In a home that provides a positive reading atmosphere the youngster will have parents who use books as a major source of pleasure. He or she will be encouraged in the development of reading readiness skills and surrounded by books that appeal to childlike concerns. Growing up in this kind of atmosphere prepares a youngster for academic interests and reading success.

In discussing the reading interests of her children, Annis Duff explains in "Bequest of Wings":

> People have often said to us, "How does it happen that your children know so many books? Mine have never asked for them." It does not just "happen"; children seldom do ask for books, as an initial stage in learning to love them. Reading, for young children, is rarely a pleasure in isolation, but comes through shared pleasure and constant discerning exposure to books so that they fall naturally into the category of pleasant necessities, along with food, sleep, music and all out-of-doors. [15]

You will want to be very sensitive about timing in presenting books to young children. You will probably get little encouragement if you try to read to your child when he or she is feeling especially active and needs to use up excess energy. Reading is for quiet times when a youngster wants to share a good story or perhaps just feel the closeness and love of parents who are willing to give of their time and to share pleasures. Good teachers are very conscious of the teachable moment when children are particularly interested in a given subject or activity. There are times when your child needs to hear books read aloud and to discuss them. Such times cannot be scheduled into a day's routine but should be caught and savored by both parents and youngsters. They are important for learning and for building secure, happy relationships. As an adult, what gives you more pleasure--remembering a beautifully run house in which you may have lived as a child, or thinking of the close, shared pleasure of reading or enjoying thoughtful moments that you may have had with a caring adult? In her book Babies Need Books, Dorothy Butler has a delightful discussion of learning to overlook the so-called essential elements of housework for the moment in order to enjoy story sessions with your child at appropriate times. She says, "Train yourself to smile confidently at neighbors' and relations' surprise or disapproval; tell them, if you need explain yourself at all, that you would be ashamed to neglect your children whereas you don't feel emotionally involved with the breakfast dishes!"[16]

The Reluctant Participant

If you have been reading to your child since he or she was a baby, the sharing of books has probably already become one of the happiest routines of everyday family life. If your little son or daughter does not have such a background, you cannot expect instant success when you first present books. Now it may take a very careful approach, but you will be giving your youngster a wonderful gift when you convince him or her of the pleasures to be found in reading.

There is an old adage which says, "We get that for which we teach." If you feel that a love of literature is essential to your child's future success and happiness, you will be willing to give both the time and the careful thought that will be necessary to snare your little boy or girl into a love of books even if he or she happens to be a reluctant pre-reader.

In their book On Learning to Read Bettelheim and Zelan say, "Children who acquire a great interest in reading in their homes have an easy time reading in school, and they form the overwhelming majority of those who later become good readers."[17]

Although the stakes are high, remember that you are dealing with very sensitive little people who can be pushed into a negative attitude easily. If your two- to three-year-old child hasn't learned to enjoy books, you might check your own approach to reading with him or her. Do you read in an interesting way; do you dramatize a bit, yet not overact? Are you genuinely interested and enthusiastic about books and pictures? Are you being careful to select reading materials to which your child can relate because of his or her experiences and background? Are you asking questions that let your youngster feel a part of the ongoing interest in the book and avoiding those that need only tiresome yes and no answers? Are you guilty of trying to fill the child's head with facts rather than trying to develop interests and enthusiasm? Remember, your goal is not to accelerate your child's growth but to help him or her thoroughly enjoy the present developmental stage. Are you being careful to avoid using a sweet, condescending voice when you read? This is as disturbing to children as it is to adults. Are you selecting books that you, too, can enjoy? Keep in mind that it is extremely difficult to present a book in an interesting manner if you can hardly stand to read it.

Are you remembering that reading for a two- to three-year-old child is not a spectator sport? Children must respond, ask questions, supply words when possible, and react to the rhythm and flow of the language, even going so far as to dance, sing, and dramatize what is being read. Are you setting the stage so that the reading experience becomes for the child a warm, happy, sharing time with a responsive adult who is willing to give the youngster the wonderful gift of time and shared enthusiasm? Don't count on a media program to supply this important ingredient in helping children love the sharing of literature. Just the opportunity to handle the book, turn the pages, and anticipate what is coming next is of great importance to a small child. Are you letting your little boy or girl direct the reading and participate actively? Keep in mind that it is not always necessary to read every word. Your child's involvement and participation is a basic goal.

Probably the best way to establish the relationship between books and pleasure is to hold the youngster on your lap and read stories, poems, or anything that he or she likes to hear, as long as the child is engaged. In this close, secure situation, your voice, which your son or daughter loves, will reflect your enjoyment of the story. Such a cozy setting should make for very happy experiences. This is one sure way to interest your child in reading. In discussing the role of literature in the education of children Helen Huss says, "If literature provided no other contribution than pleasure, it would still be sufficient, for enjoyment is the key to interest, and interest is the key to continued reading."[18]

Picture Books that Promote Understanding

The cognitive growth of the two- to three-year-old child is very important to the development of reading readiness skills. Of course we are not interested in word identification as yet, but basic to reading is understanding, which comes through experience. Certainly children need to understand something of the world about them before they can put story situations into focus. You will be gratified to discover how well really good picture books are able to show young children their everyday experiences with vitality, humor, and often beauty. Yet they go beyond simply repeating everyday happenings. They move out from well-known situations to broaden understanding and stretch imaginations.

Play With Me by Marie Hall Ets is a very satisfying story about an ordinary little girl who ventures into the woods and asks one animal after another to "Play with me." But each animal runs away frightened by her enthusiastic gestures. Finally, she sits down quietly by a pond and one by one the animals surface from their hiding places. This time they approach her and she has playmates at last. The pictures and the text are simple, childlike, and very meaningful.

Harry the Dirty Dog by Gene Zion tells a funny story which has great appeal to children of this age. Harry is a determined dog who is going to avoid baths. He hides the scrub brush in the backyard and runs away from home. His adventures lead him to greater and greater layers of dirt until finally, when he does return home, his family does not recognize him. Not until the children give Harry a bath do they realize that he is their dog. Harry's hatred for bathing and his love of dirt may be a familiar theme to many children.

Books like Grandfather and I and Grandmother and I, both written by Helen E. Buckley, often express a child's need for quiet and reassurance. The little boy thoroughly enjoys Grandfather's unhurried pace as they take all the time they want to talk, and look about, and enjoy interesting things. The little girl explains why Grandmother's lap is the best lap of all for quiet security.

Small listeners understand the wonderful feeling of accomplishment that Peter experiences when he finally learns to whistle in Ezra Jack Keats' excellent story Whistle for Willie. Momo's Kittens by Mitsu and Taro Yashima is one of many books that show the importance of pets in a child's life. City in the Winter by Eleanor Shick gives inner-city children the opportunity to see themselves and their surroundings pictured in books. Making Friends, also by Eleanor Schick, is a wordless book that shows a two- to three-year-old's interest and enthusiasm about the world he lives in. A small boy makes friends with all he meets, from an insect on the sidewalk to a little girl in the park. Sam, written by Ann Herbert Scott, shows, in beautiful sepia-and-black-pictures done by Symeon Shimin, the feelings of a little boy as he tries to be included in family activities and for a time is rejected. The Daddy Book by Robert Stewart shows daddies in all sizes and shapes doing the many things that they do in the small child's world. All Falling Down by Gene Zion is a concept book with delightful, large pictures depicting a two- to three-year-old's interest in falling things--from leaves, rain, snow, to blocks that must fall down at bedtime.

When adults take the time to read with small children, the youngsters are helped in many ways to be prepared for future school experiences. Their listening skills are enhanced and their attention spans gradually lengthen so that it is possible for them to give longer periods of thought to a learning situation. Expressive skills expand when they participate in identification and questioning games as they go through their books with adults who enjoy their thoughts and questions.

Some picture books provide fine opportunities for participation. Some supply guessing games, or puzzles, or opportunities to imitate sounds. Who Said Meow? by Maria Polushkin provides puzzles. In Pat Hutchins' Good-night Owl! the owl contends with all the noisy neighbors that keep him awake, but then at night the situation changes. It is his turn to create such a racket that he wakes the entire community. This is a noise book as each animal is given an accompanying sound. The illustrations are bold and exciting. Who Took the Farmer's Hat? by Joan L. Nodset will give a youngster a feeling of satisfaction in being able to spot the missing hat and realize its new function as a bird's nest.

Almost any well-loved book can and should become a participation story. The child soon learns to anticipate what is coming next in the plot, guess a character or a situation that is about to appear, add sound effects, or get ready for an explosive climax. There are often verses or phrases that the young listener picks up after one or two readings and repeats as they appear, or, better yet, reads them along. Maurice Sendak's Pierre provides a great opportunity with the oft-repeated, "I don't care." This book is somewhat advanced for the two- to three-year-old group, but if they catch the fun, it might help them laugh at some of their own negativism.

The Gunniwolf, retold by Wilhelmina Harper, like most folktales, is better told than read. Many young children love joining in on the song that the little girl sings, "kumkwa, khi-wa, kum-kwa, khi-wa," or in the exciting part of the story, creating the sound effects, "hunker-cha, hunker-cha, hunker-cha" as the Gunniwolf chases the little girl. This is followed by her "pit-pat, pit-pat, pit-pat, pit-pat" as she runs away. This is a very exciting story. The adult telling it should watch the response of the child listener, and if the youngster is not taking the whole episode as fun, perhaps this is one of the stories that should wait until the child is older.

Picture books do more than introduce children to the wonderful world of stories. They usually provide a first introduction to art. Good illustrations extend the enjoyment of the story, but they also help children learn to appreciate fine creative expressions. Experiencing the art found in well-illustrated books will begin to set aesthetic standards for boys and girls and give them some foundation for the enjoyment of truly beautiful things. It is true that at first children really won't know the difference between fine pictures and those that are not particularly well done; but if all they ever see in pictures is cuteness, prettiness, and stereotyped images, that may well be all they will ever appreciate.

Of course, books must speak to children. Both pictures and texts must relate to their limited experiences to be enjoyed. Small children become upset when the story and the illustrations are not synchronized. Pictures provide a visual language. Children want to "read the pictures" as the parent is reading the text to them, and they are often confused if only a part of an object or person is shown on a page. If a person has no head in the picture, a small child assumes that he or she has literally lost that part of the body. The whole essence of a story can be lost for young listeners who may have become concerned about some detail or lack of completeness in an illustration.

In selecting picture books, be careful to consider both the pictures and the text. Children will be disappointed if the only real appeal to a book is the pictures. They need a lively, swift-moving text to enjoy. Even the most careful of adults may be hoodwinked into buying a book that simply overwhelms them with lovely illustrations. Children are not so easily taken in. If the story is poorly done and uninteresting to them, they will discard the book with no further consideration.

Two- to three-year-old children have a whole world of picture books opening up for their enjoyment as they grow in their own experiences and their ability to comprehend stories and illustrations. Careful selection of such books can give them the opportunity to experience the best books we have from the standpoint of both literature and artistic qualities.

Old Verses and Songs from Our Oral Tradition

The old nursery rhymes, folk songs and verses, lullabies, and very simple folk games provide some of the best literature that we have for two- to-three-year-olds. These children are ready to encounter a wide variety of books that hark back to the old oral tradition. We are fortunate to have such a rich heritage which has been well preserved for us in excellent books.

Periodically we run across criticisms of Mother Goose. Some people ask why we use these old rhymes with modern children--their texts are old, the language is outdated, and, they say, the stories are not relevant to children today. (They forget that although the rhymes are old, children are always fresh and new!) Some say they are not rational, just complete nonsense. (So what is wrong with fun and a stretch of the imagination?) Others call them doggerel. Paul Hazard's comment seems appropriate here: "For if, by an act of impiety, we should try to put these nursery rhymes into prose, we would no longer have anything but ashes left from a fire. The magic quality of cadence, of rhyme, is seen here at its best.... They are the poetry exactly suited to childhood, pictures in rhyme."[19]

Chukovsky gives us some idea as to why these rhymes have lived for many generations and continue to please our children in his statement:

> Although each new generation of parents, grandfathers, and grandmothers sings and recites to children both the good and the inferior, only that which best serves the children's needs and tastes remains in their memories. And when he reaches old age, everyone who heard in his childhood these folk chants passes on to his grandchildren, in his turn, the very best, the most vivid and vital. Any everything that is out of tune and incongruous with the psychology of the young child is gradually forgotten and becomes extinct.... In this way an exemplary children's folklore has come into existence--exemplary in its language and rhythm, as well as ideally suited to the intellectual needs of the young child. Thus it is one of the strongest means of using the greatness of folklore for educational purposes.[20]

As a parent you want only the best for your children.
You may have reservations about some of the verses that
display violence or sexism.   You can be selective and simply omit those that seem offensive to you, but your child
will miss a very enjoyable part of his or her literary heritage if you ignore the bulk of these great old verses.

Much of the appeal of the old rhymes is still the enjoyment of the sound and cadence of the language.   At this two-
to three-year-old period of intensive language learning, children are sensitive to language patterns.   The rhymes sing
their way into their memories with an hypnotic sound.
Rhymes such as these sensitize children to the sounds of
words, the very essence of phonetic analysis in beginning
reading.

Sing, Sing

Sing, sing,
What shall I sing?
That cat's run away
With the pudding string!
Do, do,
What shall I do?
The cat's run away,
With the pudding too!

* * *

The Flying Pig

Dickery, dickery, dare,
The pig flew up in the air;
The man in brown
Soon brought him down,
Dickery, dickery, dare.

* * *

Diddle, Diddle, Dumpling

Diddle, diddle, dumpling, my son John,
Went to bed with his trousers on;
One shoe off, and one shoe on,
Diddle, diddle dumpling, my son John.

* * *

Sing a Song of Sixpence

Sing a song of sixpence,
  A pocket full of rye;
Four and twenty blackbirds,
  Baked in a pie.

When the pie was opened,
  The birds began to sing;
Was not that a dainty dish,
  To set before the king?

Two-to-three-year-olds are beginning to love short stories. Within their nursery rhyme books they find many of these, told quickly, presented in their entirety in a few lines. Characters in the verses begin to take on personalities. An appreciation for humor is beginning to develop with children this age. Some of the rhymes promote fun in reading, especially if the child role plays the verses.

Small children have been dramatizing verses like these for generations:

Little Miss Muffet

Little Miss Muffet
Sat on a tuffet,
  Eating her curds and whey;
Along came a big spider,
Who sat down beside her,
  And frightened Miss Muffet away.

* * *

Simple Simon

Simple Simon met a pieman,
  Going to the fair;
Says Simple Simon to the pieman,
  Let me taste your ware.

Says the pieman to Simple Simon,
  Show me first your penny;
Says Simple Simon to the pieman,
  Indeed I have not any.

Simple Simon went a-fishing,
  For to catch a whale;

All the water he had got
Was in his mother's pail.

Simple Simon went to look,
    If plums grew on a thistle;
He pricked his fingers very much,
    Which made poor Simon whistle.

He went for water in a sieve,
    But soon it all fell through;
And now poor Simple Simon,
    Bids you all adieu.

* * *

The Queen of Hearts

The Queen of Hearts
She made some tarts,
    All on a summer's day;
The Knave of Hearts
He stole those tarts,
    And took them clean away.

The King of Hearts
Called for the tarts,
    And beat the knave full sore;
The Knave of Hearts
Brought back the tarts,
    And vowed he'd steal no more.

Keep watching for nursery rhyme books that give interesting artistic interpretations of the verses. A two-and-a-half-year-old child is mature enough to begin to appreciate the humor in Raymond Briggs' The Mother Goose Treasury. This is a popular collection with its four hundred rhymes full of robust vigor and humor. The pictures are Victorian in style, yet have a very modern flavor. There is at least one picture for each rhyme, and some have an illustration for each verse, which makes for a very busy presentation, but children enjoy the fun.

Joan Walsh Anglund's In a Pumpkin Shell is a Mother Goose ABC book. The subject matter for the verses progresses through the alphabet. A is for apple, with an appropriate verse, B is for bear, C for clock, which, of course, is Hickory, Dickory, Dock. Each letter and verse is illustrated in either a one- or two-page spread with Anglund's quaint watercolor pictures that are reminiscent of Kate Greenaway's style.

Phillip Reed's Mother Goose and Nursery Rhymes is illustrated with wood engravings. This book will add variety. Your son or daughter may enjoy comparing the rustic characters found in this collection with illustrations of identical characters done in the quaint, old-fashioned style of the De Angeli or Tudor books.

Many illustrators, like Leslie Brooke with Ring O' Roses, give happy, humorous interpretations of the rhymes. This fine collection was published in 1923 and is still one of our best. It might be interesting to see which among the great variety of Mother Goose books have the most appeal to your child at this time.

You will want at least one good compilation that your little boy or girl can own, but the library will provide others to make your reading more interesting and varied. If you haven't as yet selected at least one fine collection to buy, your youngster will no doubt be able to direct you to a good choice. Choose from books that have illustrations that are representational without confusing details. Very young children need pictures that tell the story of the rhyme literally. Such pictures make it possible for them to feel that the story they are hearing read is being confirmed by the illustrations.

For a change of pace, see how your child will react to some of the books that present only one rhyme or folk song. He or she may enjoy following the development of a favorite nursery rhyme through many pages of pictures. Also, these books often include little games or participation ideas that help the child become really involved.

Drummer Hoff, a Caldecott winner, adapted by Barbara Emberley and illustrated by Ed Emberley, is a lively folk verse telling how different soldiers bring parts for the construction of a cannon. But it is Drummer Hoff who has the duty of firing the cannon, and the cumulative rhyme always ends with "Drummer Hoff fired it off." The book ends with a final illustration of the cannon covered with growing grass, flowers, grasshoppers, a spider web, birds, and even a bird's nest. Thus, the illustrator has given the folk verse a presumably new interpretation in its ending. It is too bad that small children are too young to understand the meaning of the last picture, but they respond with enthusiasm to the great "Kahbahbooom!" when "Drummer Hoff fired it off."

Simon's Song is the Simple Simon story also adapted by Barbara Emberley and enlivened by fun-provoking woodcuts by Ed Emberley. The song is included in the book with many different verses and adventures. Billy Boy has verses selected by Richard Chase and illustrated by Glen Rounds. It is a rustic, often humorous presentation of the old story with the music included in the end.

There are some picture books that present lullabies. These are interesting to look at by day, and reassuring when sung together with your child as goodnight songs. Margot Zemach presents the familiar old lullaby Hush, Little Baby in pictures that show a family in a Victorian setting. Aliki has illustrated Go Tell Aunt Rhody in bright, beautiful, realistic farm scenes of long ago. The accompaniment for this song is included, as well as an explanation of the origin of the words and the music. Many people think of "Go Tell Aunt Rhody" as a folk song, but the melody was composed over two hundred years ago by Jean Jacques Rousseau for part of the opera, The Village Soothsayer. When the melody reached America, the words that we know were put to it and it became a favorite lullaby.

Sing It Again

Two- to three-year-old children are ready to make the step from folk songs and verse to simple poetry. It is not necessary to limit a child's experience with poetry to only those selections that might be classified as children's poems. All poetry that appeals to a child because of its musical words, its content, or just the fact that it is shared by a trusted person who loves the poem can be a fine literary experience for a youngster. Fortunate is the child who often hears lovely poetry quoted at just the right moment. A poem like "Night" by Sara Teasdale adds quiet beauty to a child's experience.

> Stars over snow,
>   And in the west a planet,
> Swinging below a star--
>   Look for a lovely thing and you will find it,
> It is not far--
>   It never will be far. [21]

Or there are many to consider from the beautiful poetry of the Bible. Of course small children will not understand all the content, but the beauty of the language is a part of Judeo-Christian children's heritage. Quotations like these vibrate with a kind of simple grandeur:

> He who dwells in the shelter of the Most High,
> Who abides in the Shadow of the Almighty
> Will say to the Lord, "My refuge and my fortress;
> My God, in whom I trust.

Psalms 91:1

* * *

> But they that wait upon the Lord shall renew
>   their strength;
> They shall mount up with wings as eagles;
> They shall run, and not be weary;
> And they shall walk, and not faint.

Isaiah 40:31

* * *

> For God hath not given us the spirit of fear;
> But of power, and of love, and of a sound mind.

II Timothy 1:7

For now, this stately language can bring children the reassurance of beauty and joy shared by someone they love. Perhaps later this same poetry will surface from the depth of their minds with real meaning.

Poetry is made to be heard and to be spoken. Those of us who cannot command a wealth of it to express our thoughts at just the right moment can rely on excellent books to share with our children.

In writing of children and poetry Arbuthnot says, "Not to prepare them to enjoy some part of this special area of literature is to deprive them of one of their richest legacies." In speaking of the music and dance of the words in poetry, she makes this statement:

> The nursery jingles dance, skip, run, hop, or swing

gently. Other poems make a joyful noise or have a solemn quietness. They may sound powerful or as fluttery as a butterfly. Over and over again, the music and the dance of words and lines reflect or reinforce the mood of the meaning of a poem from <u>Mother Goose</u> to Browning and Dylan Thomas. Also, this movement in words and lines makes little melodies that are as ear-catching as a song. [22]

First poems should be marked with meter and rhythm that will entice the child to respond by clapping the verse in time or even to act out the poem as one might with Dorothy Baruch's "Merry-Go-Round."

> I climbed up on the merry-go-round,
> And it went round and round.
> I climbed up on a big brown horse,
> And it went up and down.
>   Around and round,
>   And up and down,
>   Around and round,
>   And up and down,
>   I sat high up,
>   On a big brown horse,
>   And rode around,
>   On the merry-go-round,
>   And rode around,
>   On the merry-go-round,
>   I rode around,
>   On the merry-go-round,
>   Around,
>   And round,
>   And
>   Round. [23]

Myra Cohn Livingston is a poet who has a real sensitivity to small children's feelings and what is important to them. Her tiny books fit well into a child's hands and world. She has published several books of poems for the very young. These selections are all from <u>Whispers</u>:

Just Watch

> Watch
>   how high
>   I'm jumping,
> Watch
>   how far

```
     I hop,
Watch
     how long
     I'm skipping,
Watch
     how fast
     I stop!
```

* * *

I Know A Place

```
I know a place,
Where you turn on the hose,
And take off your shoes,
And wiggle your toes.
     And the mud is oozy,
     And sort of sloozy ...
(There's no one else who knows!)
```

* * *

Cooking

```
This will be a chocolate cake,
     This a cherry pie,
This will be a doughnut,
     When the mud is dry.
```

* * *

Discovery

```
Round and round and round I spin,
Making a circle so I can fall in. 24
```

Don't be discouraged if you do not receive an immediate positive reaction to books of poetry.   Perhaps you will find that it is better to put the books away for a time and just say or sing rhymes and poems when they seem appropriate. While pushing your child in a swing at the park, it is fun to chant:

The Swing
Robert Louis Stevenson

```
How do you like to go up in a swing,
     Up in the air so blue?
```

> Oh, I do think it the pleasantest thing,
>   Ever a child can do!
>
> Up in the air and over the wall,
>   Till I can see so wide,
> Rivers and trees and cattle and all,
>   Over the countryside--
>
> Till I look down on the garden green,
>   Down on the roof so brown--
> Up in the air I go flying again,
>   Up in the air and down![25]

Many a reluctant three-year-old has been enticed on toward home by dramatizing the rhythm of A. A. Milne's "Christopher Robin goes Hoppity, hoppity, hoppity, hoppity, hop...."[26] Or for some galloping musical accompaniment try:

Windy Nights
Robert Louis Stevenson

> Whenever the moon and stars are set,
>   Whenever the wind is high,
> All night long in the dark and wet,
>   A man goes riding by.
> Late in the night when the fires are out,
>   Why does he gallop and gallop about?[27]

Little goodnight poems can help end the day with the ritual and routine that two-to-three-year-olds like. You might try these:

Going to Sleep
Dorothy Aldis

> The safest feeling
> In the world
> Is to be lying
> Warm and curled
> In bed while in
> The room next door
> They talk; and then
> Don't any more....[28]

* * *

The Star

Jane Taylor

Twinkle, twinkle, little star,
How I wonder what you are!
Up above the world so high,
Like a diamond in the sky.

Mozart wrote the music for "The Star" when he was five years old.

Fingerplays affirm the fun of verse. They are not great poetry, but they are a door to an appreciation of intriguing verse. In case you are looking for a new book to try, you might consider Fingerplay Poems for Children by Helen J. Fletcher or Finger Plays and Action Rhymes by Frances E. Jacobs.

Interest in Concepts

Don't expect your two-year-old to be a mathematical whiz. Even a second cookie will probably be "more cookie" or possibly "other cookie" rather than "two cookies." Children often do not get the concept of three objects until they are about three years old. They need to see and handle real objects to understand the most rudimentary counting processes. However, very simple number books make good identification experiences, and gradually a child will learn to transfer from a concrete object to the picture on the page, and may even try counting a few illustrated objects if the pictures are very clear. Some books that have already been used as participation stories can now be used as number books. In The Very Hungry Caterpillar by Eric Carle, we have some groupings of food that a small child might count as he or she goes over the caterpillar's menu for each day. Helen Oxenbury's Numbers of Things is fun to study and can provide some counting experiences.

Ten Bears in My Bed by Stanley Mack is a countdown book. When a little boy retires for the night, he finds ten bears in his bed. He keeps saying, "Roll over, roll over," and they leave one at a time through the window. When his mother peeks into the room, he is in bed and the bears are gone. Then he dreams of bears.

Hippos Go Berserk by Sandra Boynton is a rhyming story

with many hippo characters. A lonely hippo calls friends
who soon arrive in groups for a party. They go beserk having a grand time, but at break of day they go away in groups,
again leaving the first hippo alone.

Count the Cats has great expressive full-color pictures of
cats. There is a very limited text in this book, but the fun
is in counting the cats on double-page spreads. Erika Weihs,
the artist who created these pictures, is from Vienna, Aus-
tria. Her book provides children with a fine aesthetic experience in addition to any knowledge of number concepts
that they may gain.

1 Is One by Tasha Tudor is a simple but beautiful counting book with the numbers placed on the left-hand side of a
double-page spread and a lovely picture on the right to expand the idea of the number concept. One Dancing Drum by
Gail Kredenser and Stanley Mack is a counting book about
interesting little musicians. The alliteration adds to the fun
of this book.

ABC, number, and concept books are sometimes called
specialized texts. MacCann and Richards have made a good
observation on the evaluation of such books:

> A pragmatic approach is required in judging these texts
> because they succeed when their limited purpose is
> achieved. If the book is basically a type of game
> rather than a story, the child must be capable of play-
> ing it successfully. An adult cannot judge the book by
> his own reactions; he can best judge it in the company
> of young children at the suitable age level, observing
> children's responses and joining them in the spirit of
> play. 29

Children are usually very interested in colors, but they
may not learn to differentiate among even basic colors until
the end of their second year or later. There are many picture books that will help in color recognition. They may or
may not have a little story; in fact, for very young children
it is probably better if they simply concentrate on the colors
themselves.

My Very First Book of Colors is one of Eric Carle's
matching books. It is a spiral-bound book with board pages,
each cut horizontally so that the upper and lower halves can
be turned separately and matched. The top halves have a

solid block of a given color. They are to be matched with pictures of familiar objects found on the lower halves--red goes with a red fire engine, green with a green tree, brown with a brown shoe, and so on.

What Is a Color? by Alice and Martin Provensen provides some lovely pictures for children just learning their colors. Each color is identified with different items combined creatively to bring out what might be termed the feel or personality of the color.

A basic purpose of My Slippers Are Red by Charlotte Steiner is to help distinguish colors. This book is written in rhyme and offers many examples of primary colors presented in bright, cheerful temperas.

Colors by John J. Reiss has bold, bright pictures to show different hues of both primary and secondary colors. Clear labels and familiar objects make this a good book for just looking for a tiny child.

ABC books are often good resources for identification activities which two-to-three-year-olds still enjoy. As your child labels a picture, you will often be able to show him or her the printed word that stands for the label given. This helps the child to realize that print is "talk written down" and gradually to become aware that words and letters have their own configurations. It is important for your youngster to grasp this idea early and also to realize that the text always says the same thing.

C. B. Fall's bright, forceful woodcuts illustrate his ABC Book in dramatic fashion. One animal is shown for each letter. Captions are large and done in upper-case letters. The caption and the woodcut showing the animal form a solid rectangle framed within a white border.

Celestino Piatti's Animal ABC has bold, dramatic pictures of animals done in bright poster paints, heavily outlined in black. The giraffe and the whale both stretch straight across double-page spreads. Pictures of other animals are not as large, but all are forceful, each with its rhyme to tie the animal in with the first letter of its name.

The Kittens' ABC by Clare Turlay Newberry is a very large book in which each letter of the alphabet is used in some way pertaining to cats. Admittedly, the verses of the

text are not outstanding, but Newberry's cats are so textured and real that most children simply can't resist the
appeal of the pictures.

The subtitle for Fritz Eichenberg's Ape in a Cape is An
Alphabet of Odd Animals, and so it is! Each animal representing a letter is experiencing some odd situation in complete rhyme with its name--an ape dressed in a cape, a carp
playing a harp, a hare at the fair, a pig wearing a wig, and
on through the alphabet. Children enjoy the humor and the
rhyming words. A Big City by Francine B. Grossbart is a
different alphabet book with cut paper scenes showing a setting in the city to match each letter. Karla Kuskin's
ABCDE FGHIJKLMNOPQRSTUVWXYZ is a small book with a
couplet for each letter and a picture opposite each little
verse. These, and those mentioned in Chapter II, are just
some of the ABC books you will enjoy reviewing with a two-
to-three-year-old.

Books for Other Interests

"Nursery chronicles" are books that depict everyday happenings in a young child's life. The illustrations and the
short texts make it possible for a small child to identify
closely with the simple experiences in the books. Just Me
by Marie Hall Ets tells of a small boy going about the farm
trying to imitate all the animals--just the kind of activities
children do as they study their environment in their own experimental way. The little fellow in Just Me tries to move
like each animal until he sees his father starting the motor-
boat on the pond. Then he runs like himself to get to the
boat in time for a ride.

Big Little Davy and the other books in the Davy series by
Lois Lenski are extremely simple little books that have a
real appeal to small children because they reflect the children's own experiences. The everyday happenings in Davy's
life do not seem exciting to adults, but these books have
fascinated youngsters for years because they show activities
that seem of real importance to small children.

Three stories that concern the youngster's growing processes are The Growing Story by Ruth Krauss, Benjy's
Blanket by Myra Berry Brown, and Peter's Chair by Ezra
Jack Keats. In The Growing Story a little boy is not at all
sure that he is growing as he watches both plants and animals getting larger throughout the summer. In the fall when

he tries on his last year's clothes, he sees how small they are for him. In Benjy's Blanket Benjy gradually overcomes his need for his security blanket and is able to be the hero at the end of this story by giving up his blanket to make a kitten happy. Peter's Chair shows how Peter discovers that he has grown so much that he can no longer fit into his chair, a chair that he had refused to let be painted for his little sister. With his discovery of how large he has become, he assumes a more grown-up attitude.

Books of this type are realistic to a tiny child. Such books give children the opportunity of seeing their own experiences depicted in book form. They instigate verbalization because children will talk about activities that are familiar to them. At times such stories will help a youngster through a new experience. A first ride on a train or a visit to the dentist for a check-up may not seem threatening to a parent, but often adults have no idea how strange and frightening new experiences are to a child. My Dentist by Harlow Rockwell might be just the book to help your child understand what is going on when he or she has a dental appointment. It could ease some of the apprehension. My Doctor by the same author could provide a similar preparation for visiting the doctor's office. As a child goes through such situations with book characters, some of the strangeness involved can be eliminated. Books of this kind can give a child a "pattern of expectations" for unusual situations.

Be sensitive to your child's special interests. Very often you will find information or concept books that deal with the particular subjects. Such books add to your youngster's general knowledge and help refine understanding. The discovery that his or her interests are important enough to be found in books will build the child's ego. Without a doubt experiences with such books will sharpen interest in reading.

Just watching the movement of the great trucks across the pages of the book Truck by Donald Crews can excite the child who is especially interested in vehicles. Later this book can inspire some beginning reading experiences when the youngster has become sensitive to signs along the highway and attempts to read them. Very bold signs appear in this book. Youngsters will recognize some of these.

The Supermarket by Anne and Harlow Rockwell takes a child on a shopping trip and expands the youngster's interest in such experiences. Their book The Tool Box is a simple concept book with large, clear illustrations of tools a child would see and perhaps even try to use around the house.

I Know a Lot of Things by Ann and Paul Rand is a fun experience with cut paper pictures and short interwoven texts that helps children enjoy the importance of the knowledge they have acquired.

Sun Up written by Alvin Tresselt reviews a whole day's experiences on a farm with easy text and vivid watercolor pictures by Roger Duvoisin. Rain Drop Splash, also by Alvin Tresselt, is good to read on a rainy day. In it Leonard Weisgard's pictures show the water cycle from the falling drops of a rainstorm until the water reaches the sea. White Snow, Bright Snow is a Caldecott winner that tells of winter happenings with the reassurance of spring in the end. It, too, was written by Alvin Tresselt and was illustrated by Roger Duvoisin.

The world of two- to three-year-old children is still centered in the home, and primary caretakers, usually the parents, are central figures in their lives. For this reason they enjoy family stories, especially stories that are reassuring about their parents' love for them. Margaret Wise Brown's The Runaway Bunny is an old standard book for security and love. The theme that mother is always there comes through forcefully. Baby Bunny suggests many forms of escape from Mother Bunny: he will become a fish, a rock, a crocus. But Mother can always think of a way to catch up with her baby. She will become a fisherman, a mountain climber, a gardener, etc. Finally, the baby decides to "be your little bunny" and accepts a carrot from his mother. This is an exciting book for a very small child, with full-color spreads on every other page done by Clement Hurd.

Whose Mouse Are You? by Robert Kraus is another book about belonging. The question, "Whose mouse are you?" is first answered by, "Nobody's mouse." Not until Nobody's Mouse frees his parents from captivity and rescues his sister does he have someone to belong to. He even gains a baby brother along the way. If I Were a Mother by Kazue Mizumura provides lovely pictures by a Japanese artist of many baby animals and their mothers. It ends with the child's thinking that if she were a mother, she would be just like her own mother.

These nursery chronicles bring enjoyment to young children and often promote feelings of self-worth. They add interest and even glamour to everyday life.

An Emerging Sense of Humor

We could describe a small child's sense of humor as primitive. Their experiences are far too limited to allow them to enjoy anything but the obvious in humorous situations. Topsy-turvy or completely incongruous situations strike them as fun. Animals Should Definitely Not Wear Clothing by Judi Barrett and illustrated by Ron Barrett, shows animals dressed in funny clothes and provides many laughs for small children. Many nursery rhymes tell of silly behavior, or grotesque situations that two- to-three-year-olds can appreciate. They think that silly behavior or even accidents are funny. It is not that they want Humpty Dumpty to get hurt, for example, but they laugh at his fall. One small boy, Clayton, went into almost hysterical laughter when his father demonstrated how baseball players slide into base. The incongruity of seeing his very tall father suddenly hit the floor and slide at full length was almost too much for him. Such unexpected action can be extremely funny to small children.

They also laugh at repeated words, a mispronunciation of words they know, or explosive speech. Who, Said Sue, Said Whoo? by Ellen Raskin is a cumulative story with great visual depictions in the pictures. Children can count the animals, look for little jokes tucked into the illustrations, and help imitate the sounds of the animals as the book is read. When they reach the climax and find who said, "Chitter--chitter--chatter,"--a skunk, of course, they love joining in with "Phew!" and laugh as the animals quickly terminate their ride in Sue's car.

"You Look Ridiculous," Said the Rhinoceros to the Hippopotamus by Bernard Waber is somewhat of a moral tale with its own comedy. The hippo visits each animal in the jungle only to be told she is ridiculous looking. Naturally each animal prizes his or her own uniqueness. The hippo is convinced she should have a mane, a long neck, and so on. Only after a dream does she realize how really ridiculous she would look with such appendages, and at last she is satisfied with her appearance.

May I Bring a Friend? by Beatrice de Regniers shows a

little boy bringing strange and exotic animals to the king and queen's palace for lunch, dinner, and tea. The royalty willingly accept his friends although the meal is often ruined. Finally, after many invitations on their part, the king and queen are invited by the boy to come to the zoo for tea with his friends. Beni Montresor's illustrations for this book won the Caldecott Award.

Bears by Ruth Krauss has a very simple text that is brief but effective. Bears are pictured and described in a variety of poses: "on the stairs," "under chairs," "washing hairs," and on and on. Every activity rhymes with the word "bears." The pictures are full-page spreads showing bears participating in what would match children's antics.

Small children will enjoy the bold expressive pictures in The Egg Book by Jack Kent. This is a wordless book, but the expressions on the chicken's face as she hatches one egg after another, only to find other animals but no chicks, are enough to supply a complete story and much fun.

Pancakes for Breakfast by Tomie de Paola is another funny wordless book. The woman decides to make pancakes for breakfast but lacks many of the necessary ingredients. Finally she accumulates everything for the pancakes, but while she is away purchasing syrup, the dog and cat make away with the supplies. Her solution is to go uninvited to the neighbors for breakfast. In the last picture, she, the dog, and the cat are all fat and happy. The saying framed on the wall above where they are resting reads, "If at first you don't succeed, try, try again."

My Cat Likes to Hide in Boxes by Eve Sutton is a cumulative poem which includes eccentric cats from many lands but always gets back to "my cat" who likes to sleep in boxes. Even the cats in boxes are pictured as outlandish and fun.

Books You Will Not Want Your Child to Miss

As a child nears his or her third birthday, it is time to present some of the classics or near-classics that have brought joy to very young people for years. Outstanding among these is Beatrix Potter's The Tale of Peter Rabbit. This book was written in 1893 and has become a traditional part of our literary heritage. If you were to believe that children should have only those books with easily understood

vocabulary, you would never consider The Tale of Peter
Rabbit. Beatrix Potter was never condescending in her language. As in most of her stories, this text is crisp, pre-
cise, exciting, and complete with a very satisfying ending
that brings back the warmth and security of the family, even
for a naughty little rabbit. It is illustrated with delicate
watercolors. Even though all the animalness comes through
in the illustrations, Peter is still the disobedient, venturesome child to whom all youngsters seem to relate. Arbuthnot says that the good writing along with the exquisite illustrations are "a perfect example of the synchronization of pictures with text."[30] This little book, which is ideal for a
child to hold, is not just standard reading for English-
speaking children, but it has been translated into sixteen
foreign languages and is pleasing to children in many faraway
places. As a parent you will no doubt be renewing an ac-
quaintance with an old favorite as you enjoy reading it over
and over to your child. Soon your little boy or girl will
know the text as well as you do. One grandmother was
shocked to find that her three-year-old granddaughter, Vickie, did not know the story. In fact, she was even heard
to murmur something about her granddaughter being a dis-
advantaged child in that she had missed Peter Rabbit. Immediately she began telling the story since she had it mem-
orized. Vickie's attention never wavered from the storyteller, and each time Peter received his camomile tea and
was put to bed, the little girl would simply demand, "Talk
that Peter Rabbit again!" until Grandmother became rather
tired and suddenly decided that it was time for her to go
home. Shortly thereafter, little Vickie started outside.
When her mother asked where she was going, she said,
"My stomach hurts, I need some parsley."

Another "absolutely must-be-read" book is Wanda Gág's
Millions of Cats which was first published in 1928. This
story about a little old man and a little old woman who were
lonely is told in folktale style. The little old man sets out
to get them a cat. He finds:

> Cats here, cats there,
> Cats and kittens everywhere.
> Hundreds of cats,
> Thousands of cats,
> Millions and billions and trillions of cats.[31]

But he can't make up his mind which to take. Finally he
chooses them all and starts home. After their arrival the

jealous creatures simply destroy each other, leaving only one scrawny kitten. The old man and the old lady feed and pet this cat until it becomes the most beautiful cat in the world, according to the old man, and he should know because he has seen, "Hundreds of cats, thousands of cats, millions and billions and trillions of cats!" Both the text and the illustrations for this book are beautiful, flowing rhythms that easily catch the child's imagination. By the time you finish reading the story for the first time, you will probably have your listener joining in on the repeated refrains.

Caps for Sale by Esphyr Slobodkina is "a tale of a peddler, some monkeys and their monkey business." It is a long-standing favorite with preschoolers. The peddler carries the caps he sells on his head in exact order according to their color--with the red one always on top. One day when business isn't going well, the peddler leaves town and falls asleep under a tree. The caps are still on his head for safekeeping; but when he awakes, he finds them missing. Monkeys have stolen the caps and are up in the tree, each proudly wearing new headgear. After a frustrating time the peddler rescues his caps by throwing his own down in disgust. The monkeys, who have been teasing him by imitating everything he does, follow suit. The peddler arranges the caps on his head, again with the red one on top, and returns to the town. This is a fine story for participation. In no time a child will chant along with the reader or storyteller, "Caps, caps for sale. Fifty cents a cap!" or "Tsk, tsk," "You monkeys, you!" or "No caps, no caps," during the time when the peddler is searching for his lost goods.

Curious George by H. A. Rey is the first of the Curious George series. A young monkey is captured from the African jungles by the man in the yellow hat. He is taken aboard a ship where he gets into one bizarre situation after another and is eventually rescued after he tries to fly like a bird and almost drowns. Once on dry land he remains very curious and keeps the fire department on constant alert. Finally the man in the yellow hat recaptures him, and this time takes him to the zoo. This is an all-time favorite with youngsters, perhaps because George reminds them of themselves.

Swimmy is only one of the many exceptional books that Leo Lionni has written and illustrated for children. His books are outstanding for their innovative illustrations. His artwork not only brings enjoyment to small children, but also inspires them to try some different approaches to their own artistic ventures. Swimmy is a small black fish who is almost eaten by the huge fish who lives in that part of the ocean. He meets a school of tiny, frightened fish. Swimmy becomes the organizer and together they swim the waters in a tight group, appearing to be a large fish themselves. Swimmy is their eye. They manage to scare the great fish away. Here we have a fine old theme that children enjoy, that of the weak outsmarting the strong.

The Carrot Seed by Ruth Krauss is a very simple story about persistence. Everyone discourages the little boy who planted a carrot seed, saying it won't come up, but of course with his tender, loving care a huge carrot grows. This is a fine, satisfying ending to a story for a two-year-old.

Corduroy by Don Freeman has not been in print as long as many of the above books, but is one that is dearly loved by many children. Corduroy is a toy bear who must wait in the big department store for someone to buy him. Since he has lost a button, his chances of a home and someone to love him are not good until just the right little girl comes along.

More of the Simple Folktales

Folktales are the oldest and often the best-loved stories for early childhood. Your child may already be enjoying some of the classic stories like "The Gingerbread Boy," "The Little Red Hen," and "The Elves and the Shoemaker" because they are filled with repetition, rhymes, excitement, and fun. Two- to three-year-old children will probably be ready to listen to others of the short stories because there are good retellings to be found that have delightful illustrations which interpret the plot and make it possible for youngsters to visualize developments as they hear the story read. One that you may enjoy at this time is Henny Penny which Paul Galdone has retold and illustrated. The text is succinct and the illustrations are bright and appealing. Many books tell about the three bears and also the three pigs, but it would be difficult to find any versions that could surpass those done by Leslie Brooke in his The Story of the Three Bears and The Story of the Three Little Pigs. The texts are well done and the illustrations extend the stories with creative imagination. The same retellings and illustrations are a part of The Golden Goose Book, also by Leslie Brooke. This fine collection of several old folktales was first published in 1906.   It was reissued by the Warne Company in 1977.

The Mitten, retold by Alvin Tresselt, is a well-liked old Ukrainian folktale about many forest animals trying to find shelter in a lost mitten.   The Great Big Enormous Turnip by Alexei Tolstoy, illustrated by Helen Oxenbury, is a cumulative story told in folktale style about an old man who plants a turnip.   It grows so large that he cannot pull it up. He calls upon various characters to help him: the old woman, the granddaughter, the black dog, and others.   Finally, with the mouse's help, the turnip comes out of the ground! Small children often like to dramatize this one.

The Moving Adventures of Old Dame Trott and Her Comical Cat with pictures by Paul Galdone was based on a version of Old Dame Trot and Her Comical Cat published in London in 1807.   It is a very humorous picture book that will be a companion story to Old Mother Hubbard.

Marcia Brown illustrated the Asbjornsen and Moe version of The Three Billy Goats Gruff and produced what is perhaps the best-loved interpretation of this great old folktale.   Some mothers wince at the vivid description of how the troll was crushed to bits; however, most children see this as the demolishment of evil and they are happy when the goats get to "trip-trap" on across the bridge and make themselves fat on the grass on the other side.

Some parents fear that folktales are violent or may prove to be frightening to children, especially to very young children who may not understand the difference between fantasy and reality.   Child psychologists tend to feel that folktales have therapeutic value and help youngsters deal with their fears and problems.   Some of their comments will be discussed in succeeding chapters.   Parents should observe small children carefully to evaluate the effect of any given story on them.   Certainly, adults do not want to be overprotective; but if they see their children are upset, fidgety, and nervous over any story, they will want to switch to something else.   A few months later that particular story may be greatly enjoyed.

Goodnight Rituals

The "goodnight books" or sleepytime stories provide another type of literature that has a real appeal to children of

this age. These are helpful to finish the goodnight ritual
that seems to bring an end-of-the-day security to tiny children. In addition to Goodnight Moon, Margaret Wise Brown
has also written A Child's Goodnight Book, which has a
soothing text ending with a prayer. Another quieting little
book, printed on gray paper, is The Sleepy Book by Charlotte Zolotow. In it the child sees how animals, fish, birds,
and children sleep.

Close Your Eyes by Jean Marzollo is a sleepytime poem
illustrated by lovely pictures of all the things you can see as
you close your eyes. These are done by Susan Jeffers. Interwoven in the lovely scenes are drawings of a father having a busy time of putting his child to bed.

Bedtime Mouse by Sandol Stoddard is a rollicking verse
that tells of a mouse in the house at bedtime. The situation is greatly expanded by the child's imagination. A deer,
a bear, a goose, and many others appear, even a secret elf.
On the last page the little girl is telling all these things,
"Goodnight." In reality they are her toys. I Love You,
Mouse by John Graham is a very different, quiet book in
which a little boy talks with animals before his father puts
him to bed.

In Wynken, Blynken and Nod Barbara Cooney has produced beautiful illustrations for the old Eugene Field poem.
The entire book has the effect of a lullaby with the pictures
adding to the dream feeling. All the Pretty Horses by Susan
Jeffers has the same effect. It is a lullaby that changes into an almost believable dream of beautiful horses. Here
Comes Night by Miriam Schlein tells of things that sleep
and things that do not.

For Dr. Seuss fun there is Dr. Seuss's Sleep Book in
which the child can count sleepers. Some are sleepwalkers,
some are sleeptalkers, all are shown in Seuss's usual cartoon style.

For Calf, Goodnight, Nancy Jewell has written a charming text which has a little more story than that found in
most goodnight books. A curious calf explores the night
until he finally becomes a bit frightened and is glad to go
back to the barn to sleep with his mother.

Reading to children certainly should not be limited to
bedtime; however, storytime just before sleep can become

a beautiful, quiet interval for family togetherness. Many adults look back with real nostalgia to the storytime that they shared each evening with parents and siblings. In our modern rush, this is often the only period in the day that is set aside for real family closeness, especially with the father of the family. On the other hand, if everyone is overly tired at this particular hour, there should be no feeling of compulsion to read together. The results could be more harmful than beneficial if children are fussy and parents feel exhausted and simply "plow through" a book or two in a mechanical fashion. Reading time should be a very special, happy time, and planned accordingly. With the two- to three-year-old's need for routine, it is well to decide how many books will be read, what little goodnight ceremonies will be completed, and then stop at that. Also, do not let the youngster select six or eight books so that there is a great hurry to get them all read. Limit the reading to a few selections so that the books can be discussed and shared.

Your Child's Library

A child nearing a third birthday may become very interested in making original books. Often these consist of pictures from magazines that fascinate the youngster. Sometimes there will be special snapshots that he or she likes to talk about, or even original drawings, or special souvenirs that have been collected. Any ingenious parent can staple or sew together long sheets of wrapping paper or perhaps shelf paper. It makes little difference how the book is constructed, just so it is reasonably durable. No doubt the child will want to give the book a title and certainly his or her name should appear as the author. Help the youngster label the pictures with short captions. This promotes the idea that the printed word is simply our talk to be reflected back in what is called reading.

Some children have special subjects in which they become very interested--perhaps firetrucks, busses, dolls, or anything within their environment. They may enjoy making a book on this particular subject, and a bit later they may be able to help dictate a short story to be added to the pictures they have collected. All such activities help relate reading to interesting experiences.

Many of the books that you are using should come from the library. This gives your child the opportunity to sample various kinds of literature and often saves you from the mistake of buying books that you feel are excellent, yet, for some unknown reason, they do not appeal to your child. However, every child should own some books. This is important! Certain ones become treasured companions to be played with, studied, and enjoyed for their reassuring sameness. Such enjoyment reinforces interest in literature and in learning to read.

Books take on their own personalities. Someone has compared owning a book to owning a piece of the language. At this particular age, youngsters are quite possessive. Having, holding, and reading a book that is their property seems to add to their own stature. You will want to consider buying at least some of the ones which your child hugs tightly to his or her tummy and treats with admiration.

We are fortunate that we can get many good books in paperback, but try to stretch the budget enough to buy very special ones with lovely illustrations in a regular book form. There is nothing like the real thing! Children need such books to cherish.

By now your child's library will be growing. Try to have shelves on which the books are stored that will let your son or daughter see as many of the books as possible. If they are nicely displayed, they tempt the child to look at the pictures and relive the stories even in the midst of regular playtime activities. Try to repair tears and reinforce worn spots as soon as they develop. It is a good idea to solicit your child's help in doing this to build the idea of caring for things we love.

Progress Toward Reading

When a boy or girl reaches the age of three, he or she is moving rapidly toward the time when reading instruction will begin; however, as yet we are not interested in teaching reading as such. Rather, we should be continually helping the youngster understand the pleasures that books and reading offer. The child is still learning to learn and is gradually becoming acquainted with a variety of reading materials.

The most amazing development of this period is that of language growth. Vocabulary at age two may be limited to some fifty words, but by the end of the year, not only has vocabulary increased greatly, but the child is now making short sentences and learning the structure of the language. He or she is rapidly acquiring the abilities needed to communicate with others, to ask questions, and to gain cognitive skills by means of dialogue. Through this communication and through the sharing of books the youngster is extending his or her ability to listen and to formulate ideas.

Children enjoy learning new words. They engage in language games as they talk to themselves or share stories and poetry with others. They are beginning to understand like sounds in words--alliteration and rhyme--which are the bases for phonetic skills that will be necessary later when they start decoding the printed page. They are continually developing their language potential through listening to stories and books and by talking with thoughtful adults. Three-year-old children have probably realized that the marks on the paper are the means of communicating a story or title of a picture, especially if parents have taken time to show them what is being said as they go through books together. While children cannot read as yet, they are beginning to formulate a desire to do so, especially if reading is a part of their natural environment and they see those around them enjoying books. They are continuing to develop visual discrimination as they look at the illustrations and realize how these pictures confirm the text of stories.

"That a child should read life before he reads books is a belief held by most teachers concerned with reading readiness and beginning reading.... Only out of a reservoir of experiences is a fledgling reader able to bring meaning to the printed page."[32] Day-to-day experiences in a child's life build this essential background for reading. If parents provide a stimulating, enjoyable environment, the child's cognitive growth develops in leaps and bounds. Language skills go along with experiences. The youngster learns rapidly to communicate with others and to use his or her own encounters with reality to extend cognitive development and reasoning skills.

Children also learn to connect their own experiences with those of characters in stories so that books become more meaningful. They begin to identify with characters and extend their own experiences vicariously through those that book characters may have. In a story like Madeline by Ludwig Bemelmans, they can easily relate to everyday happenings like brushing their teeth and going to bed, going for a walk, and even visiting the zoo; but Madeline takes them one step further. She goes to the hospital. Indeed, there is confusion and some sense of fear, but then Madeline recovers rapidly. She receives a great deal of attention, and later when her friends come to see her, she shows them that "on her stomach was a scar!" All this might help convince a child, as it did Madeline's friends, that hospitals aren't all that bad.

In one way, the child who is really involved with books is reading already--not decoding words, of course, but at least he or she is often able to follow a well-loved story through the pages, using the pictures as clues. The youngster can do a kind of "creative reading" as a result of the remarkable language facility that has developed in just three short years, and because of personal experiences that help him or her interpret the story. In addition, the child who has been read to knows the joy of reading and is becoming more and more interested in learning to gain meaning from print.

As a parent, perhaps your most important contributions to your child's intellectual growth this past year have been giving him or her the freedom and desire to learn through experiences, supplying help and encouragement where it was needed, and providing that all-important home foundation for language growth. Sharing and contributing to your child's development during this critical growth period has no doubt been an interesting and rewarding experience for you. As Burton White, director of the Harvard Preschool Project, said, "I honestly cannot think of any task more exciting and more valuable that any of us do in our daily work than the task of providing an early education for one's own child under three years of age."[33]

Notes

[1]A. A. Milne, ed., "Halfway Down," in When We Were Very Young (New York: E. P. Dutton, 1924), p. 81.

[2]Joan Beck, How to Raise a Brighter Child: The Case for Early Learning, rev. ed. (New York: Pocket Books, 1975), p. 38.

[3]T. H. Bell, "Early Childhood Experiences Should Concern Educators," The National Observer, February 22, 1975, p. 14.

[4]Mary Ann Spencer Pulaski, Understanding Piaget: An

Introduction to Children's Cognitive Development (New York: Harper & Row, 1971), pp. 38-52.

5Genevieve Painter, Infant Education (San Rafael, CA: Dimensions Publishing Co., 1968), p. 16.

6Maya Pines, Revolution in Learning: The Years from Birth to Six (New York: Harper & Row, 1967), p. 7.

7Walter de la Mare, comp., "The Cupboard," in Peacock Pie (Chippewa Falls, WI: E. M. Hale and Co., 1941), p. 42.

8Marie Louise Allen, "The Mitten Song," in Sung Under the Silver Umbrella, ed. Literature Committee of the Association for Early Childhood (New York: Macmillan Company, 1935), p. 33.

9Kornei Chukovsky, From Two to Five, trans. and edited by Miriam Morton (Berkeley: University of California Press, 1966), pp. 7-10.

10Margaret C. Gillespie and John W. Conner, Creative Growth through Literature for Children and Adolescents (Columbus, OH: Charles E. Merrill Publishing Co., 1975), p. 30.

11Mary Lukens Coxon, "Learning to Read Is Doing What Comes Naturally," in Claremont Reading Conference Thirty-sixth Yearbook, ed. Malcolm P. Douglas (Claremont, CA: Claremont School Curriculum Laboratory, 1972), p. 164.

12Robert L. Doan, "Preschool Profile: Development Aspects of Young Children," in Start Early for an Early Start, ed. Ferne Johnson (Chicago: American Library Association, 1976), p. 6.

13Evelyn Pickarts and Jean Fargo, Parent Education: Toward Parental Competence (New York: Appleton-Century-Crofts, 1971), p. 7.

14David Townsend, "Reading in the Home," Reading, 15, No. 2 (July 1981), p. 48.

15Annis Duff, "Bequest of Wings": A Family's Pleasures with Books (New York: The Viking Press, 1944), p. 17.

16Dorothy Butler, Babies Need Books (New York: Atheneum Publishers, 1980), p. 60.

17Bruno Bettelheim and Karen Zelan, On Learning to Read: The Child's Fascination with Meaning (New York: Alfred A. Knopf, 1982), p. 9.

18Helen Huss, "The Role of Literature in Children's Education," Educational Horizons, Spring 1972, p. 140.

19Paul Hazard, Books Children and Men, trans. Marguerite Mitchell (Boston: Horn Book Co., 1944), p. 84.

20Chukovsky, p. 94.

21Sara Teasdale, comp., "Night," in Stars Tonight,

illus. by Dorothy Lathrop (New York: Macmillan Company, 1934), p. 2.

[22]May Hill Arbuthnot, Children's Reading in the Home (Glenview, IL: Scott, Foresman and Co., 1969), pp. 242-243.

[23]Dorothy Baruch, "Merry-Go-Round," in I Like Machinery, (New York: Harper and Brother, 1933), n. p.

[24]Myra Cohn Livingston, ed., "Just Watch," "I Know a Place," "Cooking," and "Discovery," in Whispers (New York: Harcourt, Brace, 1958), pp. 12, 17, 37, 27.

[25]Robert Louis Stevenson, ed., "The Swing," in A Child's Garden of Verses, illus. by Alice Provensen and Martin Provensen (New York: Simon & Schuster, 1951), p. 51.

[26]A. A. Milne, ed., "Hoppity," in When We Were Very Young, illus. by Ernest Shepard (New York: E. P. Dutton, 1924), p. 60.

[27]Robert Louis Stevenson, ed., "Windy Night," in A Child's Garden of Verses, illus. by Alice Provensen and Martin Provensen (New York: Simon & Schuster, 1951), p. 30.

[28]Dorothy Aldis, ed., "Going to Sleep," in All Together: A Child's Treasury of Verse, illus. by Helen D. Jameson and others (New York: G. P. Putnam's Sons, 1952), p. 88.

[29]Donnarae MacCann and Olga Richards, The Child's First Books: A Critical Study of Pictures and Texts (New York: H. W. Wilson Co., 1973), p. 107.

[30]Arbuthnot, p. 62.

[31]Wanda Gág, Millions of Cats (New York: Coward-McCann & Geoghegan, 1928), n. pag.

[32]Betty Coddy, Using Literature with Young Children, 2nd ed. (Dubuque, IA: William C. Brown, 1980), p. 66.

[33]Burton White, The First Three Years (Englewood Cliffs, NJ: Prentice-Hall, 1975), p. 255.

Books Discussed in This Chapter

Aliki. Go Tell Aunt Rhody. New York: Macmillan Company, 1974.

Anglund, Joan Walsh. In a Pumpkin Shell: A Mother Goose ABC. New York: Harcourt Brace Jovanovich, 1960.

Barrett, Judi. Animals Should Definitely Not Wear Clothing. Illus. by Ron Barrett. New York: Atheneum Publishers, 1970. (Paperback. 1980.)

Bemelmans, Ludwig. Madeline. New York: The Viking
    Press, 1939. (Paperback. New York: Penguin,
    1977.)
Boynton, Sandra. Hippos Go Berserk. Boston: Little,
    Brown, 1977.
Briggs, Raymond. The Mother Goose Treasury. New York:
    Coward-McCann, 1966. (Paperback. New York:
    Dell, 1980.)
Brooke, Leslie. The Golden Goose Book. New York:
    Frederick Warne & Co., 1905; rpt. 1977.
_____. Ring O' Roses. New York: Frederick Warne &
    Co., 1977.
_____. The Story of the Three Bears. New York:
    Frederick Warne & Co., 1905; rpt. 1977.
_____. The Story of the Three Little Pigs. New York:
    Frederick Warne & Co., 1905.
Brown, Marcia. The Three Billy Goats Gruff. New York:
    Harcourt Brace Jovanovich, 1957. (Paperback. 1972.)
Brown, Margaret Wise. A Child's Goodnight Book. Illus.
    by Jean Charlot. New York: W. R. Scott, 1943.
_____. Goodnight Moon. Illus. by Clement Hurd. New
    York: Harper & Row, 1947. (Paperback. 1977.)
_____. The Runaway Bunny. Illus. by Clement Hurd.
    New York: Harper & Row, 1942.
Brown, Myra Berry. Benjy's Blanket. Illus. by Dorothy
    Marino. New York: Franklin Watts, Inc., 1962.
Buckley, Helen E. Grandfather and I. Illus. by Paul Gal-
    done. New York: Lothrop, Lee & Shepard, 1959.
_____. Grandmother and I. Illus. by Paul Galdone.
    New York: Lothrop, Lee & Shepard, 1961.
Carle, Eric. My Very First Book of Colors. New York:
    Thomas Y. Crowell, 1974.
_____. The Very Hungry Caterpillar. Cleveland:
    Collins-World, 1969.
Chase, Richard. Billy Boy. Illus. by Glen Rounds. San
    Carlos, CA: Golden Gate Junior Books, 1966.
Crews, Donald. Truck. New York: Greenwillow, 1980.
De Paola, Tomie. Pancakes for Breakfast. New York:
    Harcourt Brace Jovanovich, 1978.
De Regniers, Beatrice Schenk. May I Bring A Friend?
    Illus. by Beni Montresor. New York: Atheneum
    Publishers, 1964. (Paperback. 1974.)
Eichenberg, Fritz. Ape in a Cape: An Alphabet of Odd
    Animals. New York: Harcourt, Brace & World,
    1952. (Paperback. 1973.)
Emberley, Barbara, adapted by. Drummer Hoff. Illus. by
    Ed Emberley. Englewood Cliffs, NJ: Prentice-Hall,
    1967.

_____, adapted by. Simon's Song. Illus. by Ed Ember-
      ley. Englewood Cliffs, NJ: Prentice-Hall, 1969.
Ets, Marie Hall. Just Me. New York: The Viking Press,
      1965. (Paperback. New York: Penguin, 1978.)
_____. Play With Me. New York: The Viking Press,
      1955. (Paperback. New York: Penguin, 1976.)
Falls, C. B. ABC Book. Garden City, NY: Doubleday
      and Company, 1957.
Field, Eugene. Wynken, Blynken and Nod. Illus. by Bar-
      bara Cooney. New York: Hastings House, 1980.
Fletcher, Helen J. Fingerplay Poems for Children. New
      York: Teachers College Press, 1964.
Freeman, Don. Corduroy. New York: The Viking Press,
      1968. (Paperback. New York: Penguin, 1976.)
Gág, Wanda. Millions of Cats. New York: Coward-McCann
      & Geoghegan, 1928. (Paperback. 1977.)
Galdone, Paul, retold by. Henny Penny. Boston: Houghton
      Mifflin, 1968. (Paperback. New York: Scholastic
      Book Services, 1980.)
_____. The Moving Adventures of Old Dame Trott and
      Her Comical Cat. New York: McGraw-Hill, 1973.
Graham, John. I Love You, Mouse. Illus. by Tomie de
      Paola. New York: Harcourt Brace Jovanovich, 1976.
      (Paperback. 1978.)
Grossbart, Francine B. A Big City. New York: Harper &
      Row, 1966.
Harper, Wilhelmina, retold by. The Gunniwolf. Illus. by
      William Wiesner. New York: E. P. Dutton, 1967.
Hoban, Tana. Dig-Drill Dump-Fill. New York: Green-
      willow, 1975.
Hutchins, Pat. Good-night, Owl! New York: Macmillan
      Company, 1972.
Jacobs, Frances E. Finger Plays and Action Rhymes.
      New York: Lothrop, Lee & Shepard, 1941.
Jeffers, Susan. All the Pretty Horses. New York: Mac-
      millan Company, 1974. (Paperback. New York:
      Scholastic Book Services, 1977.)
Jewell, Nancy. Calf, Goodnight. Illus. by Leonard Weis-
      gard. New York: Harper & Row, 1973.
Keats, Ezra Jack. Peter's Chair. New York: Harper &
      Row, 1967.
_____. Whistle for Willie. New York: The Viking
      Press, 1964.
Kent, Jack. The Egg Book. New York: Macmillan Com-
      pany, 1975.
Kraus, Robert. Whose Mouse Are You? Illus. by Jose
      Aruego. New York: Macmillan Company, 1970.
      (Paperback. New York: Macmillan Company, 1972.)

Krauss, Ruth. Bears. Illus. by Phyllis Rowand. New
York: Scholastic Book Services, 1948. (Paperback.
1970.)
_____. The Carrot Seed. Illus. by Crockett Johnson.
New York: Harper & Row, 1945. (Paperback. New
York: Scholastic Book Services, 1971.)
_____. The Growing Story. Illus. by Phyllis Rowand.
New York: Harper, 1947.
_____. A Very Special House. Illus. by Maurice Sendak.
New York: Harper, 1953.
Kredenser, Gail, and Stanley Mack. One Dancing Drum.
Illus. by Stanley Mack. New York: S. G. Phillips,
1971.
Kuskin, Karla. ABCDEFGHIJKLMNOPQRSTUVWXYZ. New
York: Harper & Row, 1963.
Lenski, Lois. Big Little Davy. New York: Henry Z.
Walck, 1956.
Lionni, Leo. Swimmy. New York: Pantheon, 1963.
MacDonald, Golden. Red Light, Green Light. Illus. by
Leonard Weisgard. Garden City, NY: Doubleday
and Company, 1944.
Mack, Stanley. Ten Bears in My Bed: A Goodnight Count-
down. New York: Pantheon, 1974.
Marzollo, Jean. Close Your Eyes. Illus. by Susan Jeffers.
New York: Dial Press, 1978.
Mizumura, Kazue. If I Were a Mother. New York:
Thomas Y. Crowell, 1968.
Newberry, Clare Turlay. Kittens' ABC. New York: Har-
per & Row, 1964.
Nodset, Joan L. Who Took the Farmer's Hat? Illus. by
Fritz Siebel. New York: Harper & Row, 1963.
Oxenbury, Helen. Numbers of Things. New York: Frank-
lin Watts, Inc., 1968.
Piatti, Celestino. Celestino Piatti's Animal ABC. New
York: Atheneum Publishers, 1966.
Polushkin, Maria. Who Said Meow? Illus. by Giulio
Maestro. New York: Crown Publishers, 1975.
Potter, Beatrix. The Tale of Peter Rabbit. New York:
Frederick Warne & Co., 1903. (Paperback. New
York: Dover Publications, Inc., 1972.)
Provensen, Alice, and Martin Provensen. What is a Color?
Racine, WI: Western Publishing Co., 1967.
Rand, Ann, and Paul Rand. I Know a Lot of Things. Illus.
by Paul Rand. New York: Harcourt, Brace &
World, 1956. (Paperback. 1973.)
Raskin, Ellen. Who, Said Sue, Said Whoo? New York:
Atheneum Publishers, 1973. (Paperback. 1976.)

Reed, Phillip. Phillip Reed's Mother Goose and Nursery Rhymes. New York: Atheneum Publishers, 1963.

Reiss, John J. Colors. Scarsdale, NY: Bradbury Press, 1969.

Rey, H. A. Curious George. Boston: Houghton Mifflin, 1941. (Paperback. 1973.)

Rockwell, Anne. The Tool Box. Illus. by Harlow Rockwell. New York: Macmillan Company, 1971. (Paperback. 1974.)

_____, and Harlow Rockwell. The Supermarket. New York: Macmillan Company, 1979.

Rockwell, Harlow. My Dentist. New York: Greenwillow, 1975.

_____. My Doctor. New York: Macmillan Company, 1973.

Schick, Eleanor. City in the Winter. New York: Macmillan Company, 1970. (Paperback. 1973.)

_____. Making Friends. New York: Macmillan Company, 1969.

Schlein, Miriam. Here Comes Night. Illus. by Harvey Weiss. Chicago: Albert Whitman & Co., 1957.

Scott, Ann Herbert. Sam. Illus. by Symeon Shimin. New York: McGraw-Hill, 1967.

Sendak, Maurice. Pierre. New York: Harper & Row, 1962.

Seuss, Dr. Dr. Seuss's Sleep Book. New York: Random House, 1962.

Simon, Mina, and Howard Simon. If You Were an Eel, How Would You Feel? Chicago: Follett Publishing Co., 1963.

Slobodkina, Esphyr. Caps for Sale. Reading, MA: Addison-Wesley, 1947. (Paperback. New York: Scholastic Book Services, 1976.)

Spier, Peter. Tin Lizzie. Garden City, NY: Doubleday and Company, 1975. (Paperback. 1978.)

Steiner, Charlotte. My Slippers Are Red. New York: Alfred A. Knopf, 1957.

Stewart, Robert. The Daddy Book. Illus. by Don Madden. New York: American Heritage Press, 1972.

Stoddard, Sandol. Bedtime Mouse. Illus. by Lynn Munsinger. Boston: Houghton Mifflin, 1981.

Sutton, Eve. My Cat Likes to Hide in Boxes. Illus. by Lynley Dodd. New York: Parents' Magazine Press, 1974.

Tolstoy, Alexei. The Great Big Enormous Turnip. Illus. by Helen Oxenbury. New York: Franklin Watts, Inc., 1969.

Tresselt, Alvin. The Mitten. Illus. by Yaroslava Mills.
New York: Lothrop, Lee & Shepard, 1964.
_____. Rain Drop Splash. Illus. by Leonard Weisgard.
New York: Lothrop, Lee & Shepard, 1947.
_____. Sun Up. Illus. by Roger Duvoisin. New York:
Lothrop, Lee & Shepard, 1949.
_____. White Snow, Bright Snow. Illus. by Roger Du-
voisin. New York: Lothrop, Lee & Shepard, 1947.
Tudor, Tasha. 1 is One. New York: Henry Z. Walck,
1956.
Waber, Bernard. "You Look Ridiculous, " Said the Rhinoc-
eros to the Hippopotamus. Boston: Houghton Miff-
lin, 1966. (Paperback. 1979.)
Weihs, Erika. Count the Cats. Garden City, NY: Double-
day and Company, 1976.
Yashima, Mitsu, and Taro Yashima. Momo's Kittens. Illus.
by Taro Yashima. New York: The Viking Press,
1961. (Paperback. 1977.)
Zemach, Margot. Hush, Little Baby. New York: E. P.
Dutton, 1976.
Zion, Gene. All Falling Down. Illus. by Margaret Bloy
Graham. New York: Harper, 1951.
_____. Harry the Dirty Dog. Illus. by Margaret B.
Graham. New York: Harper, 1956. (Paperback.
1976.)
Zolotow, Charlotte. The Sleepy Book. Illus. by Vladimir
Bobri. New York: Lothrop, Lee & Shepard, 1958.

Additional Nursery Songs, Games and Fingerplays

Berrien, Polly, ed. Games to Play with the Very Young.
Illus. by D. Hampson. New York: Random House,
1967.
Boni, Margaret Bradford. Fireside Book of Folk Songs.
Illus. by Alice Provensen and Martin Provensen.
New York: Simon & Schuster, 1974.
Dean's New Gift Book of Nursery Rhymes. Illus. by Janet
Johnstone and Anne Grahame Johnstone. London:
Dean & Son, 1971.
Fletcher, Margaret I., and Margaret Conkay Denison. The
New High Road of Song for Nursery Schools and Kin-
dergarten. Scarborough, Ontario: W. J. Gage, 1960.
Graham, Mary Nancy. 50 Songs for Children. Chicago:
Albert Whitman & Co., 1964.

Grayson, Marion. Let's Do Fingerplays. Illus. by Nancy
    Weyl. Washington: Robert B. Luce, 1962.
Kapp, Paul, ed. A Cat Came Fiddling and Other Rhymes of
    Childhood. Illus. by Irene Haas. New York: Har-
    court, Brace, 1956.
Keats, Ezra Jack. John Henry: An American Legend.
    New York: Pantheon, 1965.
Landeck, Beatrice, and Elizabeth Cook. Wake Up and Sing.
    New York: William Morrow, 1969.
Langstaff, John. On Christmas Day in the Morning. Illus.
    by Antony Groves-Raines. New York: Harcourt,
    Brace, 1959.
Lloyd, Norman, arranger. The New Golden Song Book.
    Illus. by Mary Blair. New York: Simon & Schuster,
    1963.
Matterson, Elizabeth, comp. Games to Play with the Very
    Young: A Treasury of Nursery Songs and Finger-
    plays. New York: McGraw-Hill, 1969.
Milne, A. A. The Pooh Song Book. Music by H. Fraser-
    Simson. New York: E. P. Dutton, 1961.
Mitchell, Donald. Every Child's Book of Nursery Songs.
    New York: Crown Publishers, 1969.
Moss, Jeffery, and Joseph G. Raposo. The Sesame Street
    Song Book. New York: Simon & Schuster, 1971.
Panabaker, Lucile. Lucile Panabaker's Second Song Book.
    Illus. by Pat Dacey. Toronto: Martin Associates,
    1975.
Paulson, Emilie. Fingerplays for Nursery and Kindergar-
    ten. Boston: D. Lathrop, 1963.
Pointer, Priscilla. Ten Little Fingers: A Book of Finger-
    plays. New York: Treasure Books, 1954.
Seeger, Pete, and Charles Seeger. The Foolish Frog.
    Illus. by Miloslar Jagr. New York: Macmillan
    Company, 1973.
Thomas, Marlo. Free to Be ... You and Me. New York:
    McGraw-Hill, 1974.
Wilkin, Esther. Play With Me. Illus. by Eloise Wilkin.
    Racine, WI: Western Publishing Co., 1967.
Yamaguchi, Marianne. Finger Plays. New York: Holt,
    Rinehart & Winston, 1970.

Other Book Suggestions for This Age Level

Alexander, Martha. I'll Protect You From the Jungle
    Beasts. New York: Dial Press, 1973.

Anglund, Joan Walsh. The Brave Cowboy. New York:
    Harcourt, Brace, 1959.
_____. Cowboy and His Friend. New York: Harcourt,
    Brace, 1961.
Austin, Margot. Growl Bear. New York: E. P. Dutton,
    1951.
Bank Street College of Education. Green Light Go. Rev.
    ed. Illus. by Jack Endewelt and others. New York:
    Macmillan Company, 1972.
Barton, Byron. Buzz, Buzz, Buzz. New York: Macmillan
    Company, 1973.
Bayley, Nicola. Nicola Bayley's Book of Nursery Rhymes.
    New York: Albert A. Knopf, 1975.
Blake, Pamela, ed. Peep-Show: A Little Book of Rhymes.
    New York: Macmillan Company, 1973.
Bornstein, Ruth. Little Gorilla. New York: Seabury
    Press, 1976.
Bridwell, Norman. Clifford's Good Deeds. New York:
    Four Winds Press, 1975. (Paperback. New York:
    Scholastic Book Services, 1976.)
Bright, Robert. Me and the Bears. Garden City, NY:
    Doubleday and Company, 1951.
Brock, Emma Lillian. To Market! To Market! New York:
    Alfred A. Knopf, 1930.
Brown, Marc. One, Two, Three: An Animal Counting Book.
    Boston: Little, Brown, 1976.
Brown, Marcia. All Butterflies. New York: Charles
    Scribner's Sons, 1974.
Brown, Margaret Wise. Nibble, Nibble, Poems for Chil-
    dren. Illus. by Leonard Weisgard. Reading, MA:
    Addison-Wesley, 1959.
_____. Wait Till the Moon is Full. Illus. by Garth
    Williams. New York: Harper, 1948.
Brustlein, Janice. Little Bear's Pancake Party. Illus. by
    Marian Curtis Foster. New York: Lothrop, Lee &
    Shepard, 1960.
_____. Little Bear's Thanksgiving. Illus. by Marian
    Curtis Foster. New York: Lothrop, Lee & Shepard,
    1967.
Budney, Blossom. N Is for Nursery School. Illus. by
    Vladimir Bobri. New York: Lothrop, Lee & Shep-
    ard, 1956.
Byars, Betsy. Go and Hush the Baby. Illus. by Emily
    McCully. New York: The Viking Press, 1971.
Carle, Eric. The Grouchy Ladybug. New York: Thomas
    Y. Crowell, 1977.
_____. Have You Seen My Cat? New York: Franklin
    Watts, Inc., 1973.

Chaffin, Lillie D. Bear Weather. Illus. by Helga Aichinger. New York: Macmillan Company, 1969.

Chardiet, Bernice. C Is for Circus. Illus. by Brinton Turkle. New York: Walker and Company, 1971.

Coker, Gylbert. Naptime. New York: Delacorte Press, 1978.

Cole, Brock. No More Baths. Garden City, NY: Doubleday and Company, 1980.

Davis, Alice V. Timothy Turtle. Illus. by Guy B. Wiser. New York: Harcourt Brace Jovanovich, 1972.

De Paola, Tomie. Charlie Needs a Cloak. Englewood Cliffs, NJ: Prentice-Hall, 1974.

_____. Nana Upstairs and Nana Downstairs. New York: G. P. Putnam's Sons, 1973.

De Regniers, Beatrice S. A Little House of Your Own. Illus. by Irene Haas. New York: Harcourt, Brace, 1954.

Domanska, Janina. Spring Is. New York: Greenwillow, 1976.

Emberley, Barbara. Simon's Song. Illus. by Ed Emberley. Englewood Cliffs, NJ: Prentice-Hall, 1969.

Ets, Marie Hall. Elephant in a Well. New York: The Viking Press, 1973.

Flack, Marjorie. Angus and the Cat. Garden City, NY: Doubleday and Company, 1931.

_____. Angus and the Ducks. Garden City, NY: Doubleday and Company, 1939.

Fujikawa, Gyo. A Child's Book of Poems. New York: Grosset & Dunlap, 1969. (Paperback. 1977.)

_____. Oh, What a Busy Day. New York: Grosset & Dunlap, 1976.

Gág, Wanda. Snippy and Snappy. New York: Coward-McCann, 1931.

Galdone, Paul. Tom, Tom the Piper's Son. New York: McGraw-Hill, 1964.

Garten, Jan. The Alphabet Tale. Illus. by Muriel Batherman. New York: Random House, 1964.

Getz, Arthur. Hamilton Duck. Racine, WI: Western Publishing Co., 1972.

Ginsburg, Mirra. Mushroom in the Rain. Trans. and adapted from Russian story by A. Suteyev. Illus. by Jose Aruego and Ariane Dewey. New York: Macmillan Company, 1978.

Hargreaves, Roger. Mr. Bounce's Numbers. Los Angeles: Price, Stern, Sloan Publishers, 1981.

Hazen, Barbara S. The Gorilla Did It! Illus. by Ray Cruz. New York: Atheneum Publishers, 1974.

Hoberman, Mary Ann. A Home Is a House for Me. Illus. by Betty Fraser. New York: The Viking Press, 1978.

Holdsworth, W. The Little Red Hen. New York: Farrar, Straus and Giroux, 1969.

Holzenthaler, Jean. My Hands Can. Illus. by Nancy Tafuri. New York: E. P. Dutton, 1978.

Jenkins, William A. My First Picture Dictionary. Rev. ed. Illus. by Andrew Schillar. New York: Lothrop, Lee & Shepard, 1977.

Johnson, Crockett. Harold's ABC's. New York: Harper & Row, 1963.

Keats, Ezra Jack. Jennie's Hat. New York: Harper & Row, 1966.

_____. A Letter to Amy. New York: Harper & Row, 1968.

_____. Psst, Doggie. New York: Franklin Watts, Inc., 1973.

Kessler, Ethel, and Leonard Kessler. Big Red Bus. Garden City, NY: Doubleday and Company, 1964.

Kraus, Robert. Herman the Helper. Illus. by José Aruego and Ariane Dewey. New York: E. P. Dutton, 1974.

_____. Milton the Early Riser. Abr. ed. Illus. by José Aruego and Ariane Dewey. New York: Windmill, 1981.

Krauss, Ruth. The Happy Egg. Illus. by Crockett Johnson. Chicago, IL: J. Phillip O'Hara, Inc., 1972. (Paperback. New York: Scholastic Book Services, 1972.)

Kroll, Steven. If I Could Be My Grandmother. Illus. by Lady McCrady. New York: Pantheon, 1977.

Kuskin, Karla. A Boy Had a Mother Who Bought Him a Hat. Boston: Houghton Mifflin, 1976.

LaFontaine, Jean de. The Lion and the Rat. Illus. by Brian Wildsmith. New York: Franklin Watts, Inc., 1963.

_____. The North Wind and the Sun. Illus. by Brian Wildsmith. New York: Franklin Watts, Inc., 1964.

Lang, Andrew, ed. Nursery Rhyme Book. Illus. by L. Leslie Brooke. New York: Dover Publications, Inc., 1972. (Paperback.)

Langstaff, John. Hot Cross Buns and Other Old Street Cries. Illus. by Nancy Winslow Parker. New York: Atheneum Publishers, 1978.

Lenski, Lois. Little Train. New York: Henry Z. Walck, 1940.

Lexau, Joan M. Emily and the Klunky Baby and the Next-Door Dog. Illus. by Martha Alexander. New York: Dial Press, 1972.

Livermore, Elaine. Find the Cat. Boston: Houghton Mifflin, 1973.

Long, Ruthanna. Ten Little Chipmunks. Illus. by June Goldsborough. Racine, WI: Western Publishing Co., 1971.

Maestro, Betsy. Where Is My Friend? Illus. by Giulio Maestro. New York: Crown Publishers, 1976.

Marshall, James. Yummers! Boston: Houghton Mifflin, 1973.

Mayer, Mercer, and Marianne Mayer. One Frog Too Many. Illus. by Mercer Mayer. New York: Dial Press, 1975.

McDermott, Gerald. The Stonecutter: A Japanese Folk Tale. New York: The Viking Press, 1975.

McMillan, Bruce. The Alphabet Symphony: An ABC Book. New York: Greenwillow, 1977.

McPhail, David. The Bear's Toothache. Boston: Little, Brown, 1972. (Paperback. New York: Penguin, 1978.)

Miles, Miska. Swim Little Duck. Illus. by Jim Arnosky. Boston: Little, Brown, 1975.

Miller, Mitchell. One Misty Moisty Morning: Rhymes From Mother Goose. New York: Farrar, Straus and Giroux, 1971.

Mizumura, Kazue. If I Were a Cricket ... New York: Thomas Y. Crowell, 1973.

Moffett, Martha. A Flower Pot is Not a Hat. Illus. by Susan Perl. New York: E. P. Dutton, 1972.

Munari, Bruno. Bruno Munari's Zoo. Cleveland: Collins-World, 1963.

Nakatani, Chiyoko. My Day on the Farm. New York: Thomas Y. Crowell, 1977.

Newberry, Clare Turlay. The Kittens' ABC. New York: Harper & Row, 1965.

Orbach, Ruth. Apple Pigs. Cleveland: Collins-World, 1977.

Ormondroyd, Edward. Theodore. Illus. by John Larrecq. Oakland, CA: Parnassus, 1966.

Oxenbury, Helen. Shopping Trip. New York: Dial Press, 1982.

Payne, Emmy. Katy No-Pocket. Illus. by H. A. Rey. Boston: Houghton Mifflin, 1944. (Paperback. 1973.)

Peppé, Rodney. Simple Simon. New York: Holt, Rinehart & Winston, 1973.

Peterson, Jeanne Whitehouse. While the Moon Shines Bright. Illus. by Margot Apple. New York: Harper & Row, 1981.

Politi, Leo. Little Leo. New York: Charles Scribner's Sons, 1951.

Pomerantz, Charlotte. The Piggy in the Puddle. Illus. by James Marshall. New York: Macmillan Company, 1974.

Potter, Beatrix. The Sly Old Cat. London: Frederick Warne, 1972.

Provensen, Alice, and Martin Provensen. The Mother Goose Book. New York: Random House, 1976.

Rice, Eve. Goodnight, Goodnight. New York: Greenwillow, 1980.

Rockwell, Harlow. My Nursery School. New York: Greenwillow, 1976.

Roy, Ron. Three Ducks Went Wandering. Illus. by Paul Galdone. Boston: Houghton Mifflin. (Paperback. New York: Scholastic Book Services, 1980.)

Sendak, Maurice. Chicken Soup with Rice. A Book of Months. New York: Harper & Row, 1962. (Paperback. New York: Scholastic Book Services, 1970.)

Shulevitz, Uri. Oh, What a Noise. New York: Macmillan Company, 1971.

_____. Rain Rain Rivers. New York: Farrar, Straus and Giroux, 1969.

Smith, Jessie Willcox. The Little Mother Goose. New York: Dodd, Mead & Co., 1912.

Spier, Peter. Bill's Service Station. Garden City, NY: Doubleday and Company, 1981.

_____. The Toy Store. Garden City, NY: Doubleday and Company, 1981.

Stone, Elberta. I'm Glad I'm Me. Illus. by Margaret Wise Brown. New York: G. P. Putnam's Sons, 1971.

Sutton, Jane. What Should a Hippo Wear? Illus. by Lynn Munsinger. Boston: Houghton Mifflin, 1979.

Tanz, Christine. An Egg Is to Sit On. Illus. by Rosekrans Hoffman. New York: Lothrop, Lee & Shepard, 1978.

Ungerer, Tomi. Crictor. New York: Harper, 1958. (Paperback. New York: Scholastic Book Services, 1969.)

Wahl, Jan. Push Kitty. Illus. by Garth Williams. New York: Harper & Row, 1968.

Ward, Andrew. Baby Bear and the Long Sleep. Illus. by John Walsh. Boston: Little, Brown & Company, 1980.

Wells, Rosemary. Don't Spill It Again, James. New York: Dial Press, 1977.

_____. Noisy Nora. New York: Dial Press, 1973.

Wildsmith, Brian. Brian Wildsmith's ABC. New York: Franklin Watts, Inc., 1963.

———. Brian Wildsmith's Circus. New York: Franklin Watts, Inc., 1970.

———. Brian Wildsmith's Wild Animals. New York: Franklin Watts, Inc., 1967.

Winthrop, Elizabeth. I Think He Likes Me. Illus. by Denise Saldutti. New York: Harper & Row, 1980.

Yeoman, John. Mouse Trouble. Illus. by Quentin Blake. New York: Macmillan Company, 1973.

Ylla. Two Little Bears. New York: Harper, 1954.

Zagone, Theresa. No Nap for Me. Illus. by Lillian Hoban. New York: E. P. Dutton, 1978.

Zhenya, Gay. Look. New York: The Viking Press, 1952.

Zion, Gene. Hide and Seek Day. Illus. by Margaret Bloy Graham. New York: Harper, 1954.

Zolotow, Charlotte. The Quarreling Book. Illus. by Arnold Lobel. New York: Harper & Row, 1963.

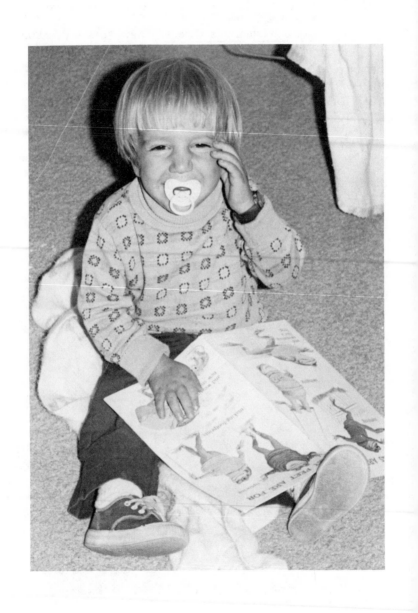

CHAPTER IV

A POSITIVE LEARNING ENVIRONMENT
--Three-to-Four-Year-Olds--

Changing Developmental Patterns

"The parents of just-turned three-year-olds must be for-
given for assuming, with incredulous relief and joy, that they
have now mastered the art of parenthood."[1] The "just-three
tranquility" is wonderful while it lasts. To the three-year-
old, life is good and to be enjoyed! Six months later the
little person may be filled with doubts, fears, and anxieties.
However, do not despair. By the time the fourth birthday
comes around, things are lovely once again. Self-confidence
seems to return, along with enthusiasm and joy. If nothing
else, one can count on variety in the developmental growth
of preschool children! Never are parents allowed to become
too smug. Just as they think everything is going beautifully
for their child, his or her world seems to fall apart; but
then, after a time on a downbeat plateau, almost miraculous-
ly things come back into focus, and their son or daughter is
again adding real joy to each day. At least this is the general pattern; of course every child is an individual. There
is no such thing as a universal pattern of development.

A prevalent characteristic of most children of this age
which affects their intellectual development is a growing interest in adults. They respond freely to adult suggestions
and enjoy conversing with them. They love imitative play
and will pretend to be grown up. Dressing up is great fun,
and often youngsters dramatize parts of favorite stories and
poems. They gradually move from their self-centered world
to an enjoyment of friends, a sharing of toys, and an ability
to feel and express sympathy for others in times of difficulty. Three-year-olds usually conform quite well; however,
often they still seem to be simply watching what is happening. At three-and-a-half children become doers, anxious
and demanding. Oddly enough, the routine that was of such

great importance a year ago is now a very bothersome aspect of life. Imagination develops rapidly. Many children have imaginary companions and talk with storybook characters in their play. They begin enjoying simple guessing games and love to try out new words. Although vocabularies expand at a surprising rate, children will at times get so excited in trying to tell something, that their thoughts run ahead of their ability to verbalize, and they may stumble over words in the rush. Wise parents understand that these youngsters are not displaying a speech defect, but simply a desire to communicate faster than they are capable of doing.

Frequently a three- to four-year-old child whose development has been average or even somewhat slow will demonstrate a sudden spurt of growth. A late talker, for example, will often start speaking quite fluently. There is a delightful book, Leo the Late Bloomer by Robert Kraus, in which the little tiger, Leo, cannot do anything right. He can't read, or write, or draw. He is a sloppy eater, and he never says a word. His father worries about him, but his sensible mother insists that nothing is wrong. Leo is just a late bloomer. She tells his father to quit watching him for signs of growth. Time passes and Leo is left alone. Finally there comes the day when Leo blooms! He can do all of the things that had been expected of him! This book is probably more reassuring to parents than to children, but the entire family will enjoy it.

One of the strongest fears or anxieties that usually mark the second half of the fourth year of life is the fear of separation, the anxiety of being parted from parents. The assurance that loved ones will always return is not gained through one or two experiences. Such an adjustment will probably take time. One way of helping a child gain this understanding can be through reading and talking about certain books in which the characters face the same anxiety. Children's reasoning usually moves back and forth freely between reality and book situations. Just knowing that book characters have suffered the same fears that they have--and have survived--can be very reassuring. The vicarious experience of living through fears of separation with a book character who eventually finds that his or her fears were groundless may help develop feelings of security for children. Even discussing the fact that a character is having more difficulty than the listener/reader in overcoming fears can help build self-reliance and a feeling of competence in solving one's own problems. Perhaps the most important asset of such books is the opportunity to talk over the story with an adult and learn that problems can be solved.

There are many books that can be helpful in situations of this kind. Waiting by Nicki Weiss is a simple little story showing a small girl waiting for her mother to return. The diminutive block pictures express the anguish that a child endures, and, of course, there is the reassuring ending.

Be Good, Harry by Mary Chalmers is the story of a cat family. In this book the mother leaves Harry with a baby-sitter, telling him that she will be back in one hour. Harry is unhappy at first, but adjusts slowly. Naturally his mother does return. This is a true-to-life situation, and it could be reassuring to see it depicted in a book. I'd Rather Stay with You by Charlotte Steiner is about a baby kangaroo whose mother encourages him to leave her protective pouch and venture out on his own. It takes a great deal of time and patience to help the little fellow learn that he is capable of going out alone, but finally he becomes brave enough even to go to kindergarten. This sensitive story reinforces the fact, for parents as well as for children, that the break away from a mother's "protective pouch" cannot be made quickly. A Drink for Little Red Diker by Jane Thayer is a similar story about a little deer.

If going to nursery school is causing your child separation anxiety, there are many books about early school experiences that could be helpful. Cathy's First School by Betty Katzoff is a reassuring story that might help eliminate fears. The Two Friends by Grete Mannheim is illustrated by photographs and could give a child some idea of what to expect in school if the book were read and discussed before the youngster meets this new situation. Another experience book that could be helpful to read before your son or daughter ventures out to nursery school is John E. Johnson's My School Book. Will I Have a Friend? by Miriam Cohen has been a favorite concerning school experiences. In this story a little boy is reluctant about leaving his father and starting to a new school. As one might guess from the title, he does find a friend, and when the day is over, he has gained confidence.

One criticism of some books of this kind is that they make the solutions seem all too easy, but perhaps that would provide a good basis for discussion between parents

and their child. Often the fact that a book furnishes a
means of talking about deep-seated concerns is more important to a child than the story itself.

The Joy of Real Communication

Through admirable efforts on the part of the child and
real patience on the part of caring adults, the three-to-four-
year-old has developed the ability to use language in truly
functional ways. Finally, and at last, the youngster has at
hand the tools with which to express needs, interests, and
feelings, and to inquire about what heretofore has often
caused misunderstandings and frustrations. Usually a child
of this age has mastered enough of the basic skills of communication to enjoy not only talking with others, but also
listening to a variety of stories and poems, and expressing
exuberance about life itself. What a satisfaction it is when
a boy or girl reaches this developmental stage. At last,
basic communication is possible! Of course there is still
a need for vocabulary growth, better articulation, and a
greater fluency of speech, but all of these skills develop
rapidly. The youngster can now use about ninety percent of
the vowel sounds and most of the consonant sounds. He or
she is also beginning to master some shades of the language
and can employ some adjectives, adverbs, and auxiliary
verbs.

This new facility with language provides the means of
making discoveries. Parents are inundated with a bombardment of what, when, and how questions. The three-and-a-
half- to four-year-old period is probably the most prevalent
time for "why" questions. Admittedly, this demand for explanations is trying for caring adults, but it helps to remember that your child is displaying healthy curiosity and intelligence with his or her continual quest for understanding.
Chukovsky puts it rather forcefully when he says:

> Adults who irritably avoid answering the "boring"
> childish questions commit an irrevocable and cruel
> act--they forcibly retard the child's mental growth
> and thwart his spiritual development. It is true that
> with some children there is a period when they liter-
> ally wear out their grandmothers, fathers, and moth-
> ers with endless "why's" and "what for's, " but what
> is our respect for the child worth when we deprive
> him, for the sake of our personal convenience, of es-
> sential mental nourishment?

Chukovsky also tells of a little Russian girl who said to her mother, "I'm a why-er, you are a becaus-er."[2] Perhaps being a "becaus-er" is one of parents' prime responsibilities during this growth period. But caring adults should not act as traveling encyclopedias; they should turn the tables on the children and ask them questions to promote the development of reasoning powers.

Promotion of Language Growth

Oral language ability is an essential basis for reading. In his book Preparing Your Child for Reading, Miles A. Tinker says, "The greater your child's ability to comprehend material presented in oral form and the greater his proficiency in the use of oral language, the more ready he will be for success in beginning reading."[3] Since most of a child's language learning takes place before the youngster enters kindergarten, it is no wonder that educators are saying that parents are the child's most vital teachers! They are the ones who provide the all-important incidental teaching of the language that is the very foundation for future academic success.

Like authors of fine children's books, thoughtful parents do not water down their conversations and use only one- or two-syllable words. They realize that a youngster learns from being exposed to rich vocabulary and sentence patterns that reflect the structure of the language. Children understand more than they can give back in their own speech. They need the opportunity to grow through a rich language environment.

Reading aloud to children acquaints them with the sentence structures and vocabulary of a more formal language than that used in ordinary speech. It gives them a kind of feeling for the patterns of language that they will meet in reading. Carol Chomsky found in a study reported in The Harvard Educational Review that there is a positive correlation between the stage of linguistic development of pre-readers and the amount of reading aloud to which they have been exposed. [4]

In their discussion of how reading aloud to preschool children promotes language development and prepares youngsters for future academic experiences, Butler and Clay say:

It is certain that listening to stories expands the

vocabulary. The speech of children who are used to "book language" is often rich and varied. This is easy to understand; such children have a large store of words and ideas to draw on. This store just has to help when they are later trying to make sense of a line of print. They need resources to call on, then. How can a beginning reader, groping for a word, find it unless it is in his mind to begin with?[5]

One way to promote language growth is to capitalize on the fact that three- to four-year-old children simply enjoy words. They like to create crazy new words and rhyme them with ones they know. They are fascinated with the language gymnastics in the Dr. Seuss books, and they play with alliteration and rhyme in Mother Goose and in simple poetry. They love imitating sounds. Fiddle-I-Fee by Diane Stanley provides fine opportunities for such fun. This is a clever, rather modern interpretation of "Had a Cat, the Cat Pleased Me," which is often found in songbooks. The various animal noises, so important to the rhythm of this traditional American chant, are included in the pictures. A child's participation in adding the sound effects that appear in the ballooned captions can be an early reading experience. Too Much Noise by Ann McGovern and Shhhhhh, Bang by Margaret Wise Brown also provide opportunities for fun in contributing sound effects. Children who enjoy collecting words will be fascinated with the labels that Wildsmith uses for his unusual pictures in Brian Wildsmith's Birds. He names the groups of birds, giving interesting captions such as "A wedge of swans, a sedge of herons." Young listeners will often learn such labels and enjoy rolling them off their tongues.

For a book that will challenge even an adult reader, try the captions in Hosie's Alphabet, which Leonard Baskin produced with the help of his children. The pictures are stunning but the wording is so difficult that only the brave among small children will try repeating them. Alliteration like that in "Bumptious Baboon" or "A ghastly, garrulous gargoyle" is not easy to quote.

Poetry provides some of the most pleasing literature for the language connoisseur. Try some of David McCord's poems with his or her new facility with words. "Song of the Train" is a favorite.

Song of the Train

David McCord

Clickety-clack
Wheels on the track,
This is the way
They begin the attack:
Click-ety-clack
Click-ety-clack
Click-ety, clack-ety,
Click-ety
Clack.

Clickety-clack,
Over the crack,
Faster and faster
The song of the track:
Clickety-clack,
Clickety-clack
Clickety, clackety
Clackety
Clack.

Riding in front,
Riding in back,
Everyone hears
The song of the track:
Clickety-clack,
Clickety-clack,
Clickety, clickety,
Clackety
Clack. 6

* * *

Never Tease a Weasel by Jean C. Soule is a book built
around a poem that provides jolly rhymes within lines and
wonderful chants to roll off the tongue like:

You can knit a kitten mittens
And perhaps that cat would purr.
You could fit a fox with socks
That exactly matched his fur....
But never tease a weasel;
That is very good advice.
A weasel doesn't like it
And teasing isn't nice![7]

Children will spend hours poring over Richard Scarry's Great Big Air Book or The Best Word Book Ever, also by Scarry. Books of this kind may help to develop vocabularies. Many three-to-four-year-olds enjoy picture dictionaries. At first, experiences with books of this type amount to labeling and playing the identification game, but after a time children will begin to associate the labels under the pictures with the objects and may even begin to read a few words through this association.

Words like "secret" and "surprise" hold magical qualities for youngsters this age. They love secret phrases like those found in The Magic Porridge Pot by Paul Galdone and in Strega Nona by Tomie de Paola. It is fun for them to know the magic secret while the story characters are in a state of panic because they do not know what to do. A surprise climax like that found in The Camel Who Took a Walk by Jack Tworkov can be pure excitement to small children. In this cumulative plot there is a build-up to a breathtaking climax, yet nothing ever harms the innocent, unsuspecting camel.

Brian Wildsmith's Puzzles by Wildsmith is a fascinating experience in modern art for small children. The puzzles that he presents in his pictures provide real challenges for preschool children as they match designs, count groupings, and try to find missing objects in pictures.

Tana Hoban has given children one of the most interesting puzzle books to be found in Look Again! From the part of an object that can be seen through a square cut in the preceding page, the viewer of this wordless book is invited to guess what the object is. The book urges youngsters to be more observant and to enjoy the designs found in nature. Take Another Look, also by Hoban, is very similar in format and just as enjoyable.

This is just a sampling of books that will help to promote language development. Texts that present puzzling situations or an exciting climax cause children to speculate and discuss the pictures and the stories. Unusual words fascinate young listeners, help them expand their vocabularies and challenge them to use language that appeals to them because of interesting sound patterns. The language in poetry encourages them to expand vocabulary through supplying rhyming words or explosive sounds when someone reads the verses to them. And the identification games that go along with pictured words and groupings add to general language development.

Refinement of Listening Skills

One of the reading readiness skills that is greatly enhanced by sharing exciting books is the ability to listen carefully. Tinker states:

> Learning to read depends to a large degree upon good listening habits. The reader must become familiar with many sound patterns as indicated in print and be able to make such fine distinctions as the difference in the middle sounds of <u>horse</u> and <u>house</u> or <u>shall</u> or <u>shell</u>. Otherwise he cannot pronounce or comprehend what he is trying to read. [8]

You can help your child refine listening skills by calling attention to various sounds in the environment, and by playing guessing games to identify certain noises. Children enjoy onomatopoeia, words that actually imitate the natural sounds; for example, the hiss of steam, the squeak of a mouse, the screech of an owl, the clang of a chain. You can play games with words of this type just as you did with the animal sounds that fascinate toddlers. Mother Goose and simple poetry provide a great wealth of alliteration and rhyming experiences. As you are saying or reading poems, let your child guess what word completes the rhythm and rhyme or continues the alliteration in a phrase such as "One misty, moisty morning." Stories like "The Three Billy Goats Gruff" help children appreciate the importance of pitch, tone, and intensity, especially if you encourage the listener to participate in dramatizing sound effects for each character. What fun it is to get heavier and heavier "trip-traps" for each goat coming across the bridge! You will find that you will forget your inhibitions and have as much fun as your son or daughter while you enjoy these stories and lively poems together.

Three-to-four-year-olds love to make up words. Some are very clever at this. You should appreciate this talent along with the silly language that they invent. Often such experiences are an exercise in rhyming and the learning of sounds. Singing games or rhymes assist children in gaining control over language. Telling their own stories and pretending to read books helps them learn to manipulate language. All of these experiences add to a rich learning environment and help lay a foundation for reading.

You will want to encourage such activities whenever your

youngster is interested, but the wise parent will avoid the temptation to push a child into premature academic achievements. The experiences that should be fostered are those that provide anxiety-free, pleasurable learning. Through all such experiences a child will be building a language background that will be necessary for success in reading, without developing the common educational anxiety that attends forced learning and later interferes with academic success.

The Art of Reading Aloud

Leland Jacobs says, "For literature to be enjoyable to the young, it takes an appealing book, an eager child, a comfortable setting, and a sensitive, enthusiastic adult. Without any one of these components, the experience is likely to be less than satisfying."[9] Probably the best possible physical conditions are for the child to be seated on the adult's lap with an interesting book held in a way so that both can see and touch it easily. The reader should often follow the print along with his or her finger to keep reminding the child that the marks on the paper are simply talk, written down.

Oral reading is an artform and the sharing of books should be a growing experience that lets the young listener expand basic understandings. The interaction that goes on between the reader and the child is of great importance. Select times for reading when both you and your youngster feel like enjoying such an activity. Parents are human, too, and a child is sensitive to the subtle signs of that humanity. If you make yourself read when it seems like a dull chore that has to be done, you can inadvertently give your son or daughter negative feelings toward the reading process. In addition, you should take time to cultivate your talents as a reader. Be natural in your approach. One little girl, who loved her father dearly, was always a bit unnerved when he read to her because he assumed an unnatural voice that seemed to indicate that he had become a different person.

Take care with both the pronunciation and enunciation of words. When you are reading to a small child, read more slowly than you normally would. Youngsters need extra time to comprehend new or unusual vocabulary and different sentence structures. Changing your tone of voice for different characters adds fun and excitement. Soon your little boy or girl will imitate the voices of the "wee, small bear" and other characters. Your reading will be much more animated if you highlight important words, unusual vocabulary, or repeated phrases. Don't rush through lines like "Not by the hair of my chinny, chin, chin, " because you have already read this twice before. These are the pungent, vibrating expressions that "tickle the ear" and make the story exciting and memorable.

Take time to enjoy the pictures in the books, especially when your listener wants to discuss them. Talk about different items of interest and involve the child in actually putting a finger on pictures of objects. Often a youngster comprehends far less in a picture than we assume he or she does. Encourage your little boy or girl to talk and ask questions after you finish a story. Refrain from telling a child that responses to questions are wrong, but try to find something right about what has been said. Expand questions to get more verbalization. Relate a story to a child's own experiences. Eventually you will want to help the youngster in understanding story sequence by occasionally asking about the next step in the plot as you turn from page to page. Pictures are a real help here.

When you start to read, have a warm-up time. You might want to talk about the book that has been selected, perhaps why you both like it. One of the great advantages of reading to one or two children in the home is that they can interrupt with their questions and comments and not ruin the story for a group. This is important because these questions help children to understand a situation, to extend their ideas, and perhaps to relate their experiences to the story. There are times, however, when children will not be in the mood for a lot of discussion. Just listening to a good story or poem may be all they want to do. Remember there is such a thing as beating a story to death. Let listeners determine whether or not you will discuss or perhaps reread the story.

Try to interest your child in a variety of books. Your little boy or girl probably prefers what he or she knows the most about, but it is easy to overplay special interests to the extent that many of the fine books are missed. A child may become quite a little authority in some given field but have very limited areas of interest. Try to select a wide variety of books and then stimulate your listener's curiosity about them.

You will probably find that one particular book will become absolutely fascinating to your son or daughter, and it

will need to be read over and over. You must remind yourself that for some reason this book is filling a real need for
your child. Most of us do not have the training that would
enable us to guess why a certain book is very much in demand, but since it seems to be needed just at that stage of
development, you can probably continue for a few dozen readings! Even if you think you can guess why your youngster
demands a certain story over and over again, never let the
child know of your speculations. A child needs to uphold
his or her own dignity, and also has a right to privacy.
The young listener probably doesn't know why a story speaks
to special needs, but you can ruin the story by attempting to
explain what you think is the cause of such interest. Also,
it is a mistake to make disparaging remarks about such a
book. If your son or daughter loves a story greatly, you
will hurt the youngster's pride by being critical. Criticizing a favorite book can be equal to criticizing a beloved
friend.

As you read to children, don't make the mistake of trying to teach a lesson or drive home moral values that youngsters are not as yet capable of understanding. Let them
take what they can from a book on their level of comprehension. Understanding is based on experience, and three-to-
four-year-olds are limited here. The essence of the morals
that are presented in nursery chronicles, folktales, and fables may remain even though the story was first enjoyed only on a surface level. Years later it may manifest itself
with more depth of understanding. Someone suggested a fine
analogy concerning attempts to teach values prematurely by
saying that you would not tie a plastic rose onto your favorite bush early in the spring. Instead you would nurture the
bush throughout the season until it blossomed on its own
with real flowers, far more beautiful and significant than
some applied imitation.

Children must more or less join the style of living that
has already been established in a home. If a child comes
into a reading atmosphere, he or she is indeed fortunate,
for the foundation for academic success has already been
established. Members of a reading family will often read
aloud and share their interests and the knowledge and pleasure that they get from reading. They become adult cata-
lysts who bring a child and the world of books together. A
reading family prepares for special times throughout the day
when there will be opportunities to enjoy books. Naturally
there will be many trips to the local library and very early

the youngster will get the idea that libraries are fun, interesting places. Going to look at books, talking with the librarian, and perhaps attending a story hour will all be real treats. As a thoughtful parent you will not try to rush through these pleasures, nor insist on making all of the selections of books to take home. Let your son or daughter have the time to browse and to select books that are of interest. Be aware of types of literature which are attracting your child at the moment. In this way your little boy or girl will learn that reading is not just a casual pastime to be considered if there is nothing of interest on television.

Young children are sometimes attracted to books that are far beyond their comprehension level. To avoid disappointment at reading time try to interest your youngster in a variety of books and take along some that you feel are especially appropriate. However, don't be disappointed if your choices are not appreciated. If you think your child is missing some especially good books by rejecting them, just wait until another time and try them again. Keep library books in their own special place and treat them as honored houseguests. A child must realize that they are borrowed property and that many other children will also want to read them.

It is a good idea to have a special reading spot where books are kept along with art and writing materials in case the youngster wishes to extend the story into pictures. Perhaps the book will inspire other creative ideas. Some old clothes for dress-up, a good bulletin board for pictures, or some sacks and equipment for puppets can enlarge upon the fun and stretch the imagination after a little person hears a good story.

Developing Learning Potential

It is helpful to have a basic understanding of current practices in the education of young children in order to assist youngsters in their progress. Alice Yardley, one of England's best known authorities in the field of early education, states:

> Learning is usually based on personal experiences.
> Due recognition is given to the significance of individual differences. Understanding is seen as a growth process which cannot be hastened, and children are encouraged to learn fully at each stage of development

without being urged on to the next. Motivation is
recognized as the key to involvement of the whole person, and learning through personal interest is considered important. At the same time, teachers believe
that learning is enhanced by a well-organized environment. 10

As a parent you probably understand your child's needs
and interests better than anyone else does. If you have a
little self-starter who insists on knowing a great deal about
letters and words, give this youngster the help that is re-
quested. Praise the child's accomplishments but stop any
teaching activities whenever an element of strain seems to
be developing.

A few children in the three- to four-year-old age group
are already asking about letters. Sets of plastic, magnetic
letters often found in toy stores may attract them. When
they ask, you will want to tell them the names of the letters. They may go so far as to pick out certain letters
and trace them with their fingers or with a pencil. One
mother insists that her son learned to read quite early because of the attention she gave him as she worked in the
kitchen each day. He had a set of magnetic letters and enjoyed having his mother place them on the refrigerator in
the form of words which he soon came to recognize. Of
course there is a great deal more to reading than letter and
word recognition. However, researchers say that recognition of letters is a sign that a child will learn to read quickly. It may also be a sign that this child has had caring
adults or siblings who were willing to take time to help him
or her with many reading readiness skills throughout early
childhood and to interest the youngster in written symbols.

Sharing poetry and nursery rhymes has probably already
made your son or daughter sensitive to rhyming words. If
your child is interested, you can make up riddles on rhyming words, or you can work on words that begin with the
same sound, starting with tongue twisters. These are activities that children will encounter in school and through
television programs, but they are more personal and often
more enjoyable if they are treated as games with a person
who will give immediate feedback and share the enjoyment
of the play.

Don't be concerned if your youngster is not ready for any
such activities as yet. Certainly this does not mean that he

or she is any slower to learn than is the child next door who may join in with all such experiences on Sesame Street. Respect the youngster's individuality and give him or her time to discover, experiment, invent, and explore, supplementing interests with books and also with the special, loving attention that only you can give. Try to enjoy whatever seems important to your son or daughter. An interesting activity for one child may have little meaning for another.

If children are experiencing a stimulating learning environment, you can be sure that they are developing cognitive skills in their own individual ways and at their own pace. Eve Merriam puts it very well in "A Lazy Thought" in which she says that adults are so busy rushing around doing important things that they simply do not grow up anymore, but children need plenty of "slow to grow."

A Positive Environment for Learning to Read

Parents prepare their children to read as they help them learn the language and understand everyday experiences. This same preparation continues as they encourage the children's observation and listening skills. Each day as they help youngsters develop self-reliance and positive attitudes toward their ability to learn, parents are making tremendous contributions toward their children's future academic success.

Whether or not your child should attempt to recognize printed words during the preschool period depends entirely upon the youngster. Parents are often warned to avoid any temptation to exploit their children and shine in the reflected glory of what seems to be their offspring's precociousness. For example, a three-year-old's recitation of the alphabet for admiring friends may present an opportunity for parents and grandparents to preen their egos. Such an activity probably represents little more than meaningless rote learning on the part of the child and may set up a pattern of expectancy that the youngster cannot fulfill. Research indicates that children who grow into reading at their own pace seem to become the most capable readers.

William H. Teale reviewed many of the research studies that have investigated a good prereading environment. Teale found that four factors can be identified as being associated repeatedly with the environment of early readers. First, a wide range of printed material is readily available. These materials include many children's books, and there is an

exposure to everyday print, such as television program
schedules, labels on cans and commercial products, and
different types of printed material that make reading a necessary endeavor in comprehending one's surroundings. Second, "reading is done." Successful early readers live in an
environment that causes them to discover that "reading is a
pleasurable, unique, communicative experience."

"Of all the facets of the environment mentioned in the
studies of early reading, reading to children is probably the
most cited. Little wonder then that not only reading methods
authors but also early childhood educators ... put forth vir-
tually unanimous endorsement of the policy." Parents themselves are readers and of course serve as models for reading behavior.

The third environmental factor is contact with an interest
in writing tools. It seems that early readers usually start
with an interest in drawing and scribbling. Very soon they
want to write their names, and they move on to writing
other words. In fact, an early interest in reading is usually predisposed by an interest in writing. The fourth factor
is that "significant others" in the child's environment respond
to his or her interest in reading. They help the youngster,
but it is the child's needs that determine the amount and kind
of help given. Usually such needs are in response to the
reading needs of everyday living and to the reading of books
that children enjoy. Also, adults are helpful "question an-
swerers," casually supplying information and help with details such as how to write a given letter. "In short," Teale
observed from reviewing many studies, "the children got
feedback about reading in response to their felt needs and in
a manner which preserved the general language arts concept
of reading."[11]

We should encourage children's interest in written communication since they often approach reading through writing.
Most children enjoy making pictures or adding scribbles to
family letters. They often indicate to parents that labels
should be put on their pictures. When the parent writes
dictated words under pictures and shows the child that the
words express his or her ideas, a youngster is often fascinated by this process and may even attempt to read what
has been written. Soon the child will be asking to have
many ideas spelled out on paper. The next step is usually
an attempt to reproduce both letters and words. All such
experiences give real meaning to print so that the youngster

will not enter school thinking that reading is simply the repetition of isolated words, but rather a search for meaning.

It is no wonder that preschoolers try very hard to react meaningfully to the print they encounter around them. Understanding signs and labels helps them to perceive a sense of order and logic. Have you ever traveled in a foreign country and found yourself putting forth great effort to try to decipher signs written in a language that you could not comprehend? One of the joys of returning home is to realize that you can interpret your own environment.

With a little help, small children do surprisingly well. Even a two-year-old can often "read" stop lights while slightly older children will use context clues to decipher names of products. It is interesting to note that children often realize the functional use of print on products or signs, but do not understand that the print in their storybooks is also a communicating device for the reader. It is a good idea to ask your listener to show you where the words that tell the story are found in books you are reading. With stories that have interesting repeat rhymes or phrases, read until you come to a key word, point to it and see if the child can interject the right word. For example, with "The Three Bears" you should have no trouble getting the youngster to finish the questions, "Who's been sitting in my _____?" "Who's been sleeping in my _____?" This is participation in the reading process and adds interest for the listener.

A Casual Development of Reading Readiness Skills

Whether or not children should receive reading instruction during their preschool years is debatable; however, most educators would certainly agree that they should not be exposed to a rigid, formal program of instruction. Actually, parents are inadvertently teaching beginning reading skills or what may be called reading readiness skills from the time the child is born. Because children need just the type of informal, individualized attention that parents can give, this teaching is of great importance. Readiness tests usually focus on vocabulary, auditory discrimination, and visual discrimination. Children learn more vocabulary in the home than in any other place. This learning will include skills of auditory discrimination as a parent helps a child hear and say correctly sounds for letters or blends. Parents' contributions to a child's interest in pictures and eventually in letters and words will lead to the development of visual discrimination skills as well.

Writing words, captions, and labels for youngsters helps to prepare them for reading. Pointing to word order as one reads develops an understanding of left-to-right progression across the page and eventually to interest in what the print is saying to the reader. Taking advantage of signs and labels in the child's own environment makes first exposure to the reading of words personal and functional. The child sees the importance of reading. Parents have the opportunity of taking a creative approach toward these simple skill learnings and of making their informal teaching satisfying and fun. They can gear their teaching to an individual child's needs and interests. Such an approach brings feelings of satisfaction as the youngster is given the opportunity to enrich understanding on the level of his or her own developmental stage.

Many children assume the role of a reader when they are quite young. For example, Steven started lining up his stuffed animals and sharing books with them when he was less than two years old. His verbalization was not very advanced, but he went to great effort to point out details of pictures. This kind of involvement in books is important. Very few three- to four-year-old children will actually read the words, but if they follow a very simple basic plot line while turning the pages and matching the pictures and the story, this is a real accomplishment. Some children memorize a short story and feel that they are actually reading. Four-year-old Bobby's family was enchanted when he read a favorite book verbatim for them. Wanting to add to their happiness in his accomplishment, he said, "I can read it without even opening the book!" The family was a little disappointed, but this was reading to Bobby.

Small children often tell their own stories. Even two-year-olds enjoy this activity, but the three-year-old child reaches a height in creative storytelling. Naturally such experiences develop vocabulary and promote a child's understanding of plot sequence. The stories can even be a way of letting the listener understand some of the child's thinking. In conversation, even young children learn to be somewhat guarded in what they say; however, with a story, the teller often reveals many of his or her true feelings. Researchers have been surprised at how much violence surfaces in stories told by three-year-old boys and girls. Some have speculated as to how much this violence results from our modern environment. Attitudes toward parents are also revealed in children's stories.

How to Choose the Books They Like

Fine children's literature provides us with one of our best opportunities to give the best to young children who are just now forming their own standards of taste. Duff says:

> That the standard of text, pictures, and general quality in books for little children must be high goes without saying. I believe that good taste, if it is not actually instinctive in "new people," can be developed with great sureness; and there can be no possible excuse for accepting anything other than the best that is to be had.

And why should we give our children mediocre stories and illustrations when we have such a wealth of good literature that will provide them with real aesthetic experiences? Duff states two other good reasons for selecting the best of books for youngsters. One is that small people look at the books they enjoy over and over again. We need books that wear well artistically. Also she says that a book that is good enough for a child must have qualities that cause it to be acceptable to an intelligent adult. What adult wants to read and reread some of the "rubbishy, falsely conceived books" that flood the market?[12]

The pictures, the format, and the general design of the book provide our first impression of almost any selection for three-to-four-year-olds. Before investing a part of your precious book budget money into selections for your child, check them with care. Does the book provide a story that develops quickly? Is it interesting, even exciting to a small child? Is it a story which the youngster can comprehend even from a limited background of experiences? Does the story give a child a unique, worthwhile experience, or is it just another statement of dull, mundane happenings? Is the plot exciting enough to hold the child's attention, stir imagination and curiosity? Who cares about a little boy and a little girl who live in a pretty little house unless they do something of interest? On the other hand, a three-to-four-year-old will probably feel that a book like Wait for William by Marjorie Flack is an exciting story. In it children are hurrying to the circus parade and are irritated with the slowness of a small brother. Suddenly they see that same brother, whom they have left behind, riding on a huge elephant in the parade. The listener will appreciate this plot, especially if he or she happens to be the youngest in the family.

In books for very small children there is often little time for real character development. At least the characters should seem real and interesting, whether they are people, animals, mechanical objects, or even a house, as in Virginia Lee Burton's Caldecott winner, The Little House. This house sits in the country dreaming of what it would be like to live in the city. Suddenly the city begins to expand and to surround the house. The congestion and commotion that develop become unbearable until finally the house is moved back out into the country. The look of happiness on the house makes a satisfying conclusion to the story.

You will not want your children to miss the Robert McCloskey books. These are sometimes called the most reassuring of all stories for young children, but they are more. For one thing, they provide exciting plots for preschoolers. Imagine, for example, a mother and her tiny daughter in Blueberries for Sal picking blueberries to can for winter. At the same time a bear mother and her cub are on the same mission of storing up food for the winter. They are stuffing themselves on the berries. Both Sal and the baby bear wander off and lose sight of their mothers; in fact, each is suddenly following the wrong mother. There is excitement on Blueberry Hill, especially on the part of the mothers. However, soon each offspring is back with the proper parent and the preparations for winter continue. This is an exhilarating story for the three- to four-year-old set.

Since young children must have their books read to them, we need not be too concerned with vocabulary. What we want is wording within the child's range of understanding, yet it should challenge the youngster with new vocabulary and the beauty of the language. Some explanation of unfamiliar words may be necessary, but children love to pick up interesting expressions and to surprise admiring adults with them. One three-year-old boy seemed to have a great interest in ornithology as he gazed at the many birds in his city's zoo. Finally he announced in a loud, clear voice, "The birds are infinite!" Imagine the proud look on his grandmother's face when the adults around him stared at this child in surprise! Of course she knew that he had picked up the statement from one of his books, but he knew where and how to use it appropriately.

We do not need limited vocabulary for children. Let them participate in the language insofar as they can enjoy the experience and continue to be interested in their stories. Beatrix Potter's books are full of statements like, "Jemima complained of the superfluous hen" (The Tale of Jemima Puddleduck), or "But Nutkin was excessively impertinent in his manners" (The Tale of Squirrel Nutkin), or "Peter gave himself up for lost, and shed big tears, but his sobs were overheard by some friendly sparrows who flew to him in great excitement and implored him to exert himself" (The Tale of Peter Rabbit). Yet the Potter books have been great favorites with small children for three quarters of a century.

Take your children to good bookstores. Give them time to look at the fine displays of tantalizing books, and perhaps select a special treasure to take home with them. Children need books as special companions just as they need their friends. You will probably want to avoid the "flats" that are on sale at grocery stores, drugstore counters, and many inexpensive gift shops. These are usually cheap, poorly illustrated books, full of stereotypes. The stories are hurriedly written, or perhaps they are mutilated versions of fine folktales. People often ask, "Aren't they better than nothing? I can't afford the regular children's books these days." Yes, such books are inexpensive; however, why waste money on something that will not add to your child's intellectual and artistic stature when we are fortunate in now having fine children's books reproduced in paperback? They are usually about the same price as the flats, and one good paperback (like McCloskey's Make Way for Ducklings) could provide a child with more literary and artistic background than would ten cheap flats. Fortunately, good paperback editions are readily available.

When you present a book, children will not hesitate to let you know whether or not you have made a good selection. Most three-to-four-year-olds simply wiggle away and go about more interesting activities if the book you are reading is not fascinating enough to them. On the other hand, those books that have real appeal will call forth enthusiastic responses, smiles, laughs, or serious attention--even shivers in the exciting parts. What's more, they will probably bring about much discussion, and certainly the demand of "Read it again!" Often the stories will come up in conversations later. Characters in favorite books assume roles in creative play. A child may study the illustrations and even attempt to "read" the story alone or to friends. Outstanding literature enriches everyday experiences. It broad-

ens a child's scope and helps develop understanding of the
youngster's limited world.

Differentiating between Good and Poor Illustrations

In giving children the best of picture books we are giving
them an opportunity to develop a sensitivity to fine art. We
cannot expect children to appreciate the best of art if they
have never experienced it. Warren Chappell says, "When
one considers the comics, the movie cartoons, and the textbooks, it is safe to say that the average child's pictorial experience is all but bankrupt, and that a good ninety-five percent of the illustrations he sees is little more than competent
art student work."[13]

If you as a parent feel insecure in selecting worthwhile
picture books, you may want to explore the area on your
own. In fact, you can have a delightful experience as you
attempt to sensitize yourself to some of the best of art for
your child. Perhaps a good way to begin to sharpen your
own skills in critical analysis is to spend some time studying books that have received the Caldecott Award. This is
an award given each year by the American Library Association to the book they select as the most distinguished picture
book for children published in this country during the preceding year. Books that have won this award give you a feel
for the best art we have for children, and they include a
great variety of art styles and media.

One should expect far more from illustrations than simply a depiction of the text of the story. Even a small child
wants the pictures to extend the story and make it more interesting. Children are usually much more willing than are
adults to explore unfamiliar art styles. Adults who reject a
new art experience in a picture book, because they do not
immediately feel comfortable with it, can undermine children's chances of developing an appreciation of many types
of art styles.

Take time to study the pictures in children's books. Try
to relate to the artist's intention and to determine how he or
she used the elements of color, texture, line, and shape to
communicate. In which area did the artist display special
expertise? Are the colors in the pictures you are examin-
ing bold, exciting, and inventive, or do they seem to be only
an added interest, a kind of fill-in that contributes little to
the quality of the illustrations and could be removed without

harming the general impact of the pictures? Brian Wildsmith is one of our great color artists. If you look at his
pictures, you will see that they tell their stories in bold,
stimulating colors. If the element of color were removed,
we would have little left in the pictures. Wildsmith has a
wonderful ability for producing just the right color relationships to achieve vibrating effects.

Texture is produced by inventive use of various kinds of
media. Clare Newberry has created such effective fuzzy,
warm, soft textures in her pictures of cats and kittens that
children cannot resist rubbing the illustrations. In fact,
pages in her books are often worn through because they have
such an appeal to the senses. Newberry gets this striking
effect with the use of charcoal. Other artists who emphasize texture may use a variety of media. Leo Lionni
sponged on paint, dripped and rolled it, and even used paper
doilies to give the feeling of underwater scenes and textures
in Swimmy. His collages for Alexander and the Wind-Up
Mouse are made from a variety of materials, even crum-
pled newspaper. Books of this kind can promote creativity
in small children. They include art techniques which, with
the help of adults, boys and girls can try with reasonable
success. Ezra Jack Keats' books involve exciting uses of
textured materials. He incorporates textile designs, even
wallpaper, to get the interesting effects in his pictures.
Again, children might be encouraged to try some of the
same approaches. Amrei Fechner's pictures for The Day
the Rooster Didn't Crow by Max Kruse display striking texture in vivid illustrations. In the double-page spreads of
the rooster, the surface characteristics of the fowl are such
that you almost expect him to jump off the page. The artist's unique use of color and line makes each individual
feather seem to stand out from the page.

Never underestimate the great storytelling power of fine
line drawings. Randolph Caldecott was considered the "master of the line." He helped cause a revolution in the field
of illustrations for children's books over a hundred years
ago as he brought action and excitement into simple little
nursery rhymes and verses with his marvelous extension of
texts. His lines could skip, run, meander, or jerk. They
could build up to great peaks of excitement, or perhaps
create a quiet, sad mood. He used color in some of his
pictures but carried the stories along with simple line drawings throughout. For real humor, do look at his interpretation of "Hey, Diddle, Diddle" in The Hey Diddle Diddle Pic-

ture Book. What a story of a broken romance! Caldecott
was a great pioneer in the field of fine illustrations for
children's books, and of course our most prestigious award
for outstanding illustrations was named in his honor.

Marcia Brown, probably our most versatile modern illustrator, has won the coveted Caldecott Award three times.
She used forceful silhouettes against brilliantly colored backgrounds to illustrate the book Shadow by Blaise Cendrars.
Her Once a Mouse, "a fable cut in wood," is an experience
in the intense effects that are possible with striking woodcuts. For contrast, look at her illustrations for Cinderella
as told by Perrault, her first award winner. Here she created a romantic, fairytale mood by using delicate, curving
lines to give a lacy, fragile effect for scenes appropriate to
this French version of the favorite old tale.

For a very different use of lines in illustrations, notice
the heavy, massive feel that Nicolas Sidjakov obtained in his
illustrations for Baboushka and the Three Kings by Ruth Robbins, another Caldecott Award winner.

The fourth art element, shape, is used in a utilitarian
form in some concept books. Figures and designs will sometimes be made up of one or more repeated basic shapes
which are usually rigidly geometric.

The use of shape and design plays a very important part
in the illustration of some storybooks. Gerald McDermott's
Arrow to the Sun: A Pueblo Indian Tale is an outstanding
example. A small child cannot comprehend the depth of
meaning in the text of this book, but the illustrations are a
fine aesthetic experience and an introduction to the art of
the Indians of the Southwest.

For contrast, there are the interesting shapes made from
torn paper that Lionni used to animate the characters of the
two families in Little Blue and Little Yellow. He personi-
fied the characters so well in his abstract art that even
young children are not confused with the illustrations and
relate very well to the two children in the story.

In evaluating a picture book you will want to consider
these elements of color, texture, line, and shape and the
manner in which the artist has used them to state his or
her individual interpretation of a given story. Note, too,
the entire composition of the book. When you consider its

size, shape, type of print, margins, and general layout of pictures, do you have a feeling of unity, balance, rhythm, harmony, and movement? All of these aspects of the format of the book are important, even to the use of blank space. All contribute to the artistic statement which the book makes. If you take time to compare techniques, styles, and the composition of the visual language that the artists use, you will appreciate fine picture books and help your children start building their sense of artistic taste.

There are some very worthwhile books on the market that can enhance your understanding and enjoyment of the art to be found in children's books. They can bring you into a whole field of interest, and certainly your children will profit by your knowledge and ability to select fine illustrations. Several of these books are listed in the bibliography at the end of the first chapter. In one of them, Illustrations in Children's Books, Patricia Cianciolo explains:

> Children crave something that is inspired and attractive; nonetheless, they will take whatever is at hand. Good taste can be acquired, but if children are to get on the path that will lead them to recognize beautiful things, they must be given those that are well-designed, are pleasing to look at, and will enrich their lives.... A child can develop an appreciation of beauty through handling of well-illustrated books. One need not settle for the lifeless illustrations that crowd the pages of many children's books when quantities of beautiful and vital illustrations are available at bookstores merely for the asking. [14]

Parents need to be aware of the "lifeless illustrations" and the stereotypes that are found in many books on the market today. Such books should be rejected because you want more for your child in the way of exposure to good art than they offer. MacCann and Richards have an excellent discussion on stereotypes in illustrations. They say that such art follows a kind of formula because the artist is trying to appeal to a broad public acceptance. Naturally people respond to what is familiar to them. At the same time such repetitive similarities are boring. Certainly they do not educate a child in art appreciation. As you become more and more sensitive to work done by "hack" artists, you will recognize these techniques as described by MacCann and Richards. Animals are anthropomorphized or

made to look like stuffed toys. They are often "cutesy,"
soft, and fuzzy. People wear costumes that defy period
labeling. Individualization of the characters is shown by
"cartoon-like overstatement of features." Objects are outlined with heavy black lines similar to those found in pictures in coloring books. Primary colors are used. What
texture there is shows only "fuzziness, fatness, or frilli-
ness." Spatial arrangement is given little consideration;
the objects of interest in a picture are highlighted by heavy
outlining and bright color. There is an air of sweetness
and cuteness, but little feeling in the pictures.[15]

Stereotyped pictures lack personality. They seldom express the real feelings of the story characters they are
supposed to depict. They are simply not involved with the
drama of the story, nor do they show the basic qualities of
the text in any expressive way. Rather, they give one the
feeling of cheap decorations. Compare the fuzzy, soft,
saucer-eyed cows that you see in many of the grocery store
flats with Robert Lawson's depiction of Ferdinand the Bull
in Munro Leaf's The Story of Ferdinand, to get an idea of
the contrast between real and stereotyped art in children's
books. Or notice (but please don't buy for your children)
the horrible pictures to be found in some of the cheap adap-
tations of The Tale of Peter Rabbit in which Peter becomes
a glorified Bugs Bunny type and Mother Rabbit looks like
some kind of sex symbol. Compare these with "the real
thing" in Potter's book, where she gives children beautifully
detailed, simple watercolor pictures that are works of art,
a fine artistic experience for anyone.

Those Dependable Old Rhymes

Three- to four-year-old children have not outgrown their
love of Mother Goose. Instead, now with added experiences,
they not only respond to the rollicking rhythm of the old
rhymes, but also they find that the little poems deal with a
great variety of interests. They have quick little stories,
told in just a few lines, that can hold the attention of active
youngsters. There are funny songs to sing, games to play,
and episodes to dramatize. Their grotesque or incongruous
situations amuse small children whose sense of humor is
tickled by ridiculous happenings. Animal verses can be related to pets, and the childlike characters are great old
friends.

At this stage some youngsters enjoy the tongue twisters to

be found in nursery rhymes. These contribute to language development skills. Since by now your child probably has quite a repertoire of verses to draw on, he or she has the necessary foundation for little games like "fractured nursery rhymes" described by Mary Jett-Simpson in Developing Active Readers: Ideas for Parents, Teachers, and Librarians. An older person recites a rhyme but substitutes a wrong word, "Little Miss Muffet, sat on a chair," for example. It is fun for the child to catch the error, and of course such games sharpen listening skills and sensitize perception of rhyming form. 16

Many of the rhymes have been set to music and several have found their way into picture books. Ed Emberley has illustrated ten verses in London Bridge Is Falling Down. He deals with the problem: "How shall we build it up again?" Each answer warrants a full-page depiction of a possible solution. The time is the 1750's and the illustrations are accurately drawn. Emberley has also included a description of the London Bridge game with accompanying illustrations. This is followed by the musical score and a full version of the song with additional verses not included in the picture book text. Peter Spier chose to illustrate the same song in London Bridge Is Falling Down! He also gives an historical perspective, but the various remedies for the salvation of London Bridge all seem to fail in his very detailed illustrations. London is depicted in grand style with great attention paid to architecture and water traffic. For three-to-four-year-olds the book would have its appeal in the song and story, but it might be of more help later when a child is capable of appreciating the information about the setting and the time that is depicted.

Robert Quackenbush has given children several picture songbooks of Americana. Some are more appropriate for school-age children, but Skip to My Lou is one preschoolers can enjoy. The verses of the romance, explained by a mischievous little boy, are illustrated in a way that makes them extremely humorous to children. The music and the directions for the dance are given.

Yankee Doodle, by Edward Bangs, is another book from our American heritage. The pictures, done by Steven Kellogg, are crammed with details of the Revolutionary War period. A few of the verses are used as the text, but the story appears in the illustrations with a small boy as the focus of attention. He has a jolly time, not really compre-

hending the seriousness of the war situation, but seeing it
from a child's point of view. At one time he becomes
frightened and can be found running away from the scene;
in fact, he is completely outside the border of the picture
itself.

Nancy Winslow Parker's illustrations for Oh, A-Hunting
We Will Go by John Langstaff will provide young children
with much amusement. There are enough details in the pictures for a great deal of discussion.

I Know an Old Lady by Rose Bonne and Alan Mills is a
favorite cumulative song for children. In this version Abner
Graboff used cut and torn paper to illustrate the grotesque
verses. Music is provided for singing the words.

Mommy, Buy Me a China Doll is adapted from an Ozark
children's song although no music is given in the book by
Harve Zemach. Children enjoy the repetition in the rhyme
and the exaggerated fun of the pictures done by Margot Zemach. After a few readings listeners will be joining in and
probably making up their own tunes, at least for the lines,
"Do, Mommy, do!"

Children like to participate in songs with caring adults.
They enjoy a wide variety: songs that tell stories about
familiar things, songs about their family, those in which
one can substitute names--particularly the child's own name
--songs with silly words, and those that repeat rhymes.
Often a parent and child enjoy making up little tunes for
parts of stories so that they can sing refrains like, "Hundreds of cats, thousands of cats, millions and billions and
trillions of cats," or, "I won't," said the pig, and on
through the replies of all the animals in Janina Domanska's
presentation of Little Red Hen. This is a way to add to the
fun of reading or singing along.

Children can be confused with the format of some picture
songbooks. If there are several stanzas on one page with
pictures developing later, they have difficulty following the
sequence. They like to see one verse illustrated with a
picture, preferably on a double-page spread. If there is a
chorus or refrain that is repeated, it should also be included in the text. The music for the piano and perhaps
for other instruments should be included. When the youngsters know the song, they can "read" and sing the book independently. Sing-along books are a fine way to encourage

reading readiness skills. You can point to the words as you sing them, giving the children an idea of where the words that they are singing are found on the page. Youngsters may even begin to recognize some of the repeat refrains.

Often the song itself may be somewhat sketchy, but illustrations can help develop the narrative and pull the verses together in sequence. There should be a feeling of rhythm and good pacing throughout the book, with verses and text well balanced so that there is time to enjoy each picture, but also there should be a kind of movement or flow on to the next picture and verse.

Moving into Poetry

Sutherland and Arbuthnot say, "Poetry can bring warmth, reassurance, even laughter; it can stir and arouse or quiet and comfort. Above all it can give significance to everyday experience. To miss poetry would be as much of a deprivation as to miss music."17

You have probably noticed that small children respond to nursery rhymes in the same ways that they respond to music. They may clap their hands, dance, chant the words, or simply wriggle to the rhythm. This is the beginning of a love of verse which can easily be carried into other poetry, for children are already experiencing what has been called the pulse of life that comes in poetry. Perhaps the rhythm and the rhyming will not be quite as pronounced in most first poems for children as it has been in the nursery rhymes, but it should be there. Also, the poems must be simple and understandable to the child.

Small children are fascinated with word sounds and love creating rhythms which they chant just for the fun of hearing the music of their own creative language. Dorothy Aldis' "Blum" is typical of the same types of language experiences of three-to-four-year-olds.

<u>Blum</u>

Dog means dog. And cat means cat.
And there are lots of words like that.

A cart's a cart to pull or push.
A leaf's a leaf on tree or bush.

> But there's another word I say
> When I am left alone to play.
>
> The word is Blum.   Blum is a word
> That very few have ever heard.
>
> It is very nice to hum.
> Or you can shout it: BLUM BLUM BLUM.
>
> But shout or whisper, hum or sing,
> It doesn't mean a single thing. 18

Children are dependent on those who are older to read poetry to them.   Also, they need to realize that others besides themselves enjoy the rhythm of language.   Often youngsters request the same poems over and over again.   They love the familiar, of course, but some poems, like some music, seem to have great appeal to certain children.   Fortunate is the child who has an adult who loves poetry and will share his or her enjoyment.   These are the people who read poetry with that special flair that makes it come alive. Many fathers develop quite a reputation for good poetry reading and for the reading of nonsense verse.   What better way is there to dispel the foolish notion that poetry is a kind of literature that only girls enjoy than to have a father who will share in the reading!

There is a whole range of poetry that you will want your children to experience.   Usually a good point of departure from nursery rhymes into poetry is through nonsense verse and humor.

When it comes to absurd, ridiculously funny poems, no modern writer surpasses Shel Silverstein in his appeal to children.   His poems, along with the exaggerated line drawings that he uses for illustrations, make for hours of laughter and enjoyment.   Even adults who are coaxed to read his poems over and over are often heard to chuckle and laugh as much as the children do.

William Cole is one of several people who have compiled books of humorous poems for children.   One of his collections, Beastly Boys and Ghastly Girls, has a wealth of ridiculous selections that amuse youngsters.   In this book he included the poem "Nothing to Do?" which was written by Silverstein.   It contains a list of suggestions of really naughty things that a child might try, all presented with tongue-in-cheek seriousness. Children wriggle with delight when they hear the outlandish ideas on how to keep busy.

Edward Lear's limericks and poems have been entertaining children and adults alike for a long, long time and have probably served to introduce many to poetry. A book that young children can enjoy is The Owl and the Pussy Cat. In it Lear's poetic verse is set to Cooney's pen and ink with tempera illustrations. The pictures give main characters in the poems human characteristics in whimsical full-page pictures. Helen Oxenbury has illustrated Edward Lear's The Quangle-Wangle's Hat. This book provides a fine combination of Lear's creative language with large, dramatic, sometimes hilarious illustrations.

Laura Richards' poems have pleased very young children for many years. Judging from their popularity, they will continue to appeal to children who enjoy twisted, funny words like those found in poems such as "Eletelephony," or fine verse stories like "The Monkeys and the Crocodile," or the great marching cadence in poems like "The Umbrella Brigade." She is loved for the lyrical quality of her poems and the funny characters who parade in and out of ridiculous situations. Her book Tirra Lirra, first published in 1902, is excellent for bridging the gap between nursery rhymes and slightly more sophisticated verse.

A. A. Milne's poetry for children, found in the two classics, When We Were Very Young, first published in 1924, and Now We Are Six, first published in 1927, show a small child's self-sufficient egotism in a subtle, delightful manner that has not been surpassed. Some modern critics feel that Milne is still the greatest children's poet. Arbuthnot says:

> But certainly we shall never encounter a writer who understands more completely the curious composite of gravity and gaiety, or supreme egotism and occasional whimsy that is the young child. A. A. Milne has written humorous verse for children, composed with deft craftsmanship and a sure knowledge of the little child's world, which should make them live as long as people live who love light-hearted English verse at its best. [19]

For all their simplicity, Ernest H. Shepard's pen-and-ink sketches that illustrate these two books give such remarkable interpretations of the verses that according to one story, Milne gave Shepard half the credit for the success of the books. You may want to purchase your own copies of When We Were Very Young and Now We Are Six. Both are available in paperback. Milne's stories in Winnie the Pooh, first published in 1926, and The House At Pooh Corner, first published in 1928, are a wonderful part of our literature for early childhood, but the stories are more difficult for pre-school children to follow than are his little narrative poems.

Several excellent anthologies are listed at the end of this chapter as well as collections of poems written by individual poets. This is the time when you will probably want to select at least one good anthology which you will have for reading in the years to come. There are many fine possibilities. Some, like The Golden Treasury of Poetry, with poems selected by Louis Untermeyer are "to grow on," as Untermeyer says in the Foreword. There are selections for the youngest children on up to adult age.

Piper, Pipe that Song Again is more limited in scope, but Nancy Larrick has chosen poems for this book that have a real appeal to young children. Gaily We Parade is an outstanding collection by John E. and Sara Brewton. It has poetry ranging from Mother Goose to Shakespeare. The book is nicely arranged with groupings of poems based on children's interests. The groups include "Neighbors of Ours," "Funny People," "To the Shops We Go," and "Bells for Christmas."

Beginning-to-Read Poetry is Sally Clithero's collection of some of the simplest poems that appeal to very young children. The book is small but each poem is presented on a separate page with an illustration. Book Two of the small anthologies compiled by Donald J. Bissett, Poems and Verses about Animals, and Book Three of the same series, Poems and Verses about the City, are both easy to handle and have many poems that will appeal to preschool children. These books are not illustrated.

A Beginning Book of Poems, chosen by Marjory Lawrence, has a wider variety of poetry. Many of these selections would be enjoyed by children at the elementary school level. For a Child: Great Poems Old & New, compiled by Wilma McFarland, is made up of many poems to please very young children, most of which are illustrated.

There are even special collections on a given theme. For

example, Lee Bennett Hopkins' Go to Bed! A Book of Bedtime Poems is a whole array of poems about the bedtime ritual.

Three- to four-year-old children often like books that present only one poem with many illustrations. You might hesitate to choose poetry by Robert Frost for a child this age, but you and your youngster may be happily surprised with Stopping by Woods on a Snowy Evening. Susan Jeffers' soft, detailed pictures make lovely double-page spreads of small selections of this old poem. Her visual language, which goes along with Frost's lovely writing, tells the story with child-like interpretation.

The pictures with which Barbara Cooney illustrated Delmore Schwartz's "I Am Cherry Alive" the Little Girl Sang simply vibrate with a child's feelings. Another poem that expresses thoughts of a child's searching mind is How Does It Feel to Be a Tree? by Flo Morse. The words and the pictures reflect the type of questions that a little boy or girl often considers. Places I Like to Be by Evelyn M. Andre is a very inviting book with a short text and some fine photographs of secure, happy situations that children like and need.

If you are having trouble snaring your child into the enjoyment of poetry, you might try some of the pure nonsense in If Eggs Had Legs by Lisl Weil. The Bed Book by Sylvia Plath is a longer poem with jingly rhymes about the right sort of bed to have.

> Not just a white little
> tucked-in-tight little
> night-night little
> turn-out-the-light little
>   bed--
>   instead[20]

And then the suggestions follow! A bed might be a submarine, or one that is jet propelled, or a snack bed, or a spottable one that never shows jam or paint splatters. There are many imaginative ideas. A bed might be pocket size or huge enough to fit on an elephant's back, with swimming pool included, or even have "springier springs than a kangaroo." A youngster certainly could add to this book with his or her own creative imagination.

One of the first narrative or verse story poems that

children truly enjoy is "A Visit from St. Nicholas," or "The Night Before Christmas," as it is often called. This poem appears in single-poem form and has been illustrated in a variety of ways. Some versions show nostalgic, Victorian pictures that have a sentimental appeal. Other books will have a modern visual interpretation.

Enjoyment is the attitude that we want to establish when we read poetry to small children. We do not need to discuss or analyze poetry; let the youngsters talk about it all they want, of course, but don't expect them to take from any poem what you, as a much more experienced person, will. Try to choose what is of interest to them. They will quickly let you know when you have erred, but go along with their choices, slipping in a favorite of yours as you find the opportunity. You will often be surprised how meaningful a special poem will be to a small child.

Remember that poetry should be read slowly. Read a selection again and again if a child requests it. If you enjoy the poems, you will be successful in helping your children do the same. If you have been robbed of this pleasure, perhaps this is a good chance for you to make another start and learn of the joy and beauty of poetry along with your child.

A young child needs to be included in some way in the reading of poetry. Fingerplays provide such involvement for a three-to-four-year-old. These verses provide enjoyable experiences that develop a love of poetry, but they also contribute to reading readiness by the development of listening skills. The child has to listen carefully to match words with actions. Fingerplays provide a means of group communication which, at least for a three-year-old, often comes about more easily through movement than through conversation. In addition, participation in fingerplays can help to extend a child's attention span. At this time you will probably be looking for fingerplay books in which the rhymes are slightly more challenging than those you have used heretofore. Two that you might enjoy trying are Little Boy Blue: Finger Plays Old and New by Daphne Hogstrom and Rhymes for Fingers and Flannelboards by Louise B. Scott and Jesse J. Thompson. The second book is an extensive collection with a variety of fingerplays. Some are rhymes from other countries, but many were written by the authors, often for school curriculum units or special occasions.

Finally, original verses will probably interest your youngster. The two of you can make up your own little rhymes
that include your child's name and things that are important
to him or her.

Storytelling: An Art Form for Parents to Cultivate

As a parent you have a wonderful opportunity to become a
good storyteller. You will be asked to read favorite books
again and again. Before long these stories will become well
fixed in your mind. It is not that a good storyteller memo-
rizes stories, but he or she must be very well acquainted
with them and should know any rhyming schemes, unusual
phrases, and rich descriptive vocabulary, in addition to
unique beginnings and endings. What a great start you have
for developing this art as you read to your son or daughter!

Try telling a favorite story to your child and of course
let the youngster tell any parts he or she cares to fill in.
This makes the story your own special literature to share.
There is no book between you and the listener so that the
story becomes simply a you-to-me situation.

Listening to a storyteller provides especially good learning experiences for small children because the youngsters
must visualize the scenes and anticipate the plot development.
In our modern television age, children have little experience
of this kind. Even with their picture books, much of the
creative imagination is taken over by the illustrator. Picturing the scenes and action calls for creative thinking on
their part, a process that is absolutely necessary when
children are later asked to visualize what is being said in
textbooks in order to understand the essence of reading.
Another asset of storytelling is that children hear adults using powerful words that convey real meaning. This artful
use of words has a magic of communication that may not be
found in everyday speech. Such experiences contribute to
language development and to an appreciation of the wonder of
our language.

Sometimes parents enlarge upon a story that has appealed
to their children and even develop their own family serials.
Another type of storytelling that young children really enjoy
is hearing about things their parents did when they were little. Such antics seem unbelievable to them, yet such fun!
When grandparents are prompted to tell such tales, the stories are usually appreciated more by the grandchildren than
they are by the parents who become the story characters.

There is something very special about hearing stories told, especially by those one trusts and loves. It is a very intimate, personal experience that provides memories that last a lifetime. Certain stories become a basis for family literature and for sharing what has been of great importance at an extremely impressionable time in a person's life. Few people forget the family storyteller. Why not develop and enjoy this treasured art with your children? Later, when they are involved in group activities, they will be proud if you share your talents with their friends. Remember that many parents will not put forth this special effort to be a part of their children's world.

Types of Humor for This Developmental Age

"Children and laughter are just about synonymous."[21] Naturally children look for funny books, and for three-to-four-year-olds such books contain humor that is obvious and simple, perhaps silly. They like ridiculous situations or slapstick, pie-in-the-face nonsense. They love incongruity and silly language. By three-and-a-half most children share jokes and laugh with adults. They still enjoy a great deal of clowning around and think that accidents are funny.

Books that pose silly questions are favorites. Children like to feel superior in their knowledge. Joan W. Blos says, "Humor depends upon mastery that is new enough to be interesting; old enough to be firm."[22] This is the great appeal of books like Do Baby Bears Sit in Chairs? by Ethel and Leonard Kessler. This story provides many laughs as a child watches foolish cubs attempting to do just what the listener knows they cannot do.

Watch for stories that promote laughter and fun. They provide one of our best ways of developing an interest in books and reading. Folktales supply a fine resource. Many have just the kind of primitive humor that children love. The Three Wishes, retold by Paul Galdone, has dramatic pictures that almost tell the story themselves. Those that show the sausages on the end of the woodcutter's nose are especially humorous. In them only the cat appreciates the ridiculous situation. The ending reinforces the idea of being happy with the simple things in life. The Man Who Was Going to Mind the House, retold by David McKee, shows the poor man getting himself into progressively more ridiculous situations as he tries to prove that housekeeping is easy work. Margot Zemach has given children a simple version of The Three Sillies that could bring delight to those capable of comprehending the ludicrous antics of the original family in the story as well as the actions of the three sillies who are encountered by the suitor. The pictures in this book are childlike and humorous.

Richard Scarry is surely one of the best-known authors of children's books. His books come in all shapes and sizes. His humor appeals to youngsters, especially those who have little or no literary background except that which is gained from television, for his style is very similar to what they see on the screen. The books can serve as stepping stones to other literature where boys and girls will find more aesthetic appeal. Your child will enjoy some Scarry books, but try to see that they do not comprise a major part of your son or daughter's literary diet at any age.

Moving Toward an Understanding of Number Concepts

Although most three-year-olds can count only about three objects, they are beginning to realize how things in their environment relate to each other in terms of numbers and amounts. Even though the basic understanding of number concepts probably develops from the use of real objects in manipulative experiences, counting books substitute pictures for objects and can contribute to learning.

First counting books should be very simple and clear. The objects should stand out on the page and be easy to identify. The numbers should be large and plainly drawn. Open spaces should divide objects or groups of objects to be counted. A cluttered page can be very confusing. For example, a three-year-old will have difficulty counting three roses that are to be found among a page full of daisies and tulips. At this age all of the blossoms would probably be considered as just flowers since a child's generalizations at this time are far from refined.

One Snail and Me by Emilie Warren McLeod is a counting book that children will enjoy for its repetition. After each addition of a number grouping there is a countdown until, at last, there are ten little minnows, nine hippopotamuses, eight alligators, seven bears, six kangaroos, five whales, four seals, three ducks, two turtles, one snail, and me-- all in the bathtub!

Robert Allen's Numbers: A First Counting Book is illustrated with color photographs. This book can help children realize that size and position of objects does not affect the numerical value; for example, five objects in a straight line are equal to the same five objects arranged in a circle. At the end of the book realistic pictures demonstrate very simple addition. In one grouping there are two pictures, each showing one puppy. Across from it there is a picture of the two puppies together to show that one and one makes two.

George Mendoza's The Marcel Marceau Counting Book is a clever number book presenting the equivalent of a mime show with an accumulation of hats to represent the numbers.

One, Two, Three for the Library by Mary E. Little is a unique counting book in which each child attending the library's story hour is assigned a number. The brief text is in rhyme and a multiethnic group of children comprise the illustrations.

Goodnight--1, 2, 3 by Yutaka Sugita incorporates numbers through a blaze of color in the magical dreamworld of a child. Fritz Eichenberg's Dancing in the Moon: Counting Rhymes is a book of funny animals and nonsense rhymes for each number from one to twenty. Brenda Seymour's First Counting has simple, descriptive pictures with a jingly text. In Two Lonely Ducks by Roger Duvoisin, the ducks find life becomes anything but lonely with ten eggs laid and hatched. Jeanne-Marie Counts Her Sheep by Francoise has childlike drawings that show a little girl dreaming about the number of lambs her sheep may produce.

These are a few of the number books that are available. As a child develops different interests there are usually counting and concept books that will promote new understanding in an enjoyable way.

More Alphabet Books

ABC books provide a kind of organizational structure by which objects can be presented to children. They afford fine opportunities for discussion, identification, and enjoyment; however, a child needs an adult, or at least older children, with whom to share the experiences.

From the great wealth of ABC books, one can find a range from the simplest, most representational pictures to very detailed illustrations and captions that stretch even an adult's vocabulary. Some books provide riddles or puzzles; others center around a given theme and develop it with originality. For most children of this age, books should still be rather simple in style and show just a few objects on a page. One problem that sometimes develops in ABC books and causes confusion for children is that objects pictured may have more than one common name. Children often insist that "B is for rabbit," and in their way of thinking, they are perfectly right.

One of the alphabet books that deals with a given theme is ABC of Cars and Trucks by Anne Alexander. This is a unique picture book. Each letter introduces a particular form of transportation. It is written in rhyme with brief descriptions of the vehicles. Each letter merits its own separate page or a two-page spread. A criticism of the book could be that boys are seen in the active roles. Girls are somewhat stereotyped, pushing baby carriages and appearing as princesses in parades.

Annie's ABC Kitten: An Alphabetical Story about Annie and Her Pet by Charlotte Steiner is another book developed around a simple story theme. A kitten carries the movement through the alphabet and holds the book together. Pictures are large and quite simple. Our New Baby's ABC, by Beman Lord with illustrations by Velma Ilsley, tells of the new baby and its experiences. The two older children in the book feel quite grown-up as they think of the baby's needs.

Hey, Look at Me by Sandy Grant is a city ABC book with photographs that show action words for each letter. The book deals with children's experiences. Some of the settings are very urban in nature and help add stature to the inner-city child.

The Alphabeast Book, An Abecedarium by Dorothy Schmiderer is a clever book that many three-to-four-year-olds will enjoy. In it each letter in the alphabet is accompanied by a series of four boxes extending across both pages of a double-page spread. In the far left the letter appears. The letter is shaped, then it changes as the boxes progress until the final image is of an animal whose name begins with the same letter.

Ed Emberley's ABC is somewhat similar. It has humorous illustrations of animals introducing the letters of the

alphabet. Again, there are four pictures across the page.
There is a chart at the end that shows how to make capital
letters and also a list of things one should search for in the
pictures. This book could be of help to the child who is becoming interested in trying to write the letters.

Books that Help to Satisfy a Desire for Knowledge

Preschool children are the most inquisitive creatures on
the face of the earth. Fortunately their great desire to know
and to understand their environment is coupled with a sense
of wonder that can make their new discoveries exhilarating
experiences. They need much more than a knowledge of
facts. Rote learning offers little stimulus for creative thinking, reasoning, or application of knowledge to new situations.
Rachel Carson talks of children's need to retain their enjoyment of the fresh, new, and beautiful world they experience
in nature in her book A Sense of Wonder. She makes the
following comment:

> If I had influence with the good fairy who is supposed
> to preside over the christening of all children I should
> ask that her gift to each child in the world be a sense
> of wonder so indestructible that it would last through-
> out life, as an unfailing antidote against the boredom
> and disenchantments of later years, the sterile preoc-
> cupation with things that are artificial, the alienation
> from the sources of our strength.

This beautifully illustrated book is more for adults than for
children and certainly a fine addition to the library of new
parents. In it Carson tells of sharing exciting discoveries
in the natural world with her nephew, always helping him to
enjoy the wonder of the universe. She avoided making their
times together lessons, yet she was amazed at how he re-
called names and identified plants following their casual discussions. She concludes, "If a child is to keep alive his in-
born sense of wonder without any such gift from the fairies,
he needs the companionship of at least one adult who can
share it, rediscovering with him the joy, excitement and
mystery of the world we live in."23

Shared enjoyment makes the development of any interest
a happy approach to learning. The way you answer your
child's questions may be of more importance than the facts
that you state. When you select books to buy for your little boy or girl, look for those that do more than just throw

out dozens of facts with no unifying ideas or concepts. Ask yourself if a particular book will expand your child's intelligence and promote even more curiosity on a given subject.

You will want your child to realize that books provide the means of exploring his or her interests. Fortunately, there are fine informational books that can help to develop almost any subject that is fascinating to your youngster. You can share real moments of discovery by exploring such books together.

Try to avoid information books which seem to overwhelm children with too much in the way of details. As one little girl said, "That book told me more than I wanted to know." A good book provides some facts and information but also leaves a residue of curiosity and inspires youngsters to continue the search.

At the three- to four-year-old stage children are interested in colors. Some may not be able to recognize even the primary colors as yet; others are already considering shades and hues. A book that can stir imaginations is The Great Blueness and Other Predicaments by Arnold Lobel. It shows the world all in grays and black; then a wizard invents first one color and then another, and things become bright and exciting. The Adventures of the Three Colors by Annette Tison and Talus Taylor is a manipulation book that excites children. It uses transparent overlays to show the concept of mixed colors to produce yet another color as well as new objects in the pictures. What Is the Color of the Wide, Wide World? by Margaret Friskey is a little story in which each animal has a different idea as to what color the world is. While the camel is sure the world is yellow, the tiger says, no, the world is green. Of course the owl thinks it is black. The illustrations show why the animals have made their judgments. Don Freeman's A Rainbow of My Own shows a boy's imaginative play with a rainbow. In the end he finds a rainbow of his own in his own fishbowl through which the sun is shining.

Three-to-four-year-olds are usually quite sensitive to shapes. There are fine books to help develop improved understandings of basic shapes. In My Very First Book of Shapes Eric Carle has employed the same format that he used in his color book. Through the use of split pages children are asked to match solid black shapes with shapes of things they know--a kite, half of a watermelon, and many others. Shapes by John J. Reiss shows a variety of examples of a given shape on one page; on the opposite page the form is labeled and there is a picture made up of combinations of the particular shape.

You can trust photographer Tana Hoban to give children unusual experiences in concept books! Her Circles, Triangles and Squares gives them an opportunity to pick out different forms and shapes in unique photographs of everyday objects. Unusual photography provides picture puzzles in another Hoban book, Shapes and Things. Here she uses black-and-white photograms of common tools and utensils in a wordless book that challenges children to some creative guessing.

Books that show opposites help children sharpen insights. Again, Tana Hoban has supplied one of the best. Her Push-Pull, Empty-Full provides sharp, clear photographs that give excellent visual experiences in dealing with opposites. Peter Spier's Fast-Slow, High-Low is a busier book about opposites that helps children generalize in a humorous, exciting way.

Whatever your child's special interests are at this time, you will probably be able to find information books that will expand understanding and stimulate more curiosity. Such books explain concepts on a preschool child's level of understanding.

The Wonderful Realm of Fantasy

Books of fantasy probably have the most fascinating appeal of any to be found in children's literature. These are stories that bring much pleasure as they take the child from a world of immediate experiences and move out into realms of pure imagination. Here children can explore thoughts, dreams, and ideas in settings that are removed from the restrictions of daily living. There is the delightful story of the mother who asked Professor Einstein what books her sons should read to prepare them for the life of a scientist. He told her that they should read fairy tales for they cause children to wonder; they expand the imagination, and it is through imagination that creativity grows.

Some parents worry about books of fantasy in the lives of their children, thinking that perhaps such books will inhibit the children's ability to distinguish between truth and falsehood. In Honey for a Child's Heart Gladys Hunt gives suggestions for reading in a Christian home. She says, "There is nothing unspiritual about an active imagination, a token of the liberty of childhood." She tells about a discussion in which a university student said that he would never tell his own child about Santa Claus because he feared that when the child later found that this character is a fanciful one, he or she might assume that Jesus is also unreal. The author's ten-year-old son explained that he never confused Jesus with Santa Claus or any fictitious character because he could tell by his parents' talk and actions that Jesus was a real person. Gladys Hunt recommends fine stories of fantasy throughout her book and feels that the "world of pretend" is a "legitimate adventure."[24]

There are a few criteria for fantasy over and beyond the usual standards of excellence that should be considered in selecting books for children. A fantasy needs to have its own sense of logic. The reader/listener ventures into the world of imagination, but there needs to be a limit set on the suspension of disbelief. If the situation is such that anything can happen, the child encounters nothing but a series of impossible episodes as might be found in a Popeye comic strip. In a good fantasy the child is led into a fanciful situation within which certain limited happenings can and do occur. Then he or she is brought back into reality having experienced new ideas that can promote understanding.

A small child's book of fantasy should start with a situation that the youngster understands and move into the unknown. In Where the Wild Things Are by Maurice Sendak, Max is seen being sent to his room by his mother for being disruptive--a very ordinary occurrence to which almost any child can relate. But, "That very night in Max's room a forest grew and grew--and grew...." Sendak carefully leads the child from an ordinary room into a magical land, even by way of the gradual expansion of the size of the pictures. In a fantasy for small children we want to avoid really fearful objects and gruesome texts. In this story we do meet monsters who "roared their terrible roars and gnashed their terrible teeth and rolled their terrible eyes and showed their terrible claws," but throughout there is a kind of playful mood. Max is always in control using one of his mother's tricks to keep in command--that of staring into their eyes without blinking. But then Max tires of his great adventure and sails back home because he wants "to be where someone loves him best of all." This short text with its vivid pictures takes a child away from an unpleasant situation, out into the world of fantasy, lets him or her experience real control over a scary environment, but then brings the youngster back to the real security of home where supper is waiting, and is still hot. [25]

In The Tale of Peter Rabbit the little protagonist leaves his secure home and ventures out on his own into the real and dangerous world of Mr. MacGregor's garden. The events of this story stay well within the limits of suspended disbelief that Potter set. The animals communicate and think as human beings, but never do they escape their animal characteristics. Peter is a little rabbit being chased by an angry man. His only defenses are to run and to hide. His perilous adventures are breathtaking, and a child who is hearing the story shares the precarious situation in which Peter finds himself. Peter returns home a wiser little rabbit. Most children will admire his daring spirit, but his experiences may indicate to them that it is wise to be cautious when one ventures out into the world.

Our tales of fantasy have their beginnings in the old folk and fairy tales. The basic themes and motifs of these stories provide the framework of modern fantasy and of literary folk and fairy tales such as "The Three Bears." Here the protagonist ventures into a strange situation or quest, experiences a new, more exciting world, but in the end is able to return to security. Goldilocks does all the things a small child would like to do in a strange house--tasting all the food, trying the feel of the furniture, and then, childlike, making herself comfortable in the best bed before going to sleep. The bears return, and their shock at what Goldilocks has done, Goldilocks' real fright when they awaken her, and her escape all make for an exciting climax. The child may see possibilities of satisfying natural curiosity in this story, but at the same time may feel real sympathy for the bears whose home was disturbed in such a rude manner.

These are books that not only bring enjoyment to children, but also give them a means of keeping imagination, curiosity, and a sense of wonder alive and growing. They help children explore ideas, needs, and even frustrations and fears. They also make it possible to experience a happy ending of returning to security and loved ones, perhaps having gained something in the way of understanding.

Books that Can Help Deal with Emotional Needs

Children's self-image determines to a great extent their

success in meeting the developmental tasks of early childhood. Families provide children's first social contacts. The attitudes of families toward their youngsters have a great deal to do with the way the children feel about themselves. Parents need to continually let their children know that they are loved and that they are a source of pride.

A youngster needs to experience success frequently. Expectations should be geared to a child's ability and developmental level. Consideration must be given to the psychological needs of a child at any given time. Three-to-four-year-olds often experience feelings of inadequacy. Of course a book can never replace the love and assurance that is needed from one's family, but often hearing about personal fears-- how they are met or at least endured by storybook characters --can be heartening.

Danny and His Thumb by Kathryn F. Ernst deals with a problem that many small children encounter. Even though parental attitude toward thumb sucking has mellowed in the past few years, some children are still harassed because of this habit. Perhaps Danny's situation will relieve them of some of their anxieties. Jenny, the little girl in Don't Worry Dear by Joan Fassler, has many problems. She stutters, wets her bed, and sucks her thumb. Fortunately, she has an understanding family who accept her and her problems and keep reassuring her that it only takes time to outgrow such difficulties.

Three-to-four-year-olds are beginning to learn the give and take of sharing and playing with friends. Often this involves difficult adjustments. Sometimes reading a book about similar situations can help. I Do Not Like It When My Friend Comes to Visit by Ivan Sherman is very real to a small child's experiences and feelings of frustration at having to share precious possessions when a friend comes calling. However, this book ends on a real "upbeat," for the child in the story returns the friend's visit and it is time to demand reciprocation! Let's Be Enemies by Janice May Udry suggests another good resolution of unhappy feelings. Charlotte Zolotow is an expert in presenting children's inner feelings in her fine little books. The Hating Book gives a very lifelike experience of two girls who began hating each other because of a misunderstanding. Negative feelings developed very rapidly but dissolved even more quickly when they discovered the cause of their problem. In A Tiger Called Thomas she gives children more than just a Halloween story, but an understanding of how Thomas, who was shy about going out to meet friends in his new neighborhood, is able to make advances in his tiger costume. He finds that his new neighbors are already his friends. Eleanor Schick's Making Friends is an interesting wordless book about a little girl who makes friends first with animals, but finds a girl to be friends with in the end.

Some books help children understand family troubles. Are You Sad, Mama? by Elizabeth Winthrop illustrates a small child's sensitivity to her mother's feelings. She tries very hard to cheer her mother and is finally able to do so with her love. In My Mother Lost Her Job Today, Judy Delton shows how very deeply children feel insecurity. In the end of this book the mother reassures the little girl that she will be able to find other work and things can go on as usual.

I Am Adopted by Susan Lapsley tells, in a casual way, what being adopted means--the children were given to their parents and they belong to the family.

There are excellent books that deal with situations like those mentioned above and with many other problems. Some of the difficulties confronted in the books are serious in nature; others may seem ridiculous to adults, but very important to children. We never know what a child will take from a book, but very often a story will have the capacity of assisting growth, development, and understanding.

Being Replaced by the Television Set

Because children are fascinated with action on the television screen, the temptation to let it become an electronic parent is great. An amazing amount of childhood is spent watching TV and the debate continues as to how much harm is done to youngsters because of excessive viewing. "By the time today's child graduates from high school, he will have accumulated about one-third more TV watching time than the total time spent in the classroom."[26] Children spend more time watching TV before they enter school than they will spend attending four years of college classes.

We do not know at this time what the effect of watching unwholesome programs may be, but we do know that "In any media, the trivial, trashy, or predominantly violent and sensational is poor fare for children."[27] This is not to say that there are not fine programs available, but selections should be supervised and viewing time limited.   After all, parents set the standards in the home and are responsible for helping children develop reasonable habits about use of time. Children need a balance of activities.   Passive viewing adds little to the development of intellect through creative experiences.   The bombardment of most fast-action, audiovisual programs does not allow children time to assimilate the experience or to learn through discussion and organization of facts.   When parents take time to read to children, they are bringing youngsters into the academic world of books, where experiences can progress at a pace geared to the children's understanding.   There is time to go back, reread and assimilate ideas, and enjoy the experience.   In fact, in college classes students who have been read to by parents and other relatives when they were growing up are often the envy of peers who repeatedly say that the only books they had read to them as children were those they heard on the Captain Kangaroo program.   Often, however, students will conclude such a discussion with comments like, "Well, thank goodness for Captain Kangaroo and for programs like Mister Rogers where children can experience some of the warmth and understanding that they may otherwise miss."   Such wholesome programs have enriched children's lives, but parents should never let any mechanical device take away their privilege of sharing some of the best moments of their children's preschool years.

The Fascination of Folktales

Young children enjoy the here-and-now stories because such realistic events can add to the excitement of their own experiences.   These stories are easily understood because they come directly from the children's world.   But youngsters are also drawn to the old folktales.   Bernice E. Cullinan discusses what many authorities in the field of early childhood education have proposed as the reasons for such an attraction.   Because young children are in what Piaget terms the "preoperational stage" of development, their reasoning and their comprehension of story structure coincide well with that found in the simplest folktales.   They usually are not able to generalize or consider more than one aspect of an experience at a time.   Their stories must be simple. They respond to cumulative tales because of the obvious relationship of one part of the plot to the next as revealed through repetition.   Three-to-four-year-olds will enjoy stories like "The Three Billy Goats Gruff" because they are beginning to comprehend sequence and the increasing size of

the goats makes the development of the story more meaningful. Many small children think that animals can talk, and
they believe in magical creatures. To them the world is
simple and uncomplicated, just as it is in the old stories.
The old tales help children objectify their fears, and prove
to be very reassuring because the good always overcomes
the evil. Many of the stories are exciting; most expand the
creative imagination. From a literary standpoint, the plots
are easy to follow, and the characters are clearly drawn so
that the child is never confused as to which represents the
good and which the evil. Their style is direct, often con-
versational, and contains rhyming phrases, repeat passages,
and wonderful language play to which children respond whole-
heartedly. 28 Children of this age still need the simplest of
tales and enjoy picture-book editions of only one story.
Browse through library shelves with your child and let him
or her help select old tales that have real appeal at this
time. Marcia Brown's version of Stone Soup fascinates three-
to-four-year-olds. Warwick Hutton's pictures for The Sleeping Beauty from his retelling of the Grimm Brothers' story
are a fine artistic experience.

Maurice Sendak's illustrations for the Grimms' King
Grisly-Beard take an unusual turn. In this book a boy, a
girl, and a dog help re-enact the story. A regular cartoon
strip at the bottom of the pages shows their performance.
When the play is over, the Impresario says, "You were terrific," and the girl's reply is, "True." Many of the Grimm
stories have been interpreted with unusual pictures by different illustrators. See if your child will especially enjoy some
of the following: The Traveling Musicians, illustrated by
Hans Fisher; Molly Holly, with pictures by Bernadette Watts;
Tom Thumb, illustrated by Felix Hoffmann; Rumpelstiltskin,
illustrated by William Stobbs; and Three Gay Tales from
Grimm, illustrated by Wanda Gág. For a story with real
American flavor you might try Journey Cake, Ho! by Ruth
Sawyer.

Aesop's Fables, selected and adapted by Louis Untermeyer
and illustrated by Alice and Martin Provensen, could provide
a delightful introduction to the fables for your child. In this
oversize book the fables are narrated in a brief, concise
manner, and retold in large, bright pictures that easily attract children. Conversations and comments about the stories are included in the large animal cartoons and add to the
fun.

Developing Reading Readiness Skills

As you have watched your child's development in this exciting time when his or her reasoning powers are expanding daily, you have no doubt enjoyed seeing the progress that your little boy or girl has been making through stages of reading readiness. You have been able to witness the learning continuum on which the development of the abilities that are necessary to deal with written language is based. As an involved parent, you have probably consciously or unconsciously set up a positive environment for learning to read. You have made listening interesting and intriguing, and have helped your child to attain the vocabulary that will be absolutely necessary when he or she begins to grope for words that appear in reading experiences. You have helped your youngster learn that books are friends so that he or she will not be intimidated, as some children are, when faced with words in printed form in school situations. You have enjoyed poetry together, and already your child is responding to the likeness of sounds in rhyming words and the fun of creating rhyming schemes. You have continued to help your child to be visually astute by calling his or her attention to shapes of words and letters, noting likenesses and differences. Your little son or daughter probably already knows that words represent objects, feelings, and ideas. You have helped your youngster to perceive the utilitarian values of words by labeling pictures he or she has drawn. Perhaps by now your child is moving a finger across the page from left to right to help you keep your place as you read, and even starting to point out certain words and ask their meaning.

As you have read and shared some of the fine books that are available for preschool children, you have learned more about your youngster as an individual. You have discovered many things that impress your little boy or girl, and have learned what experiences appeal to his or her sense of humor. You have also encountered shared interests through books, which are one of our best tools of communication despite generation gaps. Your youngster has by now acquired a great deal of information from books, and has in this way learned something of life itself. Already he or she is beginning to develop bases for moral standards and perhaps even a foundation for the religious beliefs that you hold dear. Your child has experienced the aesthetic enjoyment that comes through literary and artistic works found in picture books. The language of storybooks has become a part of your child's language so that book wordage will not be foreign when the youngster enters school. Perhaps more important than the general knowledge that your child has accumulated is the fact that he or she has started to understand the feelings of other people, to feel empathy for others through characters in books, and to relate their experiences to his or her own.

Getting ready for academic pursuits that will come in formal school activities involves many growth experiences, including the development of very basic reading readiness skills. Because you have been interested enough to spend the necessary time to read, discuss, explore, and enjoy this exciting developmental stage with your child, you have been giving your youngster the opportunity to be well prepared for future school experiences.

Notes

[1]Dorothy Butler, Babies Need Books (New York: Atheneum Publishers, 1980), p. 84.

[2]Kornei Chukovsky, From Two to Five, trans. and edited by Miriam Morton (Berkeley: University of California Press, 1966), p. 31.

[3]Miles A. Tinker, Preparing Your Child for Reading (New York: Holt, Rinehart & Winston, 1971), p. 59.

[4]Carol Chomsky, "Stages in Language Development and Reading Exposure," The Harvard Educational Review, 42 (February 1972), pp. 1-33.

[5]Dorothy Butler and Marie Clay, Reading Begins at Home: Preparing Children for Reading Before They Go to School (Auckland, New Zealand: Heinemann Educational Books, 1979), p. 20.

[6]David McCord, "Song of the Train," in Far and Few, illus. by Henry B. Kane (Boston: Little, Brown, 1925), p. 87.

[7]Jean C. Soule, Never Tease a Weasel, illus. by Denman Hampson (New York: Parents Magazine Press, 1964), n. p.

[8]Tinker, p. 71.

[9]Leland Jacobs, ed., "Enjoying Literature with Young Children," in Using Literature with Young Children (New York: Teachers College Press, 1965), p. 1.

[10]Alice Yardley, Young Children Thinking (Englewood Cliffs, NJ: Citation Press, 1973), p. 7.

11William H. Teale, "Positive Environments for Learning to Read: What Studies of Early Readers Tell Us," Language Arts, 55, No. 8 (November-December 1978), pp. 922-932.

12Annis Duff, "Bequest of Wings": A Family's Pleasures with Books (New York: The Viking Press, 1944), p. 25.

13Warren Chappell, "Illustrations Today in Children's Books," in A Hornbook Sampler, ed. Norma R. Fryatt (Boston: The Hornbook, 1959), pp. 90-91.

14Patricia Cianciolo, Illustrations in Children's Books, 2nd ed. (Dubuque, IA: William C. Brown, 1976), p. 16.

15Donnarae MacCann and Olga Richards, The Child's First Books: A Critical Study of Pictures and Texts (New York: H. W. Wilson Co., 1973), pp. 19-20.

16Mary Jett-Simpson, "Parents and Teachers Share Books with Young Children," in Developing Active Readers: Ideas for Parents, Teachers, and Librarians, eds. Dianne L. Monson and Day Ann K. McClenathan (Newark, DE: International Reading Association, 1979), p. 74.

17Zena Sutherland and May Hill Arbuthnot, Children and Books, 5th ed. (Glenview, IL: Scott, Foresman and Co., 1977), p. 244.

18Dorothy Aldis, "Blum," in All Together (New York: G. P. Putnam's Sons, 1952), p. 163.

19May Hill Arbuthnot, Children and Books, rev. ed. (Glenview, IL: Scott, Foresman and Co., 1957), p. 120.

20Sylvia Plath, The Bed Book, illus. by Emily Arnold McCully (New York: Harper & Row, 1976), n. p.

21James Steel Smith, A Critical Approach to Children's Literature (New York: McGraw-Hill, 1967), p. 203.

22Joan W. Blos, "Getting It: The First Notch on the Funny Bone," School Library Journal, 25 (May 1979), p. 39.

23Rachel Carson, A Sense of Wonder, illus. by Charles Pratt (New York: Harper, 1956), pp. 42-43.

24Gladys Hunt, Honey for a Child's Heart (Grand Rapids, MI: Zondervan Publishing House, 1969), p. 37.

25Maurice Sendak, Where the Wild Things Are (New York: Harper & Row, 1963), n. p.

26Arnold Arnold, Teaching Your Child to Learn: From Birth to School Age (Englewood Cliffs, NJ: Prentice-Hall, 1971), p. 180.

27May Hill Arbuthnot, Children's Reading in the Home (Glenview, IL: Scott, Foresman and Co., 1969), p. 9.

28Bernice E. Cullinan, "Traditional Literature: Children's Legacy," in Literature and Young Children, eds. Bernice E. Cullinan and Carolyn W. Carmichael (Urbana, IL: National Council of Teachers of English, 1977), pp. 85-88.

Books Discussed in This Chapter

Alexander, Anne. ABC of Cars and Trucks. Illus. by
  Ninon. Garden City, NY: Doubleday and Company,
  1971. (Paperback.)
Allen, Robert. Numbers: A First Counting Book. Illus.
  by Mottke Weissman. New York: Platt and Munk,
  1968.
Andre, Evelyn M. Places I Like to Be. Nashville: Abing-
  don Press, 1980.
Bangs, Edward. Yankee Doodle. Illus. by Steven Kellogg.
  New York: Parents' Magazine Press, 1976.
Baskin, Leonard, et al. Hosie's Alphabet. New York:
  The Viking Press, 1972.
Bissett, Donald J., comp. Poems and Verses About Ani-
  mals. New York: Noble & Noble, 1967.
_____. Poems and Verses About the City. New York:
  Noble & Noble, 1968.
Bonne, Rose, and Alan Mills. I Know an Old Lady. Music
  by Alan Mills. Illus. by Abner Graboff. Chicago:
  Rand-McNally & Co., 1961.
Brewton, John E., and Sara Brewton. Gaily We Parade.
  Illus. by Robert Lawson. New York: Macmillan
  Company, 1957.
Brown, Marcia. Once a Mouse. New York: Charles
  Scribner's Sons, 1961.
_____. Stone Soup. New York: Charles Scribner's
  Sons, 1947. (Paperback.)
Brown, Margaret Wise. Shhhhhh, Bang. Illus. by Robert
  De Veyrac. New York: Harper & Row, 1943.
Burton, Virginia Lee. The Little House. Boston: Hough-
  ton Mifflin, 1942. (Paperback. 1978.)
Caldecott, Randolph. The Hey Diddle Diddle Picture Book.
  New York: Frederick Warne & Co., n.d. (Paper-
  back. New York: Franklin Watts, Inc., 1975.)
Carle, Eric. My Very First Book of Shapes. New York:
  Thomas Y. Crowell, 1974.
Cendvars, Blaise. Shadow. Illus. by Marcia Brown. New
  York: Charles Scribner's Sons, 1982.
Chalmers, Mary. Be Good, Harry. New York: Harper &
  Row, 1967.
Clithero, Sally, comp. Beginning-to-Read Poetry. Illus.
  by Eric Blegvad. Chicago: Follett Publishing Co.,
  1967.
Cohen, Miriam. Will I Have a Friend? Illus. by Lillian
  Hoban. New York: Macmillan Company, 1967.
  (Paperback. 1971.)

Cole, William, ed. Beastly Boys and Ghastly Girls. Illus.
by Tomi Ungerer. Cleveland: Collins-World, 1964.

Delton, Judy. My Mother Lost Her Job Today. Illus. by
Irene Trivas. Chicago: Albert Whitman & Co., 1980.

De Paola, Tomie. Strega Nona. Englewood Cliffs, NJ:
Prentice-Hall, 1975.

Domanska, Janina. Little Red Hen. New York: Macmillan
Company, 1973.

Duvoisin, Roger. Two Lonely Ducks: A Counting Book.
New York: Alfred A. Knopf, 1955.

Eichenberg, Fritz. Dancing in the Moon: Counting Rhymes.
New York: Harcourt, Brace, 1956. (Paperback.
1975.)

Emberley, Ed. Ed Emberley's ABC. Boston: Little,
Brown, 1978.

_____. London Bridge Is Falling Down. Boston: Little,
Brown, 1967.

Ernst, Kathryn F. Danny and His Thumb. Illus. by Tomie
de Paola. Englewood Cliffs, NJ: Prentice-Hall,
1973. (Paperback. 1975.)

Fassler, Joan. Don't Worry Dear. Illus. by Stewart Kantz.
New York: Behavioral Publishers, 1971.

Flack, Marjorie. Wait for William. Illus. by R. A. Hol-
berg. Boston: Houghton Mifflin, 1935.

Francoise. Jeanne-Marie Counts Her Sheep. New York:
Charles Scribner's Sons, 1957. (Paperback.)

Freeman, Don. A Rainbow of My Own. New York: The
Viking Press, 1966. (Paperback. New York: Penguin, 1974.)

Friskey, Margaret. What Is the Color of the Wide, Wide
World? Illus. by Mary Gehr. Chicago: Children's
Press, 1973.

Frost, Robert. Stopping by Woods on a Snowy Evening.
Illus. by Susan Jeffers. New York: E. P. Dutton,
1978.

Galdone, Paul. The Magic Porridge Pot. New York:
Seabury Press, 1976.

_____, retold by. The Three Wishes. New York:
McGraw-Hill, 1961.

Grant, Sandy. Hey, Look at Me: A City ABC. Illus.
by Larry Mulvehill. Scarsdale, NY: Bradbury
Press, 1973.

Grimm Brothers. King Grisly-Beard: A Tale from the
Brothers Grimm. Trans. Edgar Taylor. Illus. by
Maurice Sendak. New York: Farrar, Straus and
Giroux, 1973. (Paperback. New York: Penguin,
1978.)

_____. Molly Holly. Illus. by Bernadette Watts. New York: Thomas Y. Crowell, 1972.

_____. Rumpelstiltskin. Illus. by William Stobbs. New York: Henry Z. Walck, 1971.

_____. Three Gay Tales from Grimm. Illus. by Wanda Gág. New York: Coward-McCann, 1936.

_____. Tom Thumb. Illus. by Felix Hoffman. New York: Atheneum Publishers, 1973.

_____. The Traveling Musicians. Ed. and illus. by Hans Fisher. New York: Harcourt, Brace, 1956.

Hoban, Tana. Circles, Triangles and Squares. New York: Macmillan Company, 1974.

_____. Look Again! New York: Macmillan Company, 1971.

_____. Push Pull, Empty Full: A Book of Opposites. New York: Macmillan Company, 1972. (Paperback. New York: Macmillan Company, 1976.)

_____. Shapes and Things. New York: Macmillan Company, 1970.

_____. Take Another Look. New York: Greenwillow, 1981.

Hogstrom, Daphne. Little Boy Blue: Finger Plays Old and New. Illus. by Alice Schlesinger. Racine, WI: Western Publishing Co., 1976.

Hopkins, Lee Bennett, comp. Go to Bed! A Book of Bedtime Poems. Illus. by Rosekrans Hoffman. New York: Alfred A. Knopf, 1979.

Hutton, Warwick. The Sleeping Beauty. Retold from Grimm Brothers. New York: Atheneum Publishers, 1979.

Katzoff, Betty. Cathy's First School. Illus. by Sy Katzoff. New York: Alfred A. Knopf, 1964.

Kessler, Ethel, and Leonard Kessler. Do Baby Bears Sit in Chairs? Garden City, NY: Doubleday and Company, 1961.

Kraus, Max. The Day the Rooster Didn't Crow. Illus. by Amrei Fechner. New York: Methuen, 1979.

Kraus, Robert. Leo, the Late Bloomer. New York: E. P. Dutton, 1971.

Johnson, John E. My School Book. New York: Random House, 1979.

Langstaff, John. Oh, A-Hunting We Will Go. Illus. by Nancy Winslow Parker. New York: Atheneum Publishers, 1974.

Lapsley, Susan. I Am Adopted. Illus. by Michael Charlton. Scarsdale, NY: Bradbury Press, 1975.

Larrick, Nancy, comp. Piper, Pipe that Song Again. Illus. by Kelly Oechsli. New York: Random House, 1965.

Lawrence, Marjory, comp. A Beginning Book of Poems.

Reading, MA: Addison-Wesley, 1967.

Leaf, Munro. The Story of Ferdinand. Illus. by Robert Lawson. New York: The Viking Press, 1936. (Paperback. New York: Penguin, 1977.)

Lear, Edward. The Owl and the Pussycat. Illus. by Barbara Cooney. Boston: Little, Brown, 1969.

_____. The Quangle-Wangle's Hat. Illus. by Helen Oxenbury. New York: Franklin Watts, Inc., 1969.

Lionni, Leo. Alexander and the Wind-Up Mouse. New York: Pantheon, 1969.

_____. Little Blue and Little Yellow. New York: Astor-Honor, Inc., 1959.

_____. Swimmy. New York: Pantheon, 1963. (Paperback.)

Little, Mary E. One, Two, Three for the Library. New York: Atheneum Publishers, 1974.

Lobel, Arnold. The Great Blueness and Other Predicaments. New York: Harper & Row, 1968.

Lord, Beman. Our New Baby's ABC. Illus. by Velma Ilsley. New York: Henry Z. Walck, 1964.

Mannheim, Grete. The Two Friends. New York: Alfred A. Knopf, 1968.

McCloskey, Robert. Blueberries for Sal. New York: The Viking Press, 1948. (Paperback. 1976.)

_____. Make Way for Ducklings. New York: The Viking Press, 1941. (Paperback. 1976.)

McDermott, Gerald. Arrow to the Sun: A Pueblo Indian Tale. New York: The Viking Press, 1974. (Paperback. New York: Penguin, 1977.)

McFarland, Wilma, comp. For a Child: Great Poems Old & New. Illus. by Ninon. Philadelphia, PA: Westminster Press, 1947.

McGovern, Ann. Too Much Noise. Illus. by Simms Taback. Boston: Houghton Mifflin, 1967.

McKee, David, retold by. The Man Who Was Going to Mind the House. New York: Abelard-Schuman, Ltd., 1973.

McLeod, Emilie Warren. One Snail and Me. Illus. by Walter Lorraine. Boston: Little, Brown, 1961.

Mendoza, George. The Marcel Marceau Counting Book. Illus. by Milton H. Greene. Garden City, NY: Doubleday and Company, 1971.

Milne, A. A. The House at Pooh Corner. Rev. ed. Illus. by Ernest H. Shepard. New York: E. P. Dutton, 1961. (Paperback. New York: Dell, 1970.)

_____. Now We Are Six. Rev. ed. Illus. by Ernest H. Shepard. New York: E. P. Dutton, 1961. (Paperback. New York: Dell, 1975.)

_____. When We Were Very Young. Rev. ed. Illus. by Ernest H. Shepard. New York: E. P. Dutton, 1961.

(Paperback. New York: Dell, 1975.)

_____. Winnie-the-Pooh. Rev. ed. Illus. by Ernest H.
Shepard. New York: E. P. Dutton, 1961. (Paperback. New York: Dell, 1970.)

Morse, Flo. How Does It Feel to Be a Tree? Illus. by Clyde
Watson. New York: Parents' Magazine Press, 1976.

Perrault, Dharles, retold by. Cinderella. Illus. by Marcia
Brown. New York: Charles Scribner's Sons, 1954.

Plath, Sylvia. The Bed Book. Illus. by Emily Arnold
McCully. New York: Harper & Row, 1976.

Potter, Beatrix. The Tale of Jemima Puddleduck. New
York: Frederick Warne & Co., 1936.

_____. The Tale of Peter Rabbit. New York: Frederick
Warne & Co., 1902. (Paperback. 1972.)

_____. The Tale of Squirrel Nutkin. New York: Fred-
erick Warne & Co., 1903. (Paperback. New York:
Dover Publications, Inc., 1972.)

Quackenbush, Robert. Skip to My Lou. Philadelphia, PA:
J. B. Lippincott, 1975.

Reiss, John J. Shapes. Scarsdale, NY: Bradbury Press,
1974.

Robbins, Ruth, adapted by. Baboushka and the Three Kings.
Illus. by Nicholas Sidjakov. Oakland, CA: Parnassus, 1960.

Sawyer, Ruth. Journey Cake, Ho! Illus. by Robert McCloskey. New York: The Viking Press, 1953. (Paperback. 1978.)

Scarry, Richard. The Best Word Book Ever. Racine, WI:
Western Publishing Co., 1963.

_____. Richard Scarry's Great Big Air Book. New
York: Random House, 1971.

Schick, Eleanor. Making Friends. New York: Macmillan
Company, 1969.

Schmiderer, Dorothy. The Alphabeast Book: An Abecedarium.
New York: Holt, Rinehart & Winston, 1971.

Schwartz, Delmore. "I Am Cherry Alive," the Little Girl
Sang. Illus. by Barbara Cooney. New York:
Harper & Row, 1979.

Scott, Louise B., and Jesse J. Thompson. Rhymes for
Fingers and Flannelboards. Illus. by Jean Flowers.
New York: McGraw-Hill, 1960.

Seymour, Brenda. Brenda Seymour's First Counting. New
York: Henry Z. Walck, 1969.

Sherman, Ivan. I Do Not Like It When My Friend Comes
to Visit. New York: Harcourt Brace Jovanovich,
1973.

Spier, Peter. Fast-Slow, High-Low: A Book of Opposites.
Garden City, NY: Doubleday and Company, 1972.

_____. London Bridge Is Falling Down! Garden City, NY: Doubleday and Company, 1967.

Stanley, Diane. Fiddle-I-Fee. Boston: Little, Brown, 1979.

Steiner, Charlotte. Annie's ABC Kitten: An Alphabetical Story About Annie and Her Pet. New York: Alfred A. Knopf, 1965.

_____. I'd Rather Stay With You. New York: Seabury Press, 1965.

Sugita, Yutaka. Goodnight--1, 2, 3. New York: Scroll Press, 1971.

Thayer, Jane. A Drink for Little Red Diker. Illus. by W. T. Mars. New York: William Morrow, 1963.

Tison, Annette, and Talus Taylor. The Adventures of the Three Colors. Rev. ed. Columbus, OH: Charles E. Merrill Publishing Co., 1979.

Tworkov, Jack. The Camel Who Took a Walk. Illus. by Roger Duvoisin. New York: E. P. Dutton, 1951. (Paperback. 1974.)

Udry, Janice May. Let's Be Enemies. Illus. by Maurice Sendak. New York: Harper & Row, 1961. (Paperback. New York: Scholastic Book Services, 1969.)

Untermeyer, Louis, comp. and adapted by. Aesop's Fables. Illus. by Alice Provensen and Martin Provensen. Racine, WI: Western Publishing Co., 1966.

_____, comp. The Golden Treasury of Poetry. Illus. by Joan Walsh Anglund. Racine, WI: Western Publishing Co., 1959.

Weil, Lisl. If Eggs Had Legs: Nonsense and Some Sense. Garden City, NY: Doubleday and Company, 1976.

Weiss, Nicki. Waiting. New York: Greenwillow, 1981.

Wildsmith, Brian. Brian Wildsmith's Birds. New York: Franklin Watts, Inc., 1967.

_____. Brian Wildsmith's Puzzles. New York: Franklin Watts, Inc., 1971.

Winthrop, Elizabeth. Are You Sad, Mama? Illus. by Donna Diamond. New York: Harper & Row, 1979.

Zemach, Harve. Mommy, Buy Me a China Doll. Illus. by Margot Zemach. New York: Farrar, Straus and Giroux, 1975.

Zemach, Margot. The Three Sillies. New York: Holt, Rinehart & Winston, 1963.

Zolotow, Charlotte. The Hating Book. Illus. by Ben Shecter. New York: Harper & Row, 1969.

_____. A Tiger Called Thomas. Illus. by Kert Werth. New York: Lothrop, Lee & Shepard, 1963.

Additional Poetry and Verse for Young Children

Aiken, Conrad, and John Lord. Who's Zoo? New York:
Atheneum Publishers, 1977.
Belloc, Hilaire. The Yak, The Python, The Frog: Three
Beast Poems. Illus. by Steven Kellogg. New York:
Parents' Magazine Press, 1975.
Bonner, Ann, and Roger Bonner. Early Birds ... Early
Words. New York: Scroll Press, 1973.
Brewton, Sara. Birthday Candles Burning Bright. Illus.
by Vera Brock. New York: Macmillan Company,
1960.
Bright, Robert. My Hopping Bunny. Garden City, NY:
Doubleday and Company, 1971.
Brown, Margaret Wise. Four Fur Feet. Illus. by Remy
Charlip. New York: William R. Scott, 1961.
Chute, Marchette. Around and About. New York: E. P.
Dutton, 1957.
_____. Rhymes About Us. New York: E. P. Dutton,
1974.
Ciardi, John. I Met a Man. Illus. by Robert Osborn.
Boston: Houghton Mifflin, 1961.
_____. You Know Who. Illus. by Edward Gorey.
Philadelphia, PA: J. B. Lippincott, 1964.
Clifton, Lucille. Some of the Days of Everett Anderson.
Illus. by Evaline Ness. New York: Holt, Rinehart
& Winston, 1970.
Cole, William. The Birds and Beasts Were There. New
York: World Publishing Co., 1963.
_____. Oh, That's Ridiculous! Illus. by Tomi Ungerer.
New York: The Viking Press, 1972.
De Regniers, Beatrice. Catch a Little Fox. Illus. by
Brinton Turkle. New York: Seabury Press, 1968.
Ferris, Helen, ed. Favorite Poems Old and New. Garden
City, NY: Doubleday and Company, 1957.
Fisher, Aileen. Cricket in a Thicket. Illus. by Feodor
Rojankovsky, New York: Charles Scribner's Sons,
1963.
_____. Feathered Ones and Furry. Illus. by Eric Carle.
New York: Thomas Y. Crowell, 1970.
_____. I Stood Upon a Mountain. New York: Thomas Y.
Crowell, 1979.
_____. In the Middle of the Night. Illus. by Adrienne
Adams. New York: Thomas Y. Crowell, 1965.
_____. Listen Rabbit. Illus. by Symeon Shimin. New
York: Thomas Y. Crowell, 1964.

Fujikawa, Gyo, ed. A Child's Book of Poems. New York: Grosset & Dunlap, 1969.

Galdone, Paul. History of Mother Twaddle and the Marvelous Achievements of Her Son Jack. New York: Seabury Press, 1974.

Haley, Gail. One, Two, Buckle My Shoe: A Book of Counting Rhymes. Garden City, NY: Doubleday and Company, 1964.

Hopkins, Lee Bennett. Me! A Book of Poems. New York: Seabury Press, 1970.

Itse, Elizabeth M., ed. Hey Bug! and Other Poems About Little Things. Illus. by Susan Carlton Smith. New York: American Heritage Press, 1972.

Jacobs, Leland. Is Somewhere Always Far Away? Illus. by John E. Johnson. New York: Holt, Rinehart & Winston, 1967.

Kahl, Virginia. Plum Pudding for Christmas. New York: Charles Scribner's Sons, 1956.

Kroll, Steven. Sleepy Ida and Other Nonsense Poems. New York: Pantheon, 1977.

Kuskin, Karla. Rose on My Cake. New York: Harper & Row, 1964.

Larrick, Nancy. Poetry for Holidays. Illus. by Kelly Oechsli. Champaign, IL: Garrard, 1966.

Lear, Edward. The Dong with the Luminous Nose. Illus. by Edward Gorey. Reading, MA: Addison-Wesley, 1969.

_____. The Jumblies. Illus. by Edward Gorey. New York: Frederick Warne & Co., 1907.

McCord, David. Every Time I Climb a Tree. Illus. by Marc Simont. Boston: Little, Brown, 1967.

_____. One at a Time: His Collected Poems for the Young. Boston: Little, Brown, 1977.

McEwen, Catherine Schaefer. Away We Go! Illus. by Barbara Cooney. New York: Thomas Y. Crowell, 1956.

McGovern, Ann. Feeling Mad, Sad, Bad, Glad. Illus. by Hope Wurmfeld. New York: Walker and Company, 1978.

Nash, Ogden. Custard the Dragon and the Wicked Knight. Illus. by Linell Nash. Boston: Little, Brown, 1961.

Ness, Evaline. Amelia Mixed the Mustard and Other Poems. New York: Charles Scribner's Sons, 1975.

O'Neill, Mary. Hailstones and Halibut Bones. Illus. by Leonard Weisgard. Garden City, NY: Doubleday and Company, 1964.

Patrick, Gloria. A Bug in a Jug. Illus. by Joan Hanson. New York: Scholastic Book Services, 1970.

Pomerantz, Charlotte. The Piggy in the Puddle. Illus. by
James Marshall. New York: Macmillan Company,
1974.
Rawlins, Margaret G. Round About Six. Illus. by Denis
Wrigley. New York: Frederick Warne & Co., 1973.
Rossetti, Christina. Sing-Song. Illus. by Marguerite Davis.
New York: Macmillan Company, 1924.
Scheer, Julian. Upside Down Day. Illus. by Kelly Oechsli.
New York: Holiday House, 1968.
Seeger, Peter, and Charles Seeger. The Foolish Frog.
New York: Macmillan Company, 1973.
Starbird, Kaye. Don't Ever Cross a Crocodile. Philadel-
phia, PA: J. B. Lippincott, 1963.
Thomas, Patricia. There Are Rocks in My Soxs, Said the
Ox to the Fox. Illus. by Mordicai Gerstein. New
York: Lothrop, Lee & Shepard, 1979.
Tippett, James. Crickety-Cricket! Illus. by Mary Chal-
mers. New York: Harper & Row, 1973.
Trip, Wallace. A Great Big Ugly Man Came Up and Tied
His Horse to Me, A Book of Nonsense Verse. Bos-
ton: Little, Brown, 1973.
Vance, Eleanor Graham. From Little to Big. Illus. by
June Goldsborough. Chicago: Follett Publishing Co.,
1972.
Worth, Valerie. Small Poems. Illus. by Natalie Babbit.
New York: Farrar, Straus and Giroux, 1972.
Yulya. Bears Are Sleeping. Illus. by Nonny Hogrogian.
New York: Charles Scribner's Sons, 1967.

Other Book Suggestions for This Age Level

Adams, Adrienne. A Woggle of Witches. New York:
Charles Scribner's Sons, 1971.
Adams, Pam. This Old Man. New York: Grosset & Dun-
lap, 1975.
Alderson, Brian, ed. Cakes and Custard: Children's
Rhymes. Illus. by Helen Oxenbury. New York:
William Morrow, 1975.
Alexander, Martha. Nobody Asked Me If I Wanted a Baby
Sister. New York: Dial Press, 1971.
_____. No Ducks in Our Bathtub. New York: Dial
Press, 1973.
_____. Sabrina. New York: Dial Press, 1971.
_____. When the New Baby Comes, I'm Moving Out.
New York: Dial Press, 1979.

Aliki. My Five Senses. New York: Thomas Y. Crowell, 1972.

Allard, Harry. I Will Not Go to Market Today. Illus. by James Marshall. New York: Dial Press, 1979.

Anderson, Clarence W. Billy and Blaze. New York: Macmillan Company, 1962.

Anderson, Eloise A. Carlos Goes to School. Illus. by Harold Berson. New York: Frederick Warne & Co., 1973.

Ardizzone, Edward. Little Tim and the Brave Sea Captain. New York: Oxford University Press, 1978.

Aruego, Jose, and Ariane Aruego. Crocodile's Tale. New York: Charles Scribner's Sons, 1972. (Paperback. New York: Scholastic Book Services, 1976.)
_____. We Hide, You Seek. New York: Greenwillow, 1979.

Asch, Frank. Macgooses' Grocery. Illus. by James Marshall. New York: Dial Press, 1980.
_____. Turtle Tale. New York: Dial Press, 1978.

Balian, Lorna. I Love You, Mary Jane. Nashville: Abingdon Press, 1967.

Barrett, Judith. I Hate to Go to Bed. Illus. by Ray Cruz. New York: Four Winds Press, 1977.
_____. I Hate to Take a Bath. Illus. by Charles B. Slackman. New York: Four Winds Press, 1975.
_____. The Wind Thief. Illus. by Diane Dawson. New York: Atheneum Publishers, 1977.

Batherman, Muriel. Some Things You Should Know About My Dog. Englewood Cliffs, NJ: Prentice-Hall, 1976.

Battles, Edith. What Does the Rooster Say, Yoshio? Illus. by Toni Hormann. Chicago: Albert Whitman & Co., 1978.

Becker, John. Seven Little Rabbits. Illus. by Barbara Cooney. New York: Walker and Company, 1973.

Behrens, June. Where Am I? Illus. by Austin Anton. Chicago: Childrens Press, 1969.

Beim, Lorraine Levy, and Jerrold Beim. Two Is a Team. Illus. by Ernest Crichlow. New York: Harcourt, Brace, 1945. (Paperback. New York: Harcourt Brace Jovanovich, 1974.)

Bemelmans, Ludwig. Madeline's Rescue. New York: The Viking Press, 1973.

Bennett, Rainey. The Secret Hiding Place. Cleveland: Collins-World, 1960.

Berenstain, Stanley, and Janice Berenstain. Bears on Wheels. New York: Random House, 1969.
_____. Inside, Outside, Upside Down. New York: Random House, 1968.

Bester, Roger. Guess What? New York: Crown Publishers, 1980.

Blegvad, Lenore, ed. Hark! Hark! The Dogs Do Bark, and Other Rhymes About Dogs. Illus. by Eric Blegvad. New York: Atheneum Publishers, 1976.

_____. Mittens for Kittens, and Other Rhymes About Cats. Illus. by Eric Blegvad. New York: Atheneum Publishers, 1974.

_____. This Little Pig-a-Wig, and Other Rhymes About Pigs. Illus. by Eric Blegvad. New York: Atheneum Publishers, 1978.

Brandenberg, Franz. I Wish I Was Sick Too! Illus. by Aliki. New York: Greenwillow, 1976.

Breinburg, Petronella. Shawn Goes to School. Illus. by Errol Lloyd. New York: Thomas Y. Crowell, 1974.

_____. Shawn's Red Bike. Illus. by Errol Lloyd. New York: Thomas Y. Crowell, 1976.

Brenner, Barbara. The Five Pennies. Illus. by Erik Blegvad. New York: Alfred A. Knopf, 1963.

_____. Mr. Tall and Mr. Small. Reading, MA: Addison-Wesley, 1966.

Bridgman, Elizabeth. How to Travel with Grownups. Illus. by Eleanor Hazard. New York: Harper & Row, 1980.

Briggs, Raymond. The Snowman. New York: Random House, 1978.

Bright, Robert. I Like Red. Garden City, NY: Doubleday and Company, 1955.

_____. My Red Umbrella. New York: William Morrow, 1959.

Brown, Marcia. How Hippo! New York: Charles Scribner's Sons, 1969.

Brown, Margaret Wise. The Little Fireman. Reading, MA: Addison-Wesley, 1952.

_____. Winter Noisy Book. Illus. by Charles G. Shaw. New York: Harper & Row, 1947.

Brustlein, Janice. Little Bear's Christmas. Illus. by Marian Curtis Foster. New York: Lothrop, Lee & Shepard, 1964.

Budney, Blossom. A Kiss is Round. Illus. by Vladimir Bobri. New York: Lothrop, Lee & Shepard, 1954.

Burningham, John. The Shopping Basket. New York: Harper & Row, 1980.

Caldecott, Randolph. Randolph Caldecott's John Gilpin and Other Stories. New York: Frederick Warne & Co., 1977.

Carrick, Carol. Paul's Christmas Birthday. Illus. by Donald Carrick. New York: Greenwillow, 1978.

Charlip, Remy, and Jerry Joyner. Thirteen. Illus. by
Remy Charlip. New York: Parents' Magazine Press,
1975.
Child, Lydia Maria. Over the River and Through the Wood.
Illus. by Brinton Turkle. New York: Coward-
McCann & Geoghegan, 1974.
Children's TV Workshop. The Sesame Street Book of Let-
ters. In cooperation with Children's Television Work-
shop. Illus. by Charles I. Miller and James J. Har-
vin. New York: Preschool Press, 1970. (Paper-
back. New York: New American Library, 1971.)
_____. The Sesame Street Book of Numbers. In cooper-
ation with Children's Television Workshop. Illus. by
Charles I. Miller and James J. Harvin. New York:
Preschool Press, 1970. (Paperback. New York:
New American Library, 1971.)
Chorao, Kay. Lester's Overnight. New York: E. P. Dut-
ton, 1977.
Chwast, Seymour, and Martin Stephen Moskoff. Still An-
other Alphabet Book. New York: McGraw-Hill, 1970.
Cleary, Beverly. The Real Hole. Illus. by Mary Stevens.
New York: William Morrow, 1960.
Clymer, Eleanor. Horatio Goes to the Country. Illus. by
Robert Quackenbush. New York: Atheneum Publish-
ers, 1978.
_____. Leave Horatio Alone. Illus. by Robert Quacken-
bush. New York: Atheneum Publishers, 1974.
Cohen, Miriam. Best Friends. Illus. by Lillian Hoban.
New York: Macmillan Company, 1971.
Cole, Joanna. A Chick Hatches. New York: William Mor-
row, 1976.
Cole, William. What's Good for a Three-Year-Old? Illus.
by Lillian Hoban. New York: Holt, Rinehart &
Winston, 1974.
Corey, Dorothy. Tomorrow You Can. Illus. by Lois Axe-
man. Chicago: Albert Whitman & Co., 1977.
Craft, Ruth. The Winter Bear. Illus. by Erik Blegvad.
New York: Atheneum Publishers, 1974.
Crews, Donald. We Read: A-Z. New York: Harper &
Row, 1967.
Cutler, Ivor. Elephant Girl. Illus. by Helen Oxenbury.
New York: William Morrow, 1976.
D'Aulaire, Ingri, and Edgar P. D'Aulaire. Don't Count
Your Chicks. Garden City, NY: Doubleday and
Company, 1949. (Paperback. 1973.)
Dennis, Wesley. Flip. New York: The Viking Press.
(Paperback. New York: Penguin, 1977.)

De Paola, Tomie. Strega Nona. Englewood Cliffs, NJ: Prentice-Hall, 1975.

De Regniers, Beatrice Schenk. What Can You Do with a Shoe? Illus. by Maurice Sendak. New York: Harper, 1955.

Domanska, Janina. I Saw a Ship A-Sailing. New York: Macmillan Company, 1972.

_____. If All the Seas Were One Sea. New York: Macmillan Company, 1971.

_____. What Do You See? New York: Macmillan Company, 1974.

Du Bois, William Pene. Bear Circus. New York: The Viking Press, 1971.

Duvoisin, Roger A. A for the Ark. New York: Lothrop, Lee & Shepard, 1952.

Emberley, Barbara, and Ed Emberley. Night's Nice. Illus. by Ed Emberley. Garden City, NY: Doubleday and Company, 1963.

Farber, Norma. This is the Ambulance Leaving the Zoo. Illus. by Tomie De Paola. New York: E. P. Dutton, 1975.

Fassler, Joan. All Alone with Daddy. Illus. by Dorothy Lake Gregory. New York: Human Science Press, 1969.

Fatio, Louise. The Happy Lion. Illus. by Roger Duvoisin. New York: McGraw-Hill, 1954.

Field, Eugene. Wynken, Blynken, and Nod. Illus. by Barbara Cooney. New York: Hastings House Publishers, Inc., 1980.

Fisher, Aileen. Listen Rabbit. Illus. by Symeon Shimin. New York: Thomas Y. Crowell, 1964.

Fisher, Aileen Lucia. Going Barefoot. Illus. by Adrienne Adams. New York: Thomas Y. Crowell, 1960.

Flack, Marjorie. The Story About Ping. Illus. by Kurt Wiese. New York: The Viking Press, 1933. (Paperback. New York: Penguin, 1977.)

Francoise. Springtime for Jeanne-Marie. New York: Charles Scribner's Sons, 1955.

Frasconi, Antonio. See Again, Say Again. New York: Harcourt, Brace & World, 1964.

Freeman, Don. Beady Bear. New York: The Viking Press, 1954.

_____. The Chalk Box Story. Philadelphia, PA: J. B. Lippincott, 1976.

_____. Dandelion. New York: The Viking Press, 1964.

Friskey, Margaret. Seven Diving Ducks. Illus. by Jean Morey. Chicago: Childrens Press, 1965.

Gackenbach, Dick. Do You Love Me? Boston: Houghton
  Mifflin, 1975.
    . Hound and Bear. New York: Seabury Press,
  1976.
Galdone, Paul. The Town Mouse and the Country Mouse.
  New York: McGraw-Hill, 1971.
Gibson, Myra Tomback. What Is Your Favorite Thing to
  Touch? New York: Grosset & Dunlap, 1965.
Ginsburg, Mirra. Three Kittens. Trans. and adapted from
  Russian story by V. Suteyev. Illus. by Giulio Maes-
  tro. New York: Crown Publishers, 1973.
    . Where Does the Sun Go at Night? Illus. by Jose
  Aruego and Ariane Dewey. New York: Greenwillow,
  1980.
Godden, Rumer. A Kindle of Kittens. Illus. by Lynne
  Byrnes. New York: The Viking Press, 1979.
Goffstein, M. B. Fish for Supper. New York: Dial Press,
  1976.
Goodall, John Strickland. Jacko. New York: Harcourt,
  Brace & World, 1971.
    . Naughty Nancy. New York: Atheneum Publish-
  ers, 1975.
    . Paddy's Evening Out. New York: Atheneum
  Publishers, 1973.
    . The Surprise Picnic. New York: Atheneum
  Publishers, 1977.
Goudey, Alice E. The Day We Saw the Sun Come Up.
  Illus. by Adrienne Adams. New York: Charles
  Scribner's Sons, 1961.
Graham, Al. Timothy Turtle. Illus. by Tony Palazzo.
  New York: The Viking Press, 1949. (Paperback.
  New York: Penguin, 1970.)
Graham, Margaret B. Be Nice to Spiders. New York:
  Harper & Row, 1967.
Greenaway, Kate. A Apple Pie. New York: Frederick
  Warne & Co., 1886.
    . Mother Goose: Or, The Old Nursery Rhymes.
  New York: Frederick Warne & Co., 1882.
Greenfield, Eloise. She Come Bringing Me That Little
  Baby Girl. Illus. by John Steptoe. Philadelphia,
  PA: J. B. Lippincott, 1974.
Grimm, Jacob, and W. K. Grimm. Red Riding Hood.
  Retold in verse by Beatrice De Regnier. Illus. by
  Edward Gorey. New York: Atheneum Publishers,
  1972. (Paperback. New York: Atheneum Publish-
  ers, 1977.)
Grimm, Jacob, and Wilhelm Grimm. The Shoemaker and

the Elves. Trans. by W. Andrews. Illus. by
Adrienne Adams. New York: Charles Scribner's
Sons, 1960.

Hamilton, Morse, and Emily Hamilton. My Name is Emily.
Illus. by Jenni Oliver. New York: Greenwillow,
1979.

Hay, Dean. I See a Lot of Things. New York: Lion
Press, 1966.

Hazen, Barbara S. If It Weren't for Benjamin (I'd Always
Get to Lick the Icing Spoon). Illus. by Laura Hart-
man. New York: Human Science Press, 1979.

Hill, Elizabeth Starr. Evan's Corner. Illus. by Nancy
Grossman. New York: Holt, Rinehart & Winston,
1967.

Hoban, Tana. Is It Red? Is It Yellow? Is It Blue? New
York: Greenwillow, 1978.

Hogrogian, Nonny. One I Love, Two I Love: And Other
Loving Mother Goose Rhymes. New York: E. P.
Dutton, 1972.

Huges, Shirley. David and Dog. Englewood Cliffs, NJ:
Prentice-Hall, 1978.

Hutchins, Pat. Changes, Changes. New York: Macmillan
Company, 1971.

Hyman, Trina Schart, retold by. The Sleeping Beauty.
Boston: Little, Brown, 1977.

Jacobs, Joseph. Hereafterthis. Illus. by Paul Galdone.
New York: McGraw-Hill, 1973.

_____. Master of All Masters. Illus. by Anne F. Rock-
well. New York: Grosset & Dunlap, 1972.

Janice. Little Bear's Christmas. Illus. by Mariana. New
York: Lothrop, Lee & Shepard, 1964.

_____. Little Bear's Thanksgiving. Illus. by Mariana.
New York: Lothrop, Lee & Shepard, 1967.

Jones, Jessie Mae Orton, comp. A Little Child. Illus. by
Elizabeth Orton Jones. New York: The Viking Press,
1946.

Joslin, Sesyle, and Leonard Weisgard. Brave Baby Elephant. Illus. by Leonard Weisgard. New York:
Harcourt, Brace, 1960.

Kalan, Robert. Rain. Illus. by Donald Crews. New York:
Greenwillow, 1978.

Kay, Helen. One Mitten Lewis. Illus. by Kurt Werth.
New York: Lothrop, Lee & Shepard, 1955.

Keats, Ezra Jack. Hi, Cat! New York: Macmillan Company, 1970.

Kent, Jack. The Grown-Up Day. New York: Parents'
Magazine Press, 1969.

Kepes, Juliet. Lady Bird, Quickly. Boston: Little, Brown, 1964.

Kherdian, David. If Dragon Flies Made Honey. Illus. by Jose Aruego and Ariane Dewey. New York: Green-willow, 1977.

Klein, Norma. If I Had My Way. Illus. by Ray Cruz. New York: Pantheon, 1974.

Knight, Hilary. Where's Wallace? New York: Harper & Row, 1964.

Kraus, Robert. Owliver. Illus. by Jose Aruego and Ariane Dewey. New York: Windmill Books, 1974. (Paper-back).

Krauss, Ruth. I Want to Paint My Bathroom Blue. Illus. by Maurice Sendak. New York: Harper, 1956.

Langstaff, John Meredith. Oh, A-Hunting We Will Go. Illus. by Nancy Winslow Parker. New York: Athen-eum Publishers, 1974.

_____ and Anthony Groves-Raines. On Christmas Day in the Morning! Illus. by Anthony Groves-Raines. New York: Harcourt, Brace, 1959.

Lenski, Lois. When I Grow Up (A Read-and-Sing Book). Music by Clyde Robert Bulla. New York: Henry Z. Walck, 1960.

Lindman, Maj. Snipp, Snapp, Snurr and the Red Shoes. Chicago: Albert Whitman & Co., 1932.

Lionni, Leo. A Color of His Own. New York: Pantheon, 1976.

_____. Inch by Inch. New York: Astor-Honor, 1962.

Kipkind, William, and Nicolas Mordvinoff. Finders Keepers. Illus. by Nicolas Mordvinoff. New York: Harcourt, Brace, 1951.

Livermore, Elaine. Lost and Found. Boston: Houghton Mifflin, 1975.

_____. Three Little Kittens Lost Their Mittens. Bos-ton: Houghton Mifflin, 1979.

Lobel, Arnold. A Treeful of Pigs. Illus. by Anita Lobel. New York: Greenwillow, 1979.

Lystad, Mary. That New Boy. Illus. by Emily McCully. New York: Crown Publishers, 1973.

MacGregor, Ellen. Theodore Turtle. Illus. by Paul Gal-done. New York: McGraw-Hill, 1955.

Mahy, Margaret. A Lion in the Meadow. Illus. by Jenny Williams. New York: Franklin Watts, Inc., 1969.

Marshall, James. George and Martha. Boston: Houghton Mifflin, 1972.

_____. George and Martha One Fine Day. Boston: Houghton Mifflin, 1978.

Marzollo, Jean. Close Your Eyes. Illus. by Susan Jeffers. New York: Dial Press, 1978.

Mayer, Mercer. The Great Cat Chase. New York: Scholastic Book Services, 1975. (Paperback. 1977.)

McEwen, Catherine, comp. Away We Go! 100 Poems for the Very Young. Illus. by Barbara Cooney. New York: Thomas Y. Crowell, 1956.

McGovern, Ann. Black is Beautiful. Illus. by Hope Wurmfeld. New York: Scholastic Book Services, 1969.

———. Stone Soup. Illus. by Nola Langner. New York: Scholastic Book Services, 1971.

McKee, David. The Man Who Was Going to Mind the House. New York: Abelard-Schuman, Ltd., 1973.

McMillan, Bruce. The Remarkable Riderless Runaway Tricycle. Boston: Houghton Mifflin, 1978.

McPhail, David. Where Can an Elephant Hide? Garden City, NY: Doubleday and Company, 1979.

Miles, Miska. Chicken Forgets. Illus. by Jim Arnosky. Boston: Little, Brown, 1976.

———. Noisy Gander. Illus. by Leslie Morrill. New York: E. P. Dutton, 1978.

Minarik, Else Holmelund. A Kiss for Little Bear. Illus. by Maurice Sendak. New York: Harper & Row, 1968.

———. Little Bear. Illus. by Maurice Sendak. New York: Harper & Row, 1957.

Moore, Lilian. I Feel the Same Way. Illus. by Robert Quackenbush. New York: Atheneum Publishers, 1976.

Mosel, Arlene. The Funny Little Woman. Illus. by Blair Lent. New York: E. P. Dutton, 1972.

Munari, Bruno. Animals for Sale. New York: Philomel, 1980.

Murphy, Jill. Peace at Last. New York: Dial Press, 1980.

Nakatani, Chiyoko. The Zoo in My Garden. New York: Thomas Y. Crowell, 1973.

Nash, Ogden. Custard the Dragon and the Wicked Knight. Illus. by Linell Nash. Boston: Little, Brown, 1959.

Nodset, Joan L. Come Here, Cat. Illus. by Steven Kellogg. New York: Harper & Row, 1973.

———. Go Away, Dog. Illus. by Crosby Bonsall. New York: Harper & Row, 1963.

Parents' Nursery School. Kids Are Natural Cooks: Child-Tested Recipes for Home and School Using Natural Foods. Illus. by Lady McCrady. Boston: Houghton Mifflin, 1974.

Patz, Nancy. Nobody Knows I Have Delicate Toes. New York: Franklin Watts, Inc., 1980.

Peppé, Rodney. The Alphabet Book. New York: Four Winds Press, 1968.

———. Circus Numbers. New York: Delacorte Press, 1969.

Petie, Haris. Billions of Bugs. Englewood Cliffs, NJ: Prentice-Hall, 1975.

———. A Book of Big Bugs. Englewood Cliffs, NJ: Prentice-Hall, 1977.

Pienkowski, Jan. Colors. New York: Harvey House, 1975.

———. Sizes. New York: Harvey House, 1975.

Politi, Leo. The Nicest Gift. New York: Charles Scribner's Sons, 1973.

Porter, David. Mine! Boston: Houghton Mifflin, 1981.

Potter, Beatrix. The Tale of Johnny Town Mouse. New York: Frederick Warne & Co., 1918.

———. The Tale of Mrs. Tiddlemouse. New York: Frederick Warne & Co., 1910.

———. The Tale of Tom Kitten. New York: Frederick Warne & Co., 1907.

Poulet, Virginia. Blue Bugs Vegetable Garden. Illus. by Donald Charles. Chicago: Childrens Press, 1973.

Preston, Edna Mitchell. Pop Corn and Ma Goodness. Illus. by Robert Andrew Parker. New York: Penguin, 1969. (Paperback. 1972.)

——— and Barbara Cooney. Squawk to the Moon, Little Goose. Illus. by Barbara Cooney. New York: The Viking Press, 1974.

Rayner, Mary. Garth Pig and the Ice Cream Lady. New York: Atheneum Publishers, 1977.

Reiss, John. Numbers. Scarsdale, NY: Bradbury Press, 1971.

Rey, H. A. Cecily G and the Nine Monkeys. Boston: Houghton Mifflin, 1942. (Paperback. 1977.)

———. Curious George Learns the Alphabet. Boston: Houghton Mifflin, 1963. (Paperback. 1973.)

———. Curious George Rides a Bike. Boston: Houghton Mifflin, 1952.

Rockwell, Anne. Albert B. Cub and Zebra: An Alphabet Storybook. New York: Thomas Y. Crowell, 1977.

———. The Three Bears and 15 Other Stories. New York: Thomas Y. Crowell, 1975.

Russ, Lavinia. Alec's Sand Castle. Illus. by James Stevenson. New York: Harper & Row, 1972.

Schlein, Miriam. Here Comes Night. Illus. by Harvey Weiss. Chicago: Albert Whitman & Co., 1957.

_____. What's Wrong with Being a Skunk? Illus. by Ray
Cruz. New York: Scholastic Book Services, 1974.

Schweitzer, Byrd Baylor. Amigo. Illus. by Garth Williams.
New York: Macmillan Company, 1963. (Paperback.
1973.)

Seeger, Ruth C. American Folk Songs for Children in Home,
School and Nursery School: A Book for Children, Par-
ents and Teachers. Illus. by Barbara Cooney. New
York: Doubleday and Company, 1980.

Seuss, Dr. (Geisel, Theodor Seuss). Dr. Seuss's ABC.
New York: Random House, 1963.

Sharmat, Marjorie W. Goodnight, Andrew, Goodnight,
Craig. Illus. by Mary Chalmers. New York: Harper & Row, 1969.

_____. I'm Not Oscar's Friend Any More. Illus. by
Tony De Luna. New York: E. P. Dutton, 1975.

_____. I'm Terrific. Illus. by Kay Chorao. New
York: Holiday House, 1977.

_____. Sometimes Mama and Papa Fight. Illus. by Kay
Chorao. New York: Harper & Row, 1980.

_____. What Are We Going to Do About Andrew? Illus.
by Ray Cruz. New York: Macmillan Company, 1980.

Shecter, Ben. The Hiding Game. New York: Scholastic
Book Services, 1980.

Simon, Norma. I Was So Mad! Illus. by Dora Leder.
Chicago: Albert Whitman & Co., 1974.

Slobodkin, Louis. Millions and Millions and Millions! New
York: The Vanguard Press, 1955.

Stanek. Muriel. Starting School. Illus. by Betty De Luna
and Tony De Luna. Chicago: Albert Whitman & Co.,
1981.

Supraner, Robyn. It's Not Fair! Illus. by Randall Enos.
New York: Frederick Warne & Co., 1976.

Tapio. Pat Decker. The Lady Who Saw the Good Side of
Everything. Illus. by Paul Galdone. New York:
Seabury Press, 1975.

Tester, Sylvia Root. Sometimes I'm Afraid. Illus. by
Frances Hook. Elgin, Il: The Child's World, 1979.

_____. We Laughed a Lot, My First Day of School.
Illus. by Frances Hook. Elgin, IL: The Child's
World, 1979.

Thomas, Patricia. "Stand Back," Said the Elephant, "I'm
Going to Sneeze." Illus. by Wallace Tripp. New
York: Lothrop, Lee & Shepard, 1971.

Three Jovial Huntsmen: A Mother Goose Rhyme. Illus. by
Susan Jeffers. Scarsdale, NY: Bradbury Press,
1973.

To Market! To Market! Illus. by Peter Spier. Garden City, NY: Doubleday and Company, 1967.

Tobias, Tobi. Moving Day. Illus. by William Pene Du Bois. New York: Alfred A. Knopf, 1976.

Tresselt, Alvin. Hide and Seek Frog. Illus. by Roger Duvoisin. New York: Lothrop, Lee & Shepard, 1965.

Vogel, Ilse-Margaret. One Is No Fun but Twenty Is Plenty. New York: Atheneum Publishers, 1965. (Paperback. New York: Atheneum Publishers, 1972.)

Waber, Bernard. But Names Will Never Hurt Me. Boston: Houghton Mifflin, 1976.

————. I Was All Thumbs. Boston: Houghton Mifflin, 1975.

————. Lyle, Lyle, Crocodile. Boston: Houghton Mifflin, 1965. (Paperback. 1973.)

Wagner, Jenny. John Brown, Rose and the Midnight Cat. Illus. by Ron Brooks. Scarsdale, NY: Bradbury Press, 1978. (Paperback. New York: Penguin, 1980.)

Walsh, Ellen Stohl. Brunus and the New Bear. Garden City, NY: Doubleday and Company, 1979.

Wasson, Valentina P. The Chosen Baby. 3rd ed. Trans. by Glo Coalson. Philadelphia, PA: J. B. Lippincott, 1977.

Watanabe, Shigeo. How Do I Put It On? Illus. by Yasuo Ohtomi. New York: Philomel, 1979.

Welber, Robert. The Winter Picnic. Illus. by Deborah Ray. New York: Pantheon, 1970.

Wells, Rosemary. Stanley and Rhoda. New York: Dial Press, 1978.

Wildsmith, Brian. Brian Wildsmith's Puzzles. New York: Franklin Watts, Inc., 1970.

————. The Lazy Bear. New York: Franklin Watts, Inc., 1974.

————. The Owl and the Woodpecker. New York: Franklin Watts, Inc., 1972.

Williams, Barbara. Albert's Toothache. Illus. by Kay Chorao. New York: E. P. Dutton, 1974.

Yeoman, John. Sixes and Sevens. Illus. by Quentin Blake. New York: Macmillan Company, 1971.

Yolen, Jane. All in the Woodland Early: An ABC Book. Illus. by Jane Breskin Zalben. Cleveland: Collins-World, 1979.

————. An Invitation to the Butterfly Ball; A Counting Rhyme. Illus. by Jane Breskin Zalben. New York: Parents' Magazine Press, 1976.

————. No Bath Tonight. Illus. by Nancy W. Parker. New York: Thomas Y. Crowell, 1978.

Young, Miriam. If I Drove a Truck. Illus. by Robert
    Quackenbush. New York: Lothrop, Lee & Shepard,
    1967.
Yudell, Lynn. Make a Face. Boston: Little, Brown, 1970.
Zemach, Harve. Nail Soup. Illus. by Margot Zemach.
    Chicago: Follett Publishing Co., 1964.
Zolotow, Charlotte. Hold My Hand. Illus. by Thomas Di
    Grazia. New York: Harper & Row, 1972.
    _____. I Have a Horse of My Own. Illus. by Yoko
    Mitsuhaski. New York: Abelard-Schuman, Ltd.,
    1964.
    _____. It's Not Fair. Illus. by William Pene Du Bois.
    New York: Harper & Row, 1976.
    _____. My Grandson Lew. Illus. by William Pene Du
    Bois. New York: Harper & Row, 1974.
    _____. Someone New. Illus. by Erik Blegvad. New
    York: Harper & Row, 1978.
    _____. The Summer Night. Illus. by Ben Shecter. New
    York: Harper & Row, 1974.
    _____. Wake Up and Good Night. Illus. by Leonard
    Weisgard. New York: Harper & Row, 1971.

CHAPTER V

ALMOST READY FOR SCHOOL
--Four-to-Five-Year-Olds--

An Active Age

Four-year-old children are usually so eager, so uninhibited, so exuberant, and so happy with life that it seems they should be singing Walt Whitman's "Song of Myself!" These joyous, energetic children are sure of themselves. They love excitement and seem to play with new ideas with the same enthusiasm that they show when they play with a new toy. They continually ask "Why?" but they revel so much in new information that it is a joy to supply it to them.

At times it seems that four-year-olds talk incessantly. Not only do they jump from one subject to another without a break, but also they brag, tell big stories--especially about themselves, create alibis when things go wrong, and even try to shock adults with swearing. Their emotions are extreme. Despite their friendly, outgoing characteristics, these children can be very irritating if one takes all their actions seriously.

As the parent of a four-year-old it is probably better for you to accept the fact that at this time you have a happy, exuberant little whirlwind on your hands. By the time the child reaches the age of five, there will probably be an amazing change. By then this same youngster may become a rather quiet, self-contained conformist. If you remind yourself that your four-year-old is simply going through another developmental stage, you can feel free to go along with the fun. You can contribute to the conversations with your own exaggerated stories and silly talk, letting the child know that it is all in play. He or she will love your participation and may even flatter you by teaching you big words of the moppet world. Remember that the ability to create imaginative words and participate in word games is a sign of intelligence. You can stimulate fun with language with silly rhymes and stories, very simple riddles, and puns. Try A. A. Milne's "Sneezles," the story of Christopher Robin's short illness. The little narrative ends with a convergence of creative rhyming words:

> All sorts and conditions
> Of famous physicians
> Came hurrying round
> At a run.
> They all made a note
> Of the state of his throat,
> They asked if he suffered from thirst;
> They asked if the sneezles
> Came after the wheezles,
> Or if the first sneezle
> Came first.
> They said, "If you teazle
> A sneezle
> Or wheezle,
> A measle
> May easily grow.
> But humour or pleazle
> The wheezle
> Or sneezle,
> The measle
> Will certainly go.
> They expounded the reazles
> For sneezles
> And wheezles,
> The manner of measles
> When new.
> They said, "If he freezles
> In draughts and in breezles,
> Then PHTHEEZLES
> May even ensue.
>
> Christopher Robin
> Got up in the morning,
> The sneezles had vanished away.
> And the look in his eye
> Seemed to say to the sky,
> "Now, how to amuse them today?"[1]

You will be able to find collections of silly poems, games, chants, rhymes, riddles, and songs that have great appeal to children of this age and give them many opportunities for

participation activities.   One to try is <u>Juba This and Juba</u>
<u>That</u> compiled by Virginia A. Tashjian.   This book is full
of stories and verses such as "What Did You Put in Your
Pocket?" by Beatrice Schenk de Regniers.   This cumulative poem with its descriptions of a horrible, sticky mess
may be repugnant to parents, but small children think it is
great fun.

Absurd poems of this type reflect the exuberance of as-
sertive four-year-olds.   Yet these same youngsters are gen-
erally very interested in social interaction.   They are learning to take turns, and even to think about how others might
feel.   Their play is highly imaginative.   Progress in motor
skills is so rapid that children of this age take many of
their newfound abilities for granted.   They are so busy seeing the world and enjoying what is around them that they
may no longer announce, "I did it myself," when they ac-
complish something new.

The four- to five-year-old period is no time to emphasize
the efficient performance of tasks.   At this age children care
little about a practice-makes-perfect attitude, but want to
hurry through one exciting activity to get to the next.   They
develop a strong identity with their homes and will often
brag about their belongings and quote their parents as the
final authority on all subjects.

Appropriate Books for This Developmental Level

One of the joys of associating with small children is the
opportunity to observe their sense of wonder.   Of course
young children are new to the world, but how refreshing it
is to see their complete concentration as they study what to
them is a new phenomenon and respond to the excitement of
a novel experience!   It has been a long time since most
adults have enjoyed the pleasure of a great interest in such
discoveries, but the thrill of these experiences can be re-
lived by watching children's fascination with their environment.

Many of our so-called mood or experience books reflect
children's reactions to their surroundings.   In The Moon
Jumpers, four children respond to the magic of the night as
they dance and jump, somersault and play.   Janice May
Udry's text supplies the music and Maurice Sendak's pictures provide the dance that shows the children's reactions
to the mysterious mood of a beautiful summer night.

McCloskey's Caldecott winner Time of Wonder first lets
children share the safe, secure world of the woods and beach
with the youngsters in the story.   Later there is a more om-
inous tone in both the words and pictures as the family moves
into the darkness and trepidation that comes with a hurricane.
But together the mother, father, and children survive the
force of the storm.   The next day is bright again although
questions such as, "Where do hummingbirds go in a hurricane?" still arise.

Many such mood books are available.   Some are sure to
relate well to the close, personal experiences of a given
child.   They are to be shared at special times when both
the reader and the listener are in the mood to dream and
relive thoughts and feelings in quiet reflection.

Because of their own exuberant characteristics, four-to-
five-year-olds respond with enthusiasm to exciting, funny,
flamboyant books.   Fortunately, there is a great wealth of
such books for preschool children.   The 500 Hats of Bartholomew Cubbins is Dr. Seuss's dramatic presentation of
the story of a poor boy, Bartholomew Cubbins, who goes to
town, encounters the great procession that marks the king's
entrance upon the street, and finds to his terrible embarrassment that he is unable to keep his head uncovered in
the presence of the king.   Every time he removes his homey
old cap, another appears on his head.   He is taken to the
palace but no one in the court can explain the presence of
the caps.   Finally the Grand Duke, who is only a boy himself, wants to punish Bartholomew for his disrespect to the
king by pushing him off the tower.   As they are going up
the many steps to the tower, the caps that Bartholomew
keeps snatching off his head become exceedingly grand.   The
last is so marvelous that the king wants it.   In fact, he buys
it and the other four hundred ninety-nine caps that have ma-
terialized.   And that's the end of the caps!   Bartholomew is
allowed to return home with his bag of gold.   This exciting
story, with its dramatic cartoon illustrations and the marching rhythm that develops as more and more caps are counted,
has become a great favorite among young children.

Gillespie and the Guards by Benjamin Elkin is a story
showing more subtle humor.   It, too, is exciting.   Gillespie
manages to outwit the king's three guards, all of whom have
magical powers to detect the most minute objects with their
"super-extra powerful eyes."   Gillespie fools them with a
simple trick and wins a "gleaming golden medal with shim-

mering shining diamonds." James Daugherty's rollicking illustrations help make this book a happy experience.

Pinkerton, Behave! is the story of Pinkerton, a huge dog,
who fails all obedience training and is put out of dog training
classes in disgrace. That night a burglar comes to the
house. At first Pinkerton reacts foolishly, but then obeys
his interpretation of mixed-up commands and saves his mistress. The story has very little text; rather it is told
through Steven Kellogg's exaggerated, humorous pictures.

Most children who are struggling for autonomy love to
assume the authority found in decision making. In Would
You Rather ... John Burningham asks youngsters to choose
which of many ludicrous situations they would prefer. Burningham's droll pictures add extra fun to the consideration of
the bizarre choices.

Four-to-five-year-olds sympathize with The Man Who
Didn't Wash His Dishes by Phyllis Krasilovsky. This is a
funny story about a man who does not wash his dishes until
they pile so high that it is hard for him to get into his
house. He finally has to resort to eating out of the soap
dish, the ash trays, and the flower pots. At last he has a
great idea. He gets a truck, piles the dishes into it, and
leaves them outside in the rain. After they are clean, he
puts them away. From then on, he always washes the dishes
when he finishes his dinner.

Most four-to-five-year-olds can listen to fairly long stories. They pretend to read books themselves. They enjoy
action stories and often "read" their own versions of such
tales with great enthusiasm. "The Bear Hunt" has been a
favorite action story for many years. Several versions can
be found in book form. Sandra Stoner Sivulich's I'm Going
on a Bear Hunt gives a lively presentation of this narrative.
Bear Hunt by Margaret Siewert and Kathleen Savage is a
more rhythmic retelling and has a teddy bear as the main
character. Both provide good material for exciting action
through participation, and both are often used during story
hours.

Nobody Listens to Andrew by Elizabeth Guilfoile is another bear story, the plot of which is actually based on a
real event. Andrew rushes to various people trying to get
them to listen to what he has to say. Finally he shouts in
angry tones, "There is a bear upstairs in my bed." This

brings the grown-ups to quick attention. With help from the police, the fire department, the dog catcher, and the people from the zoo, the bear is removed and Andrew enjoys a wonderful moment of supremacy when his father says, "Next time we will listen to Andrew." This is one of the most exciting and satisfying stories to be found in the easy-to-read books.

Another story to which children can easily relate is The Boy Who Didn't Believe in Spring by Lucille Clifton. Two delightful little boys who live in the inner city, Tony Polito and King Shabass, keep hearing about spring. They don't believe what they hear and decide to go exploring quite a distance from home. When they discover some blooming plants and a bird's nest with four eggs, they forget the sophisticated man-about-town air that they were trying to project and exclaim, "Man, it's spring!" Brinton Turkle's bright, expressive drawings take the reader through the streets of the city, with the sights, sounds, smells, and feel of this forbidden trip, to interesting discoveries with the two likable little boys.

No longer is there a need for very simple pictures in books. Four-to-five-year-olds enjoy tiny details and will spend a great deal of time searching out minutia. Ellen Raskin provides children with many opportunities to promote the fun and enjoyment of a simple story by a careful study of illustrations. In Nothing Ever Happens on My Block Chester Filbert sits on the curb bemoaning the fact that nothing ever happens. He is completely unconscious of all the excitement that is going on behind him--fires, robberies, accidents, the descent of a parachute, and even money floating through the air. Observant children can enjoy the turbulence in the humorous line drawings that show more and more activities. Youngsters will feel quite superior to Chester, who misses all the excitement. In Spectacles this same author/illustrator gives some amusing pictures of what a nearsighted child sees when she does not wear her glasses.

Rodney Peppé's Puzzle Book contains puzzles that include finding hidden animals in pictures, spotting mistakes, deciding which head belongs with which body, and many more reasonably easy puzzles that will challenge four-to-five-year-olds to observe pictures closely.

Susan Jeffers' Three Jovial Huntsmen: A Mother Goose

Rhyme is one of several picture-puzzle books in which there are animals hidden in busy line drawings. Many children will study the pictures in this book for long periods of time, finding and counting the hidden animals, and enjoying the fact that they are much more astute in their observations than are the three self-confident huntsmen.

Julian Scheer's Rain Makes Applesauce is a highly imaginative book with detailed pictures that take a child into a world of fantasy. The scenes depicted might appear in a small child's dream world. Most double-page spreads in this book include the statement, "Rain makes applesauce," with a reminder, somewhere on the page, "Oh, you're just talking silly talk." A very observant child will find the thread of a realistic account of how rain really does make applesauce hidden in the fanciful pictures.

Topsy-Turvies: Pictures to Stretch the Imagination is an unusual wordless picture book done by Mitsumasa Anno that presents improbable scenes and situations that defy the laws of gravity. The pictures are puzzles in perspective and position that some children will enjoy.

Four- to five-year-old children vary greatly in the amount of attention they give to books during this active age. Some will seem to be entranced with pictures, stories, and poems, and they will sit and listen for long periods of time when someone reads to them. Others are so physically active that their attention spans are quite short. Adults will find that they must use a great deal of creativity and energy to help some vivacious children learn to concentrate on an activity for a reasonable length of time, but such concentration is an ability that is necessary for success in schoolwork.

You can make a terrible mistake and set up negative attitudes or even emotional blocks against reading if you force books upon some children; yet an interest in books is necessary to prepare for success in the academic world. Reading with children is important, but watch your timing. Take advantage of times when physical exuberance is worn thin and youngsters are looking for a quieter activity. Bedtime story hours can be appropriate. Perhaps nothing will appeal to some very active children but silly jokes, funny poems or stories. Start with anything that interests them. Cookbooks written especially for children or books that tell how to make simple toys may provide a focal point for youngsters who seem to be always on the move. Such books are geared to children's immediate interests and can promote the understanding that books supply one with intriguing, helpful information.

Let's Do Some Cooking by Frederick A. Rodgers and Katherine A. Larson is a book that uses a "paired visual-verbal sentence format" to present recipes and procedures for simple cookery. The authors of the book feel that this approach enhances reading readiness and math readiness skills. Young children can study the drawings and with the help of an older person they can compare their interpretation of procedures with the written instructions on the opposite page.

There are some rebus pictures with simple drawings to stand for words in Kids Cooking by Aileen Paul and Arthur Hawkins, but a certain amount of help will be required to follow the directions for simple cookery given in this book. Small children will enjoy "reading the pictures," but an older person will have to interpret the rest of the text.

Pease Porridge Hot: A Mother Goose Cookbook by Lorinda Bryan Cauley should provide real fun for preschool children. The recipes are indeed creative, with such delights as a "Catch-Me-If-You-Can Gingerbread Man" and "Hansel and Gretel's Healthy Children's Cookie House," to say nothing of "The Big Bad Wolf's Little Pigs in a Blanket!"

If your youngster is already enjoying the Winnie-the-Pooh stories, it should be fun to try some of the many recipes in The Pooh Cook Book by Virginia H. Ellison. Peter Rabbit's Natural Foods Cookbook by Arnold Dobrin is another book in which the recipes are made intriguing through references to admired storybook characters.

Interesting, inexpensive recipes are given in Cooking in the Classroom. Janet Bruno and Peggy Dakan use many symbols to make the reading of the simply stated recipes easy and fun for a small child, with a minimum of help from an older sibling or an adult.

Among the many cookbooks geared for children there are several for special occasions, like Halloween Cookbook or Christmas Cookbook, both by Susan Purdy, that can add to the fun of festive days. Since even young children often enjoy the Little House on the Prairie series on television, they will probably find Barbara M. Walker's The Little House

Cookbook exciting. Most of the recipes are too difficult for a small child to undertake, but a youngster would probably enjoy helping to make some of the foods that were common during the time of the early settlers.

Helping a youngster make his or her own cookbook can be an interesting project at this time. Favorite recipes should be included. Using a rebus form will make the book usable for a preschool child. Quickly drawn pictures representing words such as cup or spoon can help to make a recipe readable and also help with number concepts.

Prerequisite Skills for Reading

Conscientious parents of preschool children often wonder what they should be doing to help their youngsters prepare for learning the mechanics of reading. Probably their most important job is to inspire children to love literature so much that they will be ready to put forth the essential effort to learn to read once they have acquired the necessary physical, emotional, and intellectual development.

Educators do not always agree on what constitutes reading readiness, but Martin Haberman describes the converse of proper preparation for reading. He feels that children are unready when "new learnings are perceived by the child as beyond him/herself unconnected to what is already known, valueless, or too dangerous to try."[2] These are the attitudes that caring adults can inculcate in children when they try to push them into a new developmental stage before they are ready. Parents should keep in mind Nancy Larrick's excellent advice: "There is only one hard and fast rule: Don't push, lest you slow down the child's interest and inclination to learn."[3]

An evaluation of reading readiness includes the consideration of a child's physical abilities, language skills, intellectual abilities, social-emotional development, and development of perceptual skills. The youngster's background of experiences in everyday life as well as his or her exposure to books and reading materials is of great importance.

According to the Handbook for Tutors of Reading for the "Right to Read" Program, a child will need to develop the following skills in order to be ready to read:

1. The child notes likenesses and differences in the

sounds of words.

2. The child uses the basic vocabulary common to children of his age.

3. The child puts words together in the grammatical structure of his language to form sentences.

4. The child interprets or "reads" pictures.

5. The child recognizes spoken words that rhyme.

6. The child points out pictures, shapes, letters, and words that look alike.

7. The child classifies ideas.

8. The child holds a sequence of ideas in mind and retells them in the order of their occurrence.

9. The child identifies the letters of the alphabet at random and in sequence.

10. The child establishes the habit of viewing rows of pictures, numbers, letters, and words from left to right. [4]

Parents should not be overly concerned if their children have not developed all of these skills by the time they start their formal school experience. Kindergarten and first-grade teachers will work on such skills throughout the first years of school.

In order to enhance the development of reading readiness skills parents should give their youngsters the love and attention they need, helping them realize that they are capable of learning. At the same time they should provide interesting experiences through everyday activities and through the shared enjoyment of fascinating story and informational books.

Reading to children sets up positive attitudes toward books and makes it possible for the youngsters to develop many important reading readiness skills before they enter kindergarten. In fact, the books that are read to preschool children provide the best tools for preparation for success in reading.

A child who enjoys sharing nursery rhymes, verses, and poetic writings is introduced to phonics early in life. The word phonics is derived from the Greek word for sound. Think of the sound patterns that a youngster experiences in simple nursery rhymes alone--repeated beginning sounds that sing their way into a child's mind, rhyming ending sounds that add to the rhythm, and families of words, made by adding a variety of letters to a given base such as those in the following rhymes:

Hickety, pickety, my black hen,
She lays eggs for gentlemen.
Sometimes nine, sometimes ten.
Hickety, pickety, my black hen.

* * *

Three blind mice, see how they run!
They all ran after the farmer's wife,
She cut off their tails with a carving knife.
Did you ever see such a sight in your life,
As three blind mice?

Such rhymes help develop listening skills and an understanding of likenesses and differences in closely related words.

If parents point out words as they read to children, the youngsters soon realize that letters have their own sounds and words are made up of combinations of sounds. Adults can help children develop phonic understandings by encouraging them to read along, to supply rhyming words, or to participate in identification games in alphabet books. ABC books do more than help them recognize letters of the alphabet. They promote phonetic skills with their pictured repetition of words beginning with a given letter. They also help youngsters classify objects and ideas.

Children who follow along as a parent reads not only learn the left-to-right progression pattern of the text, but also learn to "read pictures" in the order they are presented. They are learning to take more and more information from pictures as they study the fine details and extend story content with stimulation from illustrations. Certainly they are building vocabulary and developing an understanding of grammatical structure. Storybooks help to teach sequencing. Discussion and retelling of stories help children learn to keep a series of happenings in mind and to retell them in order. Information books help them classify ideas.

Many educators say that the real key to academic success is concentration. Very often an intellectually gifted child is unable to progress as he or she should in school because of an inability to give careful attention to a job at hand. One experienced teacher claims that she is usually able to predict at the beginning of a school term which students will equal or excel expectations indicated by ability testing. She bases her predictions upon the children's ability to concentrate and the length of their attention spans. Reading aloud to children during their preschool years may very well contribute more than any other activity toward the development of sustained attention spans.

Shared enjoyment and discussion of good books are much more effective than structured experiences and commercial, synthetic programs in the development of language and reading readiness skills. It is no wonder that Secretary of Education Terrell H. Bell states, "The child who has been read to reads."

Who Are the Early Readers?

Some children will learn to read even before they are introduced to formal school experiences. Dolores Durkin conducted two extensive, broadly based studies on children who read before beginning formal schooling. She identified forty-nine early readers, children who had not been given help with reading in kindergarten but were able to read before they entered first grade in the Oakland, California schools. She followed the achievements of these students over a six-year period. Her second study was done in New York City. Here she worked with one hundred fifty-six early readers. These landmark studies have given us a great deal of insight, especially because of their longitudinal nature. For example, one old assumption the Durkin studies helped dispel was that children who read early will have problems in school, that they will be bored and, consequently, will not do well in other disciplines. Durkin found that even after six years the early readers maintained their lead in classroom achievement over children who were unable to read when they entered school. She also found that while these children were usually from the precocious group, within the two groups that she studied there were real variations in I. Q. scores. One child tested as low as 91 in the California study and one child scored 82 in the New York study. In fact, she hypothesized that less bright children could profit from a preschool start in reading by experiencing additional time to achieve.

Of real interest to parents is Durkin's description of the families from which the early readers came. Parents in these families were willing to give children early help. They did not feel that reading had to be taught by a trained person, especially when the child's interest in reading was high. Most of the assistance given was in answer to children's questions and requests for help.

> The research seems to indicate, however, that young children are much more responsive to help with reading that is the consequence of their own questions rather than of their parents' ambition or insecurity-- or whatever it is that prompts parents to make an arbitrary decision to teach preschoolers to read, without regard for the child's interest or for the possibility of strain developing in the parent-child relationship.

Durkin feels that the preschool child's everyday world provides plenty of opportunities to learn to read without the aid of teaching kits. She did find that older siblings, especially older sisters, influence a child's early reading, often through playschool activities.

It is interesting to note that there were no simple connections between socioeconomic status of the family and early reading. "What is much more important, the research data indicated, is the presence of parents who spend time with their children; who read to them; who answer their questions and their requests for help; and who demonstrate in their own lives that reading is a rich source of relaxation, information, and contentment."

Here is a quick review of the six significant findings from the Durkin studies as to how children learn to read at home:

1. The language arts approach (which is discussed later in this chapter) most accurately describes the way preschool children approach reading. More than half of the children studied were interested in learning to print before or simultaneously with their interest in reading. Many moved from a scribbling and drawing stage to copying letters and objects, to interest in spelling, to the ability to read.

2. Along with the child's growing ability to print came many questions about spelling particular words. (Almost invariably the child's first request was, "Show me my name.")

3. Parents were sometimes encouraged to explain sounds of letters because of the child's interest in spelling and writing. This was helpful in some cases but not productive in others.

4. Children often had "interest binges" in their pre-school scribbling and writing. They would work at great length at an activity such as copying people's names and addresses, then suddenly discard that interest for others.

5. Children became interested in knowing what a printed word says in a variety of ways. A frequent source of interest came from being read to, especially from books that were enjoyed more than once. Also commercials, labels, food packages, and words important to their world caused interest.

6. Interest in particular types of words and in reading vocabularies was correlated with sex differences in readers. Boys tended to recognize words like rocket, jet, and Chevrolet early, while girls were more interested in names of food products.

In making final statements about her research, Durkin said:

> First, in doing the research itself, it became clear that early readers are not a special brand of children who can be readily identified and sorted by tests. Rather, it would seem, it is their mothers who play the key role in effecting the early achievement. The homes they provide, the example they show, the time they give to the children, their concepts of their role as educator of the preschool child--all these dimensions of home life and of parent-child relationships appear to be of singular importance to the early reading achievement described in this report. [5]

Informal Approaches to Reading

It is difficult for adults to remember some of the problems that arise in the learning of a skill such as reading. Young children's perception of the task is immature, to say the least. For example, research shows that a youngster first perceives objects or situations in a global way. He or she might comprehend the fact that somehow reading comes from the marks on a page, but have no understanding of the meaning of terms like letter, word, and sentence. It takes time and experience to learn that words are made from letters, that these words can be combined into sentences, and that specific written words will always correspond to specific spoken words.

When you are reading with your son or daughter, you

might discuss such terms. Let the child follow with a finger for a marker to assist you in keeping your place as you read. Ask the youngster to point to special words, perhaps his or her own name if you happen to be reading a homemade book. You might point out letter arrangements if the child is interested, and discuss similarities and differences.

Seeing one's own name in print can be an ego booster. This experience often provides a first interest in learning what printed letters say. As Durkin says, small children are intrigued by labels, especially when they pertain to food. These labels provide an easy way to introduce the idea of reading. Children often become interested in attempting to read signs when they are out for a drive or a walk. You will find yourself actually teaching beginning reading in many simple ways. By following a relaxed, natural approach, you will see that it is easy to involve a self-centered, curious four-to-five-year-old in reading a few easy words.

Label things that you and your son or daughter put into scrapbooks. As you do this, point to the words you are writing or reading and show your child how the words are symbols for objects. Soon the youngster will begin suggesting short captions for pictures and watching as you write them in appropriate places. These experiences help your child conceptualize what reading is all about. Without help of this kind many children see no value or purpose to reading. They wonder why they should go to all the hard work of learning to read.

Many teachers use a language arts approach to reading. They often start by making language experience charts with the children. At first these charts are very simple. They may be nothing more than carefully printed words on large, lined tablet paper, simple statements made by children about an experience, a story, or some interest. The printing is large, often done with a felt-tipped pen. The teacher, or perhaps a parent, simply writes down what the youngsters have said and reads it back, pointing to the words. Gradually the children learn to enjoy watching someone transform their statements into symbols. When words are read back, children begin to realize that what is spoken can be written down, and it can later be retrieved by reading. This concept gives added meaning to the reading process.

Teachers take this language experience approach a step further. Using large, lined paper with an extra-large top margin, they will ask a child to draw a picture of an experience. Then the teacher asks for a description of the experience based on the child's drawing and prints the child's dictation under the picture. This technique assists the youngster in connecting elements in his or her drawing with written words.

Some four-year-olds may not have reached a level of interest appropriate for language experience chart activities. Give them time. However, for children who want to learn to write before they develop an interest in learning to read, the charts can help make the natural progression from writing to reading. For that "joyous little botheration" who has already started asking you many questions about letters and words, writing down and reading back comments and ideas is an ideal approach to first reading. Of course it takes time, but what more exciting thing can you do than help to develop your child's intellectual powers!

Language charts have a great appeal because of ego involvement. They make a child feel respected and proud that someone actually feels that what he or she says is important enough to write down! Not only is the child's name used in the writing, but also the names of friends, family, things around the house and neighborhood, favorite storybooks, and anything else that falls within the child's interests and experiences. In this way reading is introduced gradually and informally.

Some charts, especially those done on rather heavy, lined paper, can be made into books or journals that will have very personal meaning for your youngster. He or she might like one entitled "All About Me" in which snapshots are used for illustrations. You and your little boy or girl might make a personal journal in which your partner dictates items of importance in day-to-day living, including special poems and bits about stories. These can be illustrated by the author to give them more meaning. Keep the text in your child's own words. Resist the temptation to apply the master's hand to improve on a child's art or creative productions of any kind. As soon as you start changing your youngster's work, you diminish the creative process and you may make your son or daughter feel incapable of doing things well. Remember, it is not the finished product that is of real importance, but the experience of the project.

If your child is sufficiently interested, you may want to go a step beyond the writing and reading of stories in language charts to some of the activities that teachers use, as explained by Susanna Whitney Pflaum:

> Teachers use the printed story as a focus for training in prereading skills. Thus, pupils learn to recognize letters within the context of words; they learn to recognize their own names, etc. Words which begin with the same initial letter are isolated and become the material for auditory-visual discrimination. Children learn that spoken words have written equivalents and that spaces mark off printed words. When each sentence occupies a separate line, they become conscious of how punctuation parallels intonation. 6

If you feel that your child is ready to make an attempt at reading, one approach you could take is to read some simple books, ones that have very little in the way of text, perhaps only a sentence under a picture produced in rather large-size type. Read these slowly, pointing to the words as you go along, encouraging your youngster to read a word now and then. If the child becomes interested, read a phrase or sentence, pointing to the words, and then ask him or her to read it too. Select the simplest of books and try to see that first attempts have built-in success possibilities. Have your youngster point to the words and talk about how they look in print. A small child often starts trying to differentiate between words by considering just one letter, usually the first or last. Much later he or she learns to look at the entire word.

Don't be afraid to introduce long words to children. Often they are easier for youngsters to remember than are the shorter ones. They provide clues by their shapes and lengths, and give children feelings of great pride when they can recognize words like "hippopotamus," "rhinoceros," and "chimpanzee" from an animal book, for instance.

Gradually the young reader may begin to recognize a few words even when they appear in different books or are used for functional purposes such as labels or signs. Eventually you may want to write some of these words down on cards to start a word bank, printing one word on a card. Your youngster can have these cards to play with and review; however, don't be disappointed or let the child become concerned when he or she forgets the words. Introduce any such activities with caution and continue them only if they are pleasing and enjoyable to both your child and you. Ruth Lowes says, "Wanting to read should come before learning to read."[7]

When you are trying to interest your child in reading, be selective in what books you choose. Some of the easy-to-read books are probably best to use. Many have exciting little stories told very simply. These can intrigue the young reader and make him or her feel that the reading is worthwhile. Look for books that are fun or related closely to the child's interests; otherwise your experience may be similar to that of Nathaniel's grandmother, who had many years of experience in teaching young children to read. She felt that she recognized all the signs that four-year-old Nathaniel was ready to start reading. On one visit she brought several primers along and tried to interest the little boy, but she got little or no response to, "Look, look, look! See, see, see." She knew that Nathaniel's parents had a very sensible attitude about letting their child take his time in learning any skill; therefore, she simply took the books back home and accepted the failure in the reading venture. However, on her next visit she could not resist the temptation to try again. This time she took Arnold Lobel's Frog and Toad Together. Nathaniel was interested in the exciting little stories in this book and with some help was able to read many of the words and phrases. The success of Frog and Toad Together started his real interest in reading and he read quite well by the time he entered first grade. Selecting just the right book is very important.

Some of the beginning-to-read books are much more exciting than others, and of course a great deal depends upon the child's own interests. Check your library and you will probably find that books for early reading are so much in demand now that they have been given special shelves within the children's section. You will notice that they all follow pretty much the same pattern or format. The type is clear and large, the sentences are short, and the vocabulary is simple. Pages are probably uncluttered in order to avoid any distraction from the printed text. There is plenty of white space. Illustrations vary; some are much more interesting than others, but most will give clues that make reading the text easier.

Look for books with comic appeal. These are the ones that are usually greatly appreciated. At the end of this chapter there is a list of many of the best easy-to-read or beginning-to-read books available.

There is no standard time at which a child must become interested in reading. When a boy or girl starts noticing words as he or she is sharing books or starts asking questions like, "Where does the book say that?" "How do I write my name?" or "What does the sign say?" you can be quite sure that the youngster is becoming intrigued with the reading process. On the other hand, if your child doesn't show an interest in trying to learn to read when he or she is four or five years old, don't become anxious. Simply continue enjoying literature together. Play on the youngster's wild imagination with books like Come Away from the Water, Shirley, one of Burningham's stories, in which the mother makes mundane comments to her daughter while they are visiting the seashore. Shirley's literal thinking is projected onto the opposite page each time, and the reader sees her wild, inventive exploits. A similar story, Time to Get Out of the Bath, Shirley, also by Burningham, shares Shirley's exciting daydreams about knights and castles as she is having her bath.

The Dragon in the Clockbox by Jean M. Craig tells about Joshua, who informs his family that he has a dragon's egg in a sealed clockbox. At first the rest of the family asks many questions, but they are always given a logical answer from a small child's point of view, and they go along with the situation. When the dragon hatches, they aren't allowed to see it because baby dragons are shy. One day the box is empty and Josh announces that the dragon flew away "where dragons go." With a quick change of interests, so typical of a four-to-five-year-old, Josh now fills his clockbox with marbles.

Imaginative books of this type are enjoyable. They keep children's interest in literature alive. Their pictures alone promote a real desire to be able to read in order to find out about the narrative art that is displayed.

Promoting Creativity

Enjoy the delightful, creative powers that your child displays at this uninhibited, happy age. You will find many books that can help to expand these powers. Can I Keep Him? by Steven Kellogg shows great imagination on the part of a boy while his rather stereotypical, practical mother is continually explaining the difficulties of keeping various animals and eventually a child that the little boy brings home.

Mercer Mayer's What Do You Do with a Kangaroo? is a

zany book about throwing out animals that come to your home. Problems arise such as what to do with a kangaroo who comes through the window and sits on the bed. The protagonist throws him out, of course, but she meets with many funny situations.

Smith and Park describe creativity as the ability to use past experiences to produce something new, and also to see new relationships among unrelated objects. "Creativity, of itself, cannot be taught, though many of its components can."[8] One might add that it can easily be discouraged by factual, practical reactions to children's enthusiasm. Literature is the result of the work of creative people, and children's creative powers can be extended through the stimulation they receive from well-written books. For instance, you will want to encourage youngsters to enjoy poetry, but also to add to it with their own verbalization of thoughts and feelings.

Help youngsters respond to expressive pictures like those found in When Light Turns into Night by Crescent Dragonwagon. This is a mood book in which a child wanders in a field with only the wind and the darkening sky as twilight deepens into night. Guess Who My Favorite Person Is has lovely watercolor pictures of things to be found in nature and in everyday life situations. The short text by Byrd Baylor is almost a lyrical poem. Both of these books are illustrated by Robert Andrew Parker.

Eric Carle's I See a Song is an intriguing book that is introduced by a violinist's invitation: "I see a song. I paint music. I hear color. I touch the rainbow, and the deep spring in the ground. My music talks. My colors dance. Come, listen, and let your imagination see your own song."[9] Some very creative children will be delighted with the imaginary music that flows through the rest of the book in forms and bright colors. This book can provide inspiration for both musical and artistic experiences. Perhaps your child will enjoy adding his or her own drawings for books of this kind, or dramatizing parts of more moving plots with dress-up dramas or puppets.

Storytelling is another creative art that many children enjoy. It should be encouraged. A four-year-old will still probably have some trouble differentiating between fact and fantasy. It is sad to think how many children have been punished for not telling the truth when actually they were

telling what to them was a real situation. Caring adults
need to assist youngsters in understanding the difference between what is real and what is not, but certainly they need
not go about squelching children's imaginations. As parents
read books, they can talk about why a given story is real or
unreal, and how one can tell the difference. On the other
hand, they surely will not want to belabor the point to the
extent that no one enjoys excursions into the world of fantasy. When children's stories become exaggerated, parents
can also tell their own imaginative tales, letting the children
know that the adults are having fun and making up stories
too.

In spite of their love of language, four-year-olds may become self-conscious about telling original stories. However,
with a little encouragement youngsters will usually oblige.
Making up their own stories or adding to those that are already a part of their literary background encourages creative
expression of language, helps youngsters learn to deal with a
sequence of happenings, and promotes an understanding of
story structure. It is interesting to note that most children
this age adopt storytelling devices. They will begin with a
formal opening phrase like "Once upon a time," and also use
a standard closing. It may be, "They lived happily ever after," or perhaps a culturally oriented phrase like, "Snip,
snap, snout, my tale is told out." They use the past tense
and often change their tones or the pitch of their voices in
the telling.

Wordless picture books can stimulate great storytelling.
For instance, a book like Elephant Buttons by Noriko Ueno
can provide material for some really humorous ideas for
stories. In the illustrations a big stuffed elephant pops off
its buttons and a horse appears. This same process is repeated with smaller and smaller animals appearing. As a
concept book, it might be considered a book dealing with
sizes and shapes, but the whole situation is much too funny
to be taken only as a book of information.

Wordless picture books encourage children to interpret
pictures. They provide feelings of accomplishment by al-
lowing children to reproduce sustained plots with the help of
the pictures, or even make up their own bits of humor or
add details to the rather obvious story that unfolds on the
pages. Sometimes children will attempt to use formal book
structure in the language they use to develop the pictures
into a story. The use of a tape recorder can encourage

this type of verbalization. After children record a story, they enjoy listening to it and turning the pages of the book for corresponding pictures for each part they have told.

Mercer Mayer has provided some of the most humorous, and therefore most popular wordless books. A Boy, A Dog, and A Frog, Frog on His Own, and Frog Goes to Dinner are all great fun to which a mischievous child can easily respond. John Goodall's wordless books are more sophisticated. Often half-pages are inserted which, when opened, elaborate on the visual plot and make it exciting. Jacko is the story of an adventuresome organ grinder's monkey who slips in and out of pages and half-pages, causing children to enjoy his exploits. Naughty Nancy, Paddy's Evening Out, and The Adventures of Paddy Pork are some of Goodall's other little picture melodramas.

If your child becomes interested in wordless books, you will find many waiting to be enjoyed. Some are even informational books. Of course we can hardly call them literature, but they do contribute toward reading readiness skills and a child's enjoyment of books. A listing of some of the best to be found is given at the end of this chapter.

Some books are set up in a format similar to that of the wordless books, but will have a minimum of words. In Snail, Where Are You? by Tomi Ungerer, there is no text until the last two pages. Look What I Can Do by Jose Aruego has only the sentence "I can do it too" throughout, which can provide a first reading experience. Children feel they are reading, and will spend a great deal of time poring over the pictures in books of this type and repeating the words when they come to them.

Two delightful farces by Sesyle Joslin, both illustrated by Maurice Sendak, are classified as handbooks on etiquette. In What Do You Say, Dear? and What Do You Do, Dear? there are pictures showing dramatic, unusual, slapstick situations. On the page following a picture the child is asked to give the usual mundane, courteous reply expected in polite conversations. The "Excuse me," or "I'm sorry," become a spoof on the etiquette that children are forced to learn.

A variety of activities involving children's books can help to develop youngsters' creative powers. Books and journals that children make often start them toward their own creative writing through dictating captions for their pictures. Encourage children to find shapes and colors as suggested in many fine concept books, and to respond to the music and rhythm in their songbooks and their poetry collections, dancing the poems or playing the rhythms. Play simple word games as suggested by humorous verse, adding lines and refrains, and creating new characters or situations and extending stories. All these activities help to develop children's ingenuity.

Go along with imaginative adventures, and, most of all, appreciate and praise attempts. Young children create to please themselves, but they are encouraged by the praise and interest of adults. As soon as they are made to feel that their efforts are unworthy, they begin to lose interest. They may gradually become the rigid, set persons who plod through life missing most of the joy that could have been open to them if they had somehow retained something of the great childlike sense of wonder.

Capitalizing on Curiosity

Young children's curiosity is a great asset because it prompts learning on many levels. Even small children come to appreciate the value of informational books when they realize how such books tell them things they really want to know. There are books to be had on almost any subject in which children have shown real interest.

It is not necessary to take the first available book on a given subject. You will want to help your child choose those that are well illustrated and written in a good literary style. Of course information books should be accurate and appropriate to a child's level of thinking. Because you know your youngster's needs and interests along with his or her level of comprehension, you will be able to select special books that will help your little questioner find new ideas that will be fun to explore.

Small children absorb information like a sponge. They have a wealth of isolated ideas in their minds. What they need is help in learning to associate these facts with concepts in order to develop a framework for their thinking. They need assistance in order to be able to reach conclusions based on what they experience in their everyday living and through their books.

It is easy for grown-ups to assume that children's minds function on what might be considered a simplified adult level. However, as Piaget explained, up until the time children are seven or eight years old, they rely on information perceived through the senses rather than upon logical deductions to reach their conclusions. In their thinking they tend to move from one bit of information to the next without any real generalization of ideas.[10] They need help in developing new concepts and in refining those they already have. They need to be adding to their store of information. Literature becomes more and more helpful in this area. Books can provide information and vicarious experiences that would be impossible in their usual environment.

Literature can extend simple interests like those concerning pets, life in the neighborhood, activities of families and those at nursery school. It can go further and introduce new experiences. Children can meet people of other times and places through their books. Grandpa Had a Windmill, Grandma Had a Churn by Louise A. Jackson is a book written to show something of the wholesomeness of life years ago in our country. George Ancona's photographs for the book show the simple, sturdy beauty of what might be treasured roots for the modern child. Ox-Cart Man by Donald Hall tells the story of a farm family who lived long ago in New Hampshire. It shows how they worked together to make and grow things that the father took to Portsmouth Market to sell, after which he was able to buy their supplies for the coming winter. Barbara Cooney's illustrations, which won the Caldecott Award for this book, are done in a folk-art style that brings one into the quaint, old-fashioned setting for a view of the life of this industrious family.

An Edwardian Summer and An Edwardian Christmas, both wordless picture books by John Goodall, show, in intriguing ways, life in England at the beginning of this century. No text is needed to follow the happenings of this special way of life that existed during these two seasons of the year in long-ago England.

Four- to five-year-old children should be growing in their understanding that although people live in different places and have different customs, all have basic, universal characteristics. Many storybooks for young children convey these ideas. Gilberto and the Wind by Marie Hall Ets shows a little Mexican child experiencing the wind's mischief as it seems to play with him. His reactions and his experiments to understand the wind are the same as those of any child. In Um-brella, Taro Yashima shows how Momo, the Japanese-American child, reacts with joy to the new umbrella that she receives for her third birthday. The next day, and those following, bring disappointments because there is no rain and she is unable to use her gift. Then there comes that happy day with rain pounding down, singing its song of "Bon polo, bon polo, ponpolo, ponpolo, ponpolo, ponpolo. " She takes her umbrella to nursery school, and that day, for the first time in her life, she walks home without holding either her mother's or her father's hand.

Joan Lexau, Ezra Jack Keats, and Lucille Clifton have given children many books that extend knowledge of city life. Robert McCloskey shows them what it is like to live along the coast of Maine; Byrd Baylor lets them imagine living in the Southwest desert. Such books expand their informational background but also help to build empathy for other people.

Many information or concept books provide unique discovery experiences. These are often enjoyable to adults as well as to children. Anno's Animals by Mitsumasa Anno is a great puzzle book with one hundred animals and birds hidden in the pictures of forest scenes. This is a wordless picture book, but fortunately there is a list at the end of the book of what we should be able to identify in the pictures. Sam Who Never Forgets by Eve Rice has a great wealth of information about animals and is also, in its way, a counting book. It becomes a book of colors when the child is drawn to the balloons with their subtle shading of colors. Two, Four, Six, Eight: A Book About Legs by Ethel and Leonard Kessler is a fine discovery book that moves with a fast, jingly rhythm. Check Once We Went on a Picnic by Aileen Fisher. It is a delightful rhymed story, but the real challenge is to identify the seventy-six animals, birds, and plants in the illustrations.

What the Moon Saw by Brian Wildsmith is an unusual book of opposites with elaborate pictures that help children enjoy modern art. Is This a Baby Dinosaur? And Other Science Picture Puzzles by Millicent Selsam is similar in format to Tana Hoban's excellent Look Again, a photographic recognition book. In Selsam's book questions are presented. The reader/listener guesses the answer, then turns the page to confirm their guess.

There are intriguing word books for four-to-five-year-olds. In Harriet Reads Signs and More Signs by Betsy

Maestro and Giulio Maestro, the little elephant, Harriet, skates about town reading signs everywhere as she goes. In the end she comes to some favorite signs for ice cream and bakery goods--a happy ending. Actually, the child who is looking at the book is encouraged to read the signs. Although there is no text, the book involves children in reading based upon their own experiences of reading signs in their travels around town.

Play on Words by Alice and Martin Provensen is a much more difficult presentation of word puzzles, homonyms, words within words, and noisy words. Some preschool children might enjoy the challenge this book offers.

Tongue twisters like those found in Alvin Schwartz's A Twister of Twists, A Tangler of Tongues can bring on fits of laughter with the four- to five-year-old set. Youngsters always seem to enjoy silly words, rhymes, and patterns of language more than their elders do. They go along with the fun even when they do not understand the meaning of many of the words.

One small boy enjoyed Lear's "A Was Once an Apple Pie" in his Nonsense Book so much that he often begged his teacher to read it. She hesitated to do so, even though the verses gave him such pleasure, because his almost hysterical laughter was infectious and the rest of the class would reach such a pitch of excitement that it was impossible to settle them down for other work.

Tikki Tikki Tembo, retold by Arlene Mosel, is a great favorite to tell or to read. In a very short time young listeners will be repeating that marvelous name, Tikki tikki tembo-no sa rembo-chari bari ruchi-pip peri pembo, with the teller.

ABC, Number, and Color Books to Interest and Challenge Children

ABC books for four-to-five-year-olds can supply fine puzzles and games. On Market Street by the Lobels was an honor book for the Caldecott Award. The pictures that tell of an unusual shopping trip down Market Street furnish hours of fun. In this alphabet book a boy goes to market and lists what he buys. On the page for "A" there is a human figure composed of many kinds of apples. For "B" the figure emerges from a clever design of books. "C" is all clocks, and so it continues throughout the alphabet. This is one of the most distinctive ABC books to come along in years.

Miska Miles' Apricot ABC is another book that provides wonderful experiences in just looking. The flow of the beautiful pictures done by Peter Parnell and the rhyming text make it a fine aesthetic encounter. Young children will probably need help to appreciate this book and to look for the letters in the illustrations.

Peaceable Kingdom: The Shaker Abecedarius by the Provensens is a book of quaint period art showing the animal alphabet song that Shaker children are supposed to have used to learn their letters long ago.

Bruno Munari's ABC is a powerful visual experience with its bright colors and designs that bring unusual associations to the letters. Alligators All Around from the Nutshell Library has Maurice Sendak's usual charm and fun for youngsters. Phyllis McGinley's All Around the Town shows city sights and sounds with her alphabet rhymes while Mary Azarian's A Farmer's Alphabet gives us the country scene in huge woodcuts. Anno's Alphabet: An Adventure in Imagination by Mitsumasa Anno has very unusual illustrations of letters cut from wood.

Many of the alphabet books mentioned thus far are rather sophisticated. If you feel that your child still needs to be dealing with the basic shapes of the letters, some of the books discussed in earlier chapters of this book will be more appropriate.

You will be able to find exciting counting books to fit children's interests. If you are looking for simple, direct number books with patterned language, you might try Ten Little Elephants by Robert Leydenfrost. This book involves counting backward starting at ten, going down to one, with rhymes reminiscent of some of the fingerplays. The rhymes tell how each elephant disappears and then how many are left.

The Berenstain Bears' Counting Book is done with a slapstick humor that appeals to children who especially like cartoon art. Ten Black Dots by Donald Crews takes an unusual approach using graphic design with different numbers of dots making up the patterns for the rhymes as, for example, "Three can make a snowman's face," or "Beads for stringing on a lace."

Another book from Sendak's Nutshell Library, One Was Johnny, finds Johnny living by himself, but an odd assortment of visitors arrive. Finally, the congestion is too much and Johnny causes them to leave, one at a time, of course, as we count back down.

Dahlov Ipcar's Brown Cow Farm is an old standard that gives numerous opportunities to count different groups of animals. This book has many learning possibilities, but will be too advanced for many four-to-five-year-olds because the numbers go as high as one hundred and some groupings are complicated. One Old Oxford Ox by Nicola Bayley is an old counting rhyme that is known for its "slithery use of language." As one could tell from the title alone, it exudes alliteration.

Some fine concept books deal in part with numbers. Ed Emberley's The Wing on a Flea: A Book About Shapes is outstanding. Counting the number of shapes is a part of the puzzle in verses like:

> A triangle is
> The wing of a flea,
> The beak of a bird,
> If you'll just look and see. [11]

Four-to-five-year-olds are able to enjoy interesting and exciting color books. Mr. Rabbit and the Lovely Present by Charlotte Zolotow is an unusual story with illustrations that make up a rather sophisticated color book. A little girl who is searching for just the right birthday present for her mother tells Mr. Rabbit her mother's favorite colors. Mr. Rabbit enumerates many things that could provide each particular color. In the end they have brought together a lovely basket of fruit.

If You Have a Yellow Lion by Susan Purdy is a book about the effect of mixing colors. The pictures are fascinating and show how many colors are produced by mixing just a few.

The House of Four Seasons is also a study in mixing colors. Roger Duvoisin shows a family who has bought a house in the country but they can't agree on what color it should be painted. Through a simple experiment the father shows them that white is made of all colors. The house is painted white to make it a house of all seasons.

Green Says Go by Ed Emberley explains primary colors, secondary colors, and ways of mixing colors and developing different shades. Then it includes some rather humorous pictures about what different colors seem to say--"Red says, 'I'm embarrassed,' Green says, 'I'm jealous.'"

Color Seems by Ilma Haskins presents a creative approach to the feelings that colors elicit. Interesting comparisons are made and the reader has an opportunity to experience the effect of various colors and hues upon his or her own feelings.

Let's Find Out About Color by Ann Campbell shows primary colors and discusses how colors make one feel. In the illustrations hot and cold colors are mixed and there are fascinating designs made from opposite colors on the color chart.

How the World Got Its Color by Marilyn Hirsh is a color book based on an adaptation of an Oriental legend. In the story Mikki's father is given paints to make pictures, but one day Mikki uses the paints to add color to many things-- trees, the rooster, and even her dress. The gods are pleased and decide to brighten the world, which until then has been colorless.

Help in Facing Difficulties and Adjustments

Our basic goal in sharing literature with young children is to bring them enjoyment and help them to see the value in reading, but literature has other possible functions. It may help children explore and perhaps learn to cope with some basic personal and social needs. There are books that deal with most difficulties that small children encounter. Care must be exercised in the selection of such books. Avoid didactic books that do little more than moralize or instruct. A much more helpful experience for a child is to encounter an honest storybook character who is attempting to deal with the same problem that is causing difficulty to the youngster reading or hearing the story.

Self-acceptance, especially as it pertains to physical growth and change, often concerns children more than adults realize. There are several books that have to do with size that could be helpful. In Karla Kuskin's book Herbert Hated Being SMALL poor Herb says, "I'm the only person I know with nobody to talk to except knees." Eventually he meets a girl who is exceptionally tall and they come to realize that size is not of great importance. Much Bigger Than Martin by Steven Kellogg is the story of Henry, who has to deal with the frustrations of having a brother who is much bigger than he is. Henry's great desire is to outgrow his bossy brother.

Rosa-Too-Little by Sue Felt is about an appealing little Puerto Rican girl who suffers frustrations because of her size and her age. She wants to have her own library card, and with real effort and persistence she is finally able to meet the requirement of writing her name to get one.

I Want to Be Big is the title and first statement in Genie Iverson's book about a little girl who faces the usual problems of being small, but as she thinks about being big she begins to add qualifications. For instance, she wants to be big enough to cross the street alone but not too big to hold her grandfather's hand when they go walking; big enough to eat two ice cream cones, but not big enough to eat even one helping of peas; big enough to have dinner without needing to sit on the telephone book, but not too big to be sitting on mother's lap for a story.

For a much more personal approach, help your child make his or her own growth book with individual pictures. Wonderful comparisons can be made and good feelings about continued development can result from this type of book.

If you feel that you need help in making homemade books, or if you would like to give them something in the way of a finished appearance, there are several books that can give you good ideas. Either How to Make Your Own Books by Harvey Weiss or Books for You to Make by Susan Purdy could be helpful.

Not all physical changes cause anxiety for young children. For example, youngsters are often fascinated with the idea of losing their first tooth. McCloskey's One Morning in Maine tells about Sal, who lost her first tooth in the mud while she and her father were clamming along the coast of Maine. Books of this type remind parents of the great importance of such little happenings and can help build understanding within the family.

Little Rabbit's Loose Tooth by Lucy Bate is a good description of a small child's feelings. Like most children,

Little Rabbit makes quite a production of the entire affair when she loses her first tooth, even speculating as to the reality of the tooth fairy and suggesting that her mother could pretend to be the tooth fairy and leave a present. The entire experience is very childlike in approach, enough so that a youngster will quickly relate to the character. Parents reading the book will enjoy the reflection of their own child's logic in Little Rabbit's reasoning.

Many stories deal with the psychological development that is necessary when children begin to make the break away from constant parental protection and toward independence. I Can Do It By Myself by Lessie Jones Little and Eloise Greenfield is a book that shows real growth toward auton-omy. A very young boy decides that he will not only buy his mother's birthday gift, but also go by himself to get it. This is a great show of courage, especially when he meets with a frightening dog. His triumph when he completes his mission is very satisfying. If children are not accustomed to inner-city vernacular, they will be introduced to it in a positive way in this book.

Mike's House by Julia L. Sauer will be appreciated by young children, especially those who know and love the book Mike Mulligan and His Steam Shovel. Robert, a preschooler, is so attached to the Mike Mulligan book that he calls the library "Mike's House." When he gets lost in a storm try-ing to make his way into the library, he is found by a friend-ly policeman who finally unravels the mystery of where Rob-ert is trying to go. All through the story Robert remains the self-assured, independent little boy who expects all the world to understand the importance of his favorite book.

What Mary Jo Shared by Janice May Udry is the story of a rather shy black girl who dreams of having something spe-cial to share during show-and-tell time at school. She can never think of anything outstanding until one day she has a great idea--she takes her father to school and shares him with the class.

Hardie Gramatky's Little Toot is a storybook character who has been loved for many years. He is a little tugboat who doesn't care to work but also has a hard time accepting the responsibility that goes with independence and has a fine time playing about and causing trouble until he becomes the laughingstock for the other boats. In his embarrassment he wanders away only to find himself washed down to the great ocean. When he finds an ocean liner jammed between two huge rocks, he sends up an S.O.S. smoke signal. All the boats come to help the ship in the storm, but even they cannot rescue the liner until Little Toot thinks of a way and becomes the hero.

In Barbara Greenberg's The Bravest Babysitter, Lisa is happy when her favorite babysitter, Heather, comes to stay with her. A bad thunderstorm develops while the girls are involved with an art project. Heather can't hide the fact that she is afraid of the thunder and lightning. Lisa takes over and acts like the bravest babysitter until the storm is over, after which she says she doesn't need anyone to tuck her into bed!

The Maggie B. by Irene Haas is a child's dream of complete autonomy. It is a beautiful dreamworld book in which a very resourceful little girl takes her small brother on a fine excursion on the ship "The Maggie B." She handles every situation with real proficiency and has no trouble keeping her brother and herself safe and happy. The pictures are in warm colors with exciting details. The children's faces show great contentment and self-satisfaction.

Children are sometimes encouraged to become more persistent by literary experiences. Many college students laugh when they admit that the little chant, "I think I can; I think I can," from The Little Engine That Could by Watty Piper still goes through their minds when they have an especially hard task to do. This little book has been read, chanted, and dramatized by young children for many years and probably has inspired many of them.

Pelle's New Suit by Elsa Beskow, translated by Marion Letcher Woodburn, is a Swedish story of a boy who needs a new suit. He goes through all of the steps from getting the wool for it, to having the suit made. In each case he does some work in exchange for the services. This book is a lesson on where clothes come from as well as one on perseverance.

What's the Matter, Sylvie, Can't You Ride? is Karen Andersen's realistic picture of Sylvie, who tries very hard to learn to ride a bicycle and must endure the humiliating taunts of her acquaintances as she fails in her attempts. Just as she is ready to give up, she acquires the skill. Then, childlike, she cannot resist shouting out, "Can't you

ride?" as she passes a small boy who is having the same
difficulties.

Nobody's Perfect, Not Even My Mother by Nora Simon
shows children beginning to accept the fact that they will fail
at times. They rationalize their defects by remembering
that even grown-ups fail, too.

Fortunately we have many books that deal realistically
with sibling rivalry. By facing the fact that jealousies and
competition do exist we can help children overcome guilt
feelings and sometimes even help them find solutions to some
of the problems that seem very important to them. If nothing else, some books help children see that others share
their same frustrations. Judith Viorst seems to have a special talent for expressing the love/hate relationship that usually exists among siblings. I'll Fix Anthony is a younger
brother's fantasy as to how he will get even and really "fix
Anthony." In Alexander and the Terrible, Horrible, No
Good, Very Bad Day, the same author shows Alexander suffering from sibling rivalry and all the other problems that
seem to go with just such a day. Preschool children can
appreciate much of the fun as well as the frustrations that
Alexander is having. Certainly parents will enjoy reading
this one is order to get a humorous perspective on some of
their children's trials and tribulations. It is a bit helpful
to be reassured in the end of the book that there will be
such days even in Australia!

Why Couldn't I Be an Only Kid Like You, Wigger by Barbara Shook Hazen is a youngster's idea of the advantages of
being an only child. But in the end the question arises as
to why Wigger spends all of his time at the home of his
friend rather than enjoying his solitary bliss. In Stevie by
John Steptoe the little fellow causing all the irritation is not
a younger brother but a child that Robert's mother is caring
for. Most of the book is given to the worry of having this
younger child around, but after the boy is taken away, Robert begins to think that he wasn't all that bad. His monologue about Stevie is very real from a child's point of view,
ending with:

> Aw, no! I let my cornflakes get soggy thinkin'
> about him.

> He was a nice little guy.
> He was kinda like a little brother.
> Little Stevie. 12

My Brother Never Feeds the Cat by Reynold Ruffins takes
a little girl, Anna, through her day. She often reminds people of how many jobs she does, yet her brother doesn't do
any work--"None, Zero, Zip." In the last picture one sees
the brother, who is only a baby, and Anna is hugging him.

Many books can reassure a child of the love that exists in
families even when it is not expressed as often as it might
be. Friday Night Is Papa Night by Ruth A. Sonneborn shows
an appealing young Puerto Rican boy's great concern for his
father who is late coming home from work. There is the
happy ending when only he is still awake to greet the father
upon his arrival.

My Mother and I has a text by Aileen Fisher and lovely
pictures by Kazue Mizumura, both of which are poetical.
The story tells of a little girl who comes home from school
to find her mother has been called away. In a walk through
the woods she talks to the creatures who never really know
about a mother. There's the happy reunion when the mother
returns and the little girl tells her mother she is glad she
is not a bug or a lonesome frog or a butterfly.

My Mom Hates Me in January by Judy Delton is a very
different story about a modern family who is suffering from
"January blahs." The little boy is a great irritation to his
mother for an entire day, but the next day they see the first
sign of spring, a robin, and things are back to normal. The
little fellow is wise enough to realize that his Mom is simply
affected by the weather. She really loves him, even in January.

Watch Out for the Chicken Feet in Your Soup is a delightful story about Joey, who is at first a bit embarrassed to
introduce his friend Eugene to his Italian grandmother; however, Eugene and Grandmother get along so well that Joey
becomes somewhat upset. Eugene loves Grandma's cooking
and assists with the bread dolls. All is well when Grandma
gives Joey a special bread doll, "because you are my special Joey." Tomie de Paola ends the little book with what
he thinks was his old-fashioned grandmother's recipe for
bread dolls.

Abby by Jeannette Caines is a lovely family story of Abby,
an adopted child, who asks in the end if they can't adopt a
little boy to play with an older brother. If You Listen by
Charlotte Zolotow is a dreamy book in which a little girl,

whose father has been away for a long time, asks how you can know that someone who is far away loves you. Her mother says when you are lonely, you must listen. The lovely illustrations take the reader through beautiful scenes in nature while the mother explains that if you listen hard enough you feel someone sending their love to you.

My Mother Is the Most Beautiful Woman in the World is a lovely Russian folktale retold by Becky Reyher about a six-year-old girl, Varya, who goes to the fields with her mother and father. She goes to sleep in a field of uncut wheat and becomes lost from her mother. Others find her when she wakes up, but she is so frightened and upset that she can't tell them her mother's name, only that her mother is the most beautiful woman in the world. None of the women of the area who are considered beautiful have lost a child, but then Varya's mother, whom everyone but Varya considers very, very plain, appears and the little girl is overjoyed. The story verifies the old proverb, "We do not love people because they are beautiful, but they seem beautiful to us because we love them."

The divorce of parents is one of the traumatic problems that all too many children have to face. Parents sometimes fail to realize how torn a child can be in the situation of the separation of parents. Children cannot understand what is happening and often develop real guilt complexes, feeling that somehow they have caused the tragedy. Where Is Daddy? The Story of a Divorce by Beth Goff might bring some understanding to a child in this situation. Daddy by Jeannette Caines is a beautiful story of a black girl and her father who visits her every Saturday. Such a book could help reassure a youngster of an absent parent's love. A Father Like That by Charlotte Zolotow tells of a boy who is talking to his mother, dreaming about what it would be like to have a father even though his father went away before he was born. The boy dreams of what his father would say to both him and his mother and the things they would do, how his father would always be on his side. The mother's wise answer is that she likes the kind of father he is thinking about, but if he doesn't come, the boy himself can be such a father someday. In She's Not My Real Mother, Judith Vigna gives the feelings of a boy in a three-parent situation. The stepmother is trying, in a very diplomatic fashion, to be a friend to this little fellow who is determined to remain loyal to his own mother. He realizes that in order to reach out to his father, his must accept the presence of a stepmother when he visits in their home. Several books that develop such themes are available.

It is always wise to read a book before presenting it to your child, but it is even more important when the book deals with problem situations. The book may or may not be appropriate for the youngster at a given time. Some books, Me Day by Joan Lexau, for example, could do more for adults than for children. This book might help some parents appreciate the depth of a child's feelings in a broken home situation.

Will It Be Okay? by Crescent Dragonwagon is a quiet, re-assuring book concerning many children's fears. It even touches on the possibility of the mother's death.

Many children first learn about death through the experi-ence of losing a pet or perhaps through finding a dead bird. Margaret Wise Brown's The Dead Bird has a surprising fas-cination for small children. In the very simple text children find a dead bird. They have a funeral for it. The entire situation is handled from the standpoint of a small child's level of thinking. The children's reactions are honest and immediate. They express both sorrow and joy without shame. The line in the text that tells how each day they went to visit the grave--until the time when they forgot to go--expresses what may be the most important insight in the book for chil-dren. They are left with the feeling that we do grieve, but we also forget and do not need to feel guilty for doing so.

The book When Violet Died by Mildred Kantrowitz also tells of the death of a bird. The girls in this story learn that even though you can't count on anything to last forever, you can make things last "a long, long time." In The Tenth Good Thing About Barney by Judith Viorst a small boy suf-fers real grief at the loss of his cat. He tells about how he cried. He didn't watch television or even eat his chocolate pudding. His mother suggests that he think of ten good things about Barney to tell at the cat's funeral. He can list only nine. Later, after he and his father have a quiet talk and some of his hurt and rebellion come to the surface, he can add a tenth good thing. Barney is now in the ground helping the flowers grow and "... that's a pretty nice job for a cat."13

If you feel that books might help your youngster with a problem, select those that have a good story and theme,

those in which the emotional content is a valid part of the
text, not an artificial situation put in to instruct children.
Avoid "message books." Be sensitive to children's reactions. Often books that are the most help to them are what
adults might consider escape literature, stories that remove
them from worry for a time. Dorothy Butler says, "The
best book will be the one that diverts, amuses, engrosses,
stirs the imagination and warms the heart. Such a book
may well create a climate in which emotion can be expressed,
and this is infinitely more important than 'understanding.' "[14]

Ever-Popular Animal Stories

Animal stories have a wonderful appeal to children of
preschool age. The animal characters in books for very
young children, however, are usually not realistic. They
are more like people who dress in fur and have tails, according to Arbuthnot. Many fine, fanciful animal characters
are so well presented that they have the universal qualities
of children.

Both the Frances series by Russell Hoban and the Curious
George series by H. A. Rey are all-time favorites with the
moppet set. Frances is the typical child, although she is a
member of a badger family. In Bedtime for Frances she
makes all the excuses that most children use in an attempt
to delay going to bed and, once she is finally in bed, to delay going to sleep. Young children can easily identify with
her efforts. A Baby Sister for Frances finds Frances making rather a poor adjustment to the fact that she has a baby
sister. She is displeased that her mother has not ironed her
blue dress and that there are no raisins for her oatmeal.
That night she decides to run away from home. She over-
hears a conversation between her mother and her father and
realizes that she is missed and loved, after which she returns to try to accept her new family situation. In Bread
and Jam for Frances she gets her wish to have nothing but
bread and jam to eat. The problem arises when she wants
to change her menu but can't without embarrassment. These
and other books of the series present realistic situations often encountered by children. The badger family is anthropomorphized but never cute or sweet. Their "animalness"
shows through.

The character of Curious George seems to represent the
feelings and actions of all the mischievous, venturesome little children in the world. He is a little monkey who has all

kinds of irresponsible, innocent exploits and great troubles because of his curiosity. He always comes out all right in the end, usually with the support of the man in the yellow hat. Children have real empathy for him; in fact, many mothers say that one of the books in this series, Curious George Goes to the Hospital by H. A. Rey and Margaret Rey, has helped their children face a frightening situation.

Some of the especially funny animal stories could hold your child's attention even at a restless time. The Temper Tantrum Book by Edna Mitchell Preston shows different animals having tantrums. A child must turn the page to see the reason. The whole book builds to an unusual ending. In Pig Tale by Helen Oxenbury, children meet the discontented pig couple, Bertha and Briggs, who find a treasure. They begin leading the beautiful life with all the luxuries. Finally, they can stand it no longer. They cast everything aside, including their fancy clothes, and return to simplicity. The pictures are hilarious!

The Story of Babar the Little Elephant by Jean de Brunhoff and the books that follow in the series have been children's favorites. Babar starts as a little elephant who goes to live with a lady in Paris. Eventually he returns to the jungle in Africa and is so suave in his elegant clothes that he is made king of the jungle. Dr. Seuss' Horton Hatches the Egg introduces children to the persistent Horton as the hero. The book is alive with Seuss' "verbal acrobatic antics!"

An old, old favorite, Johnny Crow's Garden by Leslie L. Brooke, which was first published in 1903, may have special appeal for your child at this time. Frog and Toad Are Friends by Arnold Lobel is one of the Frog and Toad Series. This series provides some of the best easy-to-read selections we have; in fact, these are fine read-aloud stories. These books are easy for a small child to follow because they are made up of individual chapters, separate stories about the two lovable characters who think very much on a small child's level. Even four-year-olds see the fun of their droll humor.

Sylvester and the Magic Pebble is William Steig's Caldecott Award winner. It, too, is an imaginary animal story but done in folktale fashion.

Martha Alexander says that she got her inspiration for

Blackboard Bear from watching her four-year-old nephew at
play. And My Mean Old Mother Will be Sorry, Blackboard
Bear was the result of her observations when she was visiting at the home of her editor. When the little boy in the
family got into trouble, he said that his teddy bear was the
cause. In I Sure Am Glad to See You, Blackboard Bear,
Anthony, the young protagonist, is four or five years old.
In this story Blackboard Bear symbolizes Anthony's desire
for power and protection from older boys. We're in Big
Trouble, Blackboard Bear takes Anthony a bit further. He
is beginning to develop a sense of moral values and knows
that what the bear took must be restored. This little four-
book "saga" covers quite a span of preschool personality development. All four books are very simple, easy to hold,
and tell their stories so well in pictures that they hardly
need texts. Alexander is able to enter into a child's patterns of thinking, even to the dreams of magic to solve all
problems.

Because children relate easily to animal stories, there
are hundreds of these books to be found in stores and libraries. Some are outstanding, others leave much to be
desired, but the best will bring real pleasure to young children and introduce them to characters who will remain an
important part of their literary heritage. Most of the animal stories for preschool children will be fantasies. Many
will help to develop children's creative powers; some will
assist them in understanding themselves and others. The
more realistic stories will promote empathy for animals and
thoughtfulness toward the creatures who share our earth.

The Need for Folklore

Youngsters are interested in folk and fairy tales during
specific periods of childhood, according to investigators who
have studied children's preferences in literature. Before the
age of five they are especially interested in talking-beast
stories and in very simple fairy tales. Usually the greatest
enjoyment of the fairy tales comes around the age of eight.
By the time children are ten or twelve years old such interest is pretty well a thing of the past. Chukovsky explains
this by saying:

> The fairy tale has now accomplished its task. It has
> helped the child orient himself to the surrounding world,
> has enriched his spiritual life, has made him regard
> himself as a fearless participant in imaginary struggles

for justice, goodness, and freedom; and now, when his need of the fairy tale has ended, the child himself does away with it. [15]

For four-year-olds the simplest of folktales are appropriate, ones with no really frightening aspects. By the time youngsters are five, their ability to separate reality from fantasy has become somewhat refined and they may be ready to hear some more exciting stories. Nicholas Tucker, a lecturer in developmental psychology at Sussex University in England, says:

> As always, the parent is left with no very clear guide but instinct and his feeling for his children on what or what not to read to them. If he is overprotective, the very act of avoiding fear in literature can eventually leave the child more exposed than he should be both to himself as well as to reality. If the parent throws them in at the deep end straight away, then again he may not give them time to build up adequate defenses and controls. The best guide of course is the child himself. [16]

Watch your child closely and if you see negative reactions to any story you will probably want to wait until the youngster is more mature before you try sharing it again. Children should have the opportunity to talk about stories they hear. You may find your child asking for a certain folk or fairy tale again and again. In some way this particular story fills a need and perhaps provides an opportunity to deal with a fear or frustration in an indirect manner.

There is no doubt that children harbor deep fears. If we refuse to recognize this fact, we can hurt their psychological development. They need to know that fear is common to everyone. The folktales can help show them that people, even small people, are not powerless and that facing fears and difficulties can work toward their solution. Tucker states that a child needs to explore his or her own frightening fantasies and fears in ways that will modify and eventually help to control them. "Like Rumpelstiltskin, frightening things tend to lose a lot of their power when they are brought out into the open and named." [17] When a small boy or girl repeatedly sees the evil thing in the story--the troll, the witch, or whatever character it may be--completely demolished, the child is reassured.

Bruno Bettelheim tells how the folk and fairy tales help children with crucial psychological development in his book The Uses of Enchantment: The Meaning and Importance of Fairy Tales. He says that fairy tales can help the child learn to cope in a confusing, complex world:

> The child must be helped to make some coherent sense out of the turmoil of his feelings. He needs ideas on how to bring his inner house into order, and on that basis be able to create order in his life. He needs ... a moral education which subtly, and by implication only, conveys to him the advantages of moral behavior, not through abstract ethical concepts but through that which seems tangibly right and therefore meaningful to him. The child finds this kind of meaning through fairy tales.

Bettelheim tells how a child achieves understanding and the ability to cope with the psychological problems of growing up through fantasizing in daydreams. Fairy tales provide dimensions for the child's imagination and suggest images on which to structure daydreams. The message that fairy tales give to a child is that the struggle against severe difficulties is a part of human existence, but if one has the courage to continue the struggles, he or she can be victorious.

Part of the simplicity of fairy tales lies in the fact that the characters are either all good or all bad. Such delineation is typical of a child's thinking. These characters give form to the evil and the good. The evil character is always punished, thus reassuring the child that evil can be negated. Children project themselves into the noble characters and become the heroes; therefore, they are influenced to act as the good characters do. The fact that evil is overcome and that good wins out at the conclusion of each story reaffirms the advantages of moral behavior. [18]

Bettelheim suggests that parents tell the fairy tales rather than read them. If parents feel uncomfortable in their attempts to tell the stories, it might be better to read from some of the fine collections of folk and fairy tales rather than to use picture books, providing that a preschool child is ready to follow a plot without the aid of pictures. This would allow the child to visualize his or her own characters and settings and could be more helpful in developing understanding.

If your youngster needs the help of illustrations, there are many fine picture books containing one folk or fairy tale available. A Story, A Story, retold by Gail E. Haley, introduces children to Anansi, an African folk hero. This is the story of how the spider man, Anansi, pays the Sky God's price in order to bring people a chest of stories. He is required to bring to the Sky God Osebo-the-leopard-of-the-terrible-teeth, Mmboro-the-hornet-who-stings-like-fire, and Mmoatia-the-fairy-whom-men-never-see. The literary style used in the telling is fascinating with its metrical beat, and the brightly colored woodblock illustrations were outstanding enough to win the Caldecott Award.

Marcia Brown uses expressive linoleum cuts to illustrate a simple version of Dick Whittington and His Cat. The story is told in a straightforward manner that will enlarge vocabularies and preserve the English flavor of his old tale.

Salt, retold by Harve Zemach, is an exciting old Russian tale which some four-year-olds will be able to follow. It has the usual folktale theme of the simple, good person overcoming the wicked one. In this case a giant acts as the magical agent who makes the triumph of good possible.

Duffy and the Devil, also retold by Harve Zemach and illustrated by Margot Zemach, is a Cornish tale which tells the usual Rumpelstiltskin story in a very humorous way. It, too, is a Caldecott winner.

The Tale of a Pig, retold by Wallace Tripp, is a folktale that is not as well known as many. In it there is a rather usual folktale motif of the prince who marries an animal, this time a pig, who at the end of the ceremony turns into a lovely maiden. However, this part of the plot is followed by a humorous sequel in which the envious Captain of the Guards tries to do the same, with disastrous results.

The Two Stonecutters, retold by Eve Titus, is adapted from the old Japanese fable and told with interesting repetitive rhythms and metaphors that children will enjoy. The illustrations are Oriental in style, done in soft colors and interesting designs.

You will find many fine retellings of the old stories with interesting illustrations. You will want to try a variety of these. Some are presented in small collections such as Three Grimm's Fairy Tales illustrated by Bernadette. This collection is made up of three tiny books in a little box and includes "The Silver Pennies," "The Magic Porridge Pot," and "The Fox and the Geese." These would be appropriate first folktales. There is no element of fear in these stories. They are simply told, but beautifully illustrated.

Nursery Rhymes Are Still Important

A renowned professor of early childhood education, Dr. Minnie Berson, tells an interesting story about her own childhood when she first came to this country at the age of seven. Her family members were Russian refugees who were fortunate to escape with little more than the clothes they were wearing. They managed to get to Detroit where the little girl was sent to first grade although she could speak very little English. Somehow she became acquainted with the nearby branch of the public library and this was her haven. She loved looking at the children's books. One day she found what to her was an absolutely beautiful copy of a book of nursery rhymes. She could tell from the pictures what each rhyme was, and she says that this was the way she learned many English words and taught herself to read in her new language. She still laughs about the ending to this story.

She was allowed to take the precious book home; however, there was trouble when she arrived. Her younger sister had become ill with scarlet fever, and in those days everything that had been in the room with a scarlet fever patient had to be disinfected or burned. The public health nurse who was in attendance said that the book of nursery rhymes could never be returned to the library. It had to be burned. The little girl managed to hide the book and it became her most treasured possession. She did not contract scarlet fever, and the book continued to provide her with a great deal of learning and delight. When she tells this story, one can almost see a little refugee child hugging that precious book just as she describes the experience.

Even though Mother Goose will never play such a dramatic role in your children's language development, the verses are a very important part of a four- to five-year-old's literary experience. If youngsters have had a thorough background in this age-old poetry, they will now be able to do new and exciting things with the verses. For example, can you think of a better way of involving children with beginning reading than by letting them supply words and phrases as you read the rhymes together? If they know an entire rhyme, you can point to each word as it is being repeated. The feeling of accomplishment in being able to say the words in the book provides a prelude to reading and is to be promoted. You can help youngsters understand the consistency of print if you let them read the same verses, phrases, or words from different editions of Mother Goose. They will begin to realize that even though the books look different, the print itself stands for the same words in a given rhyme.

Mother Goose books provide a fine frame of reference for activities. You can have great fun dramatizing many of the rhymes like "Polly Put the Kettle On," "Little Miss Muffet," "Simple Simon," "Old Mother Hubbard," or any others you want to try. Children will act them out very naturally. Possibilities in music and singing abound with books like A Cat Came Fiddling and Other Rhymes of Childhood, presented by Paul Kapp; How Many Strawberries Grow in the Sea? A Songbook of Mother Goose Rhymes, selected by Edith Fowke with music by Earl Bichel; and Sally Go Round the Sun: Three Hundred Children's Songs, Rhymes and Games, selected by Edith Fowke.

For four-to-five-year-olds there are interesting books with just one nursery rhyme. For example, The House that Jack Built: A Picture Book in Two Languages, illustrated by Antonio Frasconi, provides an unusual art and language experience. Old Mother Hubbard and Her Dog, illustrated by Evaline Ness, supplies much humor with the dog as the clown.

We don't have to have tunes for singing the rhymes. They roll off the tongue with such lilting rhythms and jingly nonsense words that they sing for themselves in a melody of sound such as "Hickory, Dickory, Dock," "Hickety, Pickety, My Black Hen," or "Diddledy, diddledy dum tee." Their musical qualities help promote easy memorization, develop reading readiness skills, and cultivate a love of poetry.

Now is the time to look for variants of Mother Goose verses, those that are similar in style to the usual English versions. Books like Charlotte B. de Forest's The Prancing Pony: Nursery Rhymes from Japan and Robert Wyndham's Chinese Mother Goose Rhymes help children realize the universality of children's tastes in poetry. American variants lack sophistication in comparison to some other verse, but children love their rollicking, amusing, backwoods fun. For example, in Maud and Miska Petersham's The Rooster Crows: A Book of American Rhymes and Jingles, which received the Caldecott Medal in 1946, we find:

I eat my peas with honey,
I've done it all my life.
It makes the peas taste funny,
But it keeps them on my knife. [19]

Fortunately, in later editions of this book, insulting stereotypes that were included in the first editions have been eliminated. Ray Wood compiled another edition of Mother Goose rhymes from this country called The American Mother Goose. It has been bringing laughs to children for many years.

Nursery rhymes will continue to help your child develop vocabulary, enhance speech facility, listening skills, and auditory discrimination. They will also supply him or her with aid in learning numbers, days of the week, and names of the months. You and your youngster will want to look for a variety of these books just for the enjoyment of revisiting what now are old friends in verse.

Here is some good advice from The Only True Mother Goose Melodies, which was published in Boston in 1833:

Hear What Ma'am Goose Says!

My dear little Blossoms, there are now in this world, and always will be, a great many grannies besides myself, both in petticoats and pantaloons, some a deal younger to be sure, but all monstrous wise, and of my own family name. These old women, who never had a chick nor child of their own, but who always know how to bring up other people's children, will tell you with very long faces, that my enchanting, quieting, soothing volume, my all-sufficient anodyne for cross, peevish, won't-be-comforted little bairns, ought to be laid aside for more learned books, such as they would select and publish. Fudge! I tell you that all their batterings can't deface my beauties, nor their wise pratings equal my wiser prattlings; and all imitators of my refreshing songs might as well write a new Billy Shakespeare as another Mother Goose--we two great poets were born together, and we shall go out of the world together.
No, no, my Melodies will never die,
While nurses sing, or babies cry. [20]

Into the Land of Poetry

Now is the time for your child to experience many different types of poetry. It is an easy step from a foundation of

Mother Goose and humorous verse to simple narrative poems
and even some lyrical poetry. Such poetry requires youngsters to move beyond that which appeals only because of
sound effects and hypnotic language. Some children are
ready to enjoy slightly more sophisticated poems. You
might start with some concrete poetry which appeals to
children because of its shape on the page. It is actually
shaped like the subject it is about.

Two in a Bed

Abram Bunn Ross

When my brother Tommy
Sleeps in bed with me,
He doubles up
And makes
himself
exactly
like
a
V
And 'cause the bed is not so wide,
A part of him is on my side. 21

* * *

Sliding

Myra Cohn Livingston

We can slide

down

the

hill

or

down

the

stair

or

down

the

street

or anywhere.

Or down the roof
> where the shingles broke,

Or down the trunk
> of the back-yard oak.

Down
> the
>> slide
>>> or the ice
>>> or the slippery street,

We can slide on our sled
>> or our skates
>> or our feet.

Oh, it's lots of fun to go outside

And slide
> and slide
>> and slide
>>> and slide. [22]

If your child is not as yet interested in listening to different types of poetry, continue with the funny, jingly verse and participation poems. <u>Did You Feed My Cow?</u>, compiled by Margaret Burroughs, is a collection of chants and rhymes in which there are questions to be answered that bring the child into the reading. Some will be of interest to preschool children. Almost all children enjoy humorous and nonsense poems like those found in the following books: <u>Oh, What Nonsense,</u> edited by William Cole; <u>Monster Poems,</u> edited by Daisy Wallace; <u>How to Eat a Poem and Other Morsels,</u> collected by Rose Agree; and <u>I Went to the Animal Fair,</u> collected by William Cole. These are all collections that appeal to the funny bone, but gradually lead children into perceiving images and picturing happenings that are encased in poetic language. Some of the best selections of humorous verse for preschool children are found in John Ciardi's many books of light verse. You might like to try <u>I Met a Man;</u> <u>The Man Who Sang the Sillies;</u> and <u>You Read to Me, I'll Read to You,</u> at this time.

Depend on sensory appeal. In a good anthology of children's poetry you will find unusual descriptions of how things

feel, taste, smell, or sound. These poems move out from
the child's experiences, enlarging them and making them
seem important with exhilarating language. Don't be afraid
to try a great variety of poems, and don't feel that all poetry must be catalogued for children before it is appropriate
to use.

Poetry that can be recited from memory seems to have a
magical effect upon most small children, whether it is what
might be called suitable for their age or not. In Books Before Five, White tells of reciting poems like "Daffodils" and
"Ode on a Grecian Urn" to her four-and-one-half-year-old
daughter who kept asking for more. She says, "I had the
impression as I spoke that Carol would have listened to absolutely anything I said even if it had been poetry in a foreign language. It's as if she does a special kind of listening when you fix your eye on her in ancient-mariner style."23

In selecting poetry for young children look for poems that
are fresh and unhackneyed in concept, those that provide vivid sensory impressions, yet use imagery that children can
relate to and rhythmic patterns to which they will respond.
Choose poetry that you enjoy, otherwise you will not be able
to read it in a way that will intrigue your child. You will
enjoy going through collections of poems and you will probably be surprised at the quality of fine writing you find in
good anthologies. Several are listed at the end of the preceding chapter along with collections of poetry by individual
poets. Look for those with good indexes that help you find
poems of special interest easily. Check to see if a collection you are considering gives a variety of poetry for children to savor. If you are going to buy one or more anthologies at this time, you may want to look at Time for Poetry,
compiled by May Hill Arbuthnot, an excellent collection of
over seven hundred poems, or Sung Under the Silver Umbrella, selected by The Association for Childhood Education
International. All the Silver Pennies, compiled by Blanche
Jennings Thompson, is another favorite with poems for the
youngest child.

Certain poets stand out as having contributed a great deal
to the world of verse for very small children. Robert Lewis
Stevenson is still often called the Poet Laureate for Children.
A Child's Garden of Verses was first published in 1885, but
this collection still intrigues children with poems about their
everyday play and their imaginative worlds. These poems
sing with such melody and rhythm that they are real favorites

almost one hundred years after their first publication. Several artists have illustrated this collection. It is interesting to see how Brian Wildsmith's very modern pictures correspond beautifully to these old poems.

No writer has surpassed Walter de la Mare for beautiful, lyrical language in his poetry for children. Peacock Pie and Come Hither are two of his volumes that contain some poems for preschool listeners.

Aileen Fisher's Going Barefoot is delightful. William Jay Smith's Laughing Time is made up of light verse with humor that children enjoy. Harry Behn published many collections of excellent poetry for children. The Little Hill, Windy Morning, and Wizard in the Well all have poems that can be enjoyed by the younger set. In addition to the works of Myra Cohn Livingston already mentioned, The Moon and a Star and Other Poems, Happy Birthday!, and Wide Awake and Other Poems all contain poems appropriate for the preschool group. Dorothy Aldis' All Together: A Child's Treasury of Verse is a group of lively poems about everyday happenings. Something Special by Beatrice Schenk de Regniers appeals to very young children. Then There Were Three by Eleanor Farjeon is another collection for preschool youngsters' enjoyment. Both Catch a Little Rhyme and There Is No Rhyme for Silver by Eve Merriam have happy verses full of nonsense and rhythm that appeal to young children.

In Karla Kuskin's Roar and More there are simple little verses about different animals on the left side of the double-page spreads. The animal is pictured on the right side. The following two-page spread is taken up completely with the sound the animal makes. Young listeners will have fun supplying the reading on these pages.

Poetry choices are very personal in nature. There is a great wealth from which to choose, but try many types and a variety of selections. Remember the old saying, "The love of poetry is caught, not taught." As an adult reader you can "catch" a real love of children's poetry by exposure, then infect your child!

Poetry and music belong together in your child's world. When you check your library shelves, you may be surprised at the number of picture books designed around old folk songs and collections of children's songs, games, and lullabies. One of the most complete collections is Eye Winker, Tom

Tinker, Chin Chopper, compiled by Tom Glazer. This is a selection of fifty musical fingerplays complete with piano arrangements and guitar chords. It is now available in paperback. Such a book can provide hours of enjoyment for small children.

Try taping your singing sessions, poetry reading, and picture book reading. An inexpensive cassette player is a good investment and can provide help with books and songs when adults are busy with other activities. If a family is blessed with a good storyteller, he or she can supply tapes that will keep children interested for hours. And what fine, inexpensive, personal gifts these make for children!

Remember that your performance does not have to be of a professional level to please your child. When you record poems or stories you are reading from a book, use some little signal like the ding of a small bell to let your child know when to turn the pages. If you feel inhibited about recording songs, perhaps you have a friend who would supply the singing so that your youngster can sing along, march, dance, or dramatize the text. Someone has compared a story on a record to a kiss over the telephone. This is a fine analogy; however, a kiss over the telephone is better than no kiss at all and a record will suffice a part of the time to free adults for things that must be done. Of course there are fine records on the market that may also appeal to your child.

From Picture Books to Art Appreciation

Duff comments on the wonderful talent that small children have for just looking. She tells how her son simply took possession of pictures, studying each detail with complete absorption. Her daughter became interested in the works of the great painters through exposure to fine art in picture books. Because she was engrossed in Maud and Miska Petersham's The Christ Child, she became involved with Christmas art and collected cards, pictures and prints. With her family's help she began to compare the work of picture book artists with the art in fine paintings. She associated Beatrix Potter's pictures with those of William Blake and Robert Lawson's illustrations for The Story of Ferdinand with some of the Goya pictures. Kate Greenaway's work reminded her of Joshua Reynolds' The Age of Innocence. Dorothy Lathrop's The Little Mermaid seemed to have the same remote beauty as that in Botticelli's Venus. Duff tells how she and her husband eventually bought Thomas Craven's A Treasury of Art Masterpieces for their daughter's birthday and how the little girl and her friends enjoyed long sessions of sharing the book. This sharing took place after her friends had washed their hands, at the book owner's request![24]

At first you might feel that you do not have the artistic background to help your child make the leap from the good art found in picture books to that in the great paintings. It is quite easy if you rely on help from some of the better art books for young people. A retired primary teacher in California tells of how she became known as quite an authority on the works of great painters among the parents of the children in her school. They often insisted that their children be in her classes to have the opportunity to learn to love fine paintings. In fact, many parents developed a new interest in art because their children urged their families to visit various art museums and to collect prints. Of course the teacher felt gratified, but secretly she had to chuckle because her reputation as an authority had come basically from the use of one book with her classes. Each morning, if the timing seemed right, she and the children shared one or more pictures from Alice Chase's Famous Paintings: An Introduction to Art for Young People. This book gives good reproductions of many fine paintings that interest young children. Fortunately, opposite each of the pictures there is a short discussion of unique qualities of the painting along with interesting notes about the artist. Reinforced by this information, the teacher could always tell something that would involve the children and start a discussion. Because she was learning herself, she and the students shared exciting discoveries. They often made comparisons between the work of artists and the illustrations that the children had in their picture books.

The Chase book was available along with others of its kind where class members could look at it with care during the day and select a picture that they especially liked to display. They also brought in prints and pictures that they wanted to talk about or use to start a creative work of their own.

Using a book of this kind can be a rewarding experience in the home, where there is more time to enjoy the pictures in a relaxed, personal way. You might like to check your library for such art books. If your child becomes especially interested in one, you may want to purchase it for a very special gift that could sharpen a child's visual acuity and develop aesthetic enjoyment that would last for a lifetime.

There are series of art books that can be used to expand young children's interest in pictures. The Adventures in Art Series gives them the opportunity to enjoy reproductions of outstanding works of art. Each book centers on a given theme. The text is clearly written in a style that youngsters can understand. Something is told of the artist as well as of the media and techniques used in the paintings. The simplicity of presentation makes it possible for children to study various pictures without being overwhelmed by the busyness that prevails in many books of art. Looking at Horses is the first volume of the series, followed by Looking at Children and Looking at Beasties. All are written by June Behrens and the pictures were collected by Bernard Shapiro.

If your child becomes interested in the works of a particular artist, you may find the Art for Children Series by Adeline Peter and Ernest Raboff a good resource. In this series there are individual books containing a short biography and a presentation of some of the works of fifteen different artists.

Your library will probably be able to provide you with many books that will introduce great works of art to children. Famous Artists of the Past by Alice Elizabeth Chase and The Pantheon Story of Art for Young People by Ariane Ruskin Batterberry are two books that both you and your child may enjoy. Going for a walk with a line by Douglas and Elizabeth Mac Agy provides an unusual introduction to the world of modern art for children. It may inspire some to do creative work of their own.

The Importance of Honesty in Books

Research studies give strong indication that books that are read to small children do affect their social attitudes. Surely illustrations would have the same effect. This is one of the reasons that we want to avoid exposing children to books that will promote racism, sexism, or prejudice of any kind. There is strong evidence that negative attitudes begin before a child enters school.

Fortunately, we have become more sensitive to racial slurs during the past twenty to thirty years, but there are still books on the market and in libraries that you will

probably want to avoid. Helen Bannerman's The Story of
Little Black Sambo, first published in 1899, is a classic
example. On the surface this may seem like a harmless
little story, but notice the emphasis on color, and the stereotyped characters--fat, ugly Black Mumbo, gaudy Black
Jumbo, and Black Sambo, whose very name has become a
tool of racists to put down black people. Even worse than
the text are the original illustrations for the entire series of
books about this family. In them the characters have great
bushy heads of hair, thick lips, and protruding eyes. True,
the story is supposed to be set in India, but these are not
Indian characters, nor do they wear Indian dress. Rather,
they are wretched stereotypes of American blacks. Children's experience with the various groups in our pluralistic
society is often very limited. It is necessary to be extremely careful to avoid any demeaning impressions that
they could acquire.

Watch for undesirable images of different groups within
our society. The Mexican-American is sometimes pictured
as the lazy peon, the American Indian as ineffectual, the
groups living in the inner city as dirty, loud, and uncaring.
On the other hand, we may encounter the saccharine cuteness of quaint little Japanese children always wearing ki-
monos or Dutch youngsters invariably in their pointed caps
and wooden shoes. All these stereotypes are dishonest generalizations about groups within our society.

Girls are not receiving their fair share of attention even
in books for the preschool group. Fortunately, much of the
blatant sexism is disappearing from books for children, but
care needs to be exercised in the selection of all books.
Now, although over fifty percent of American women are
working outside the home and many of those who are not
are taking active roles in community life, we still find that
even in the best of picture books women very often have
passive, sometimes exclusively feminine roles or else they
simply are not in the books at all.

The authors of the article "Sex-Role Socialization in Picture Books for Preschool Children" published by the American Journal of Sociology say:

> A tabulation of the distribution of illustrations in the
> picture books is probably the single best indicator of
> the importance of men and women in these books. Be-
> cause women comprise 51 percent of our population, if

there were no bias in these books they should be presented in roughly half of the pictures. However, in our sample of 18 Caldecott winners and runners-up in the past five years we found 261 pictures of males compared with 23 pictures of females. This is a ratio of 11 pictures of males for every one picture of a female. If we include animals with obvious identities, the bias is even greater. The ratio of male to female animals is 95:1.[25]

Remember that by the time children are six years old, they have been quite well indoctrinated into the role that society expects them to assume. Rigidity of sex roles can cause both boys and girls to fail to fulfill their potential by restricting their understanding of what their possibilities may be. If girls have accepted the fact that they receive praise because of their personal attractiveness, not for their accomplishments, they can easily become dull and lack high aspirations. If boys are continually told that they are to be supportive, strong, outgoing people who never give in to emotions, they can be harmed by a false set of standards and perhaps never make proper emotional adjustments.

What we need is honesty in books for young, impressionable minds. Setting up false prototypes can be detrimental to both boys and girls. We should perceive people as people. A non-sexist view of men and women should show their intellectual as well as emotional characteristics.

There are books on the market that make statements such as these: boys are doctors, girls are nurses; boys are principals, girls are teachers; boys fix things, girls break things. Books of this type probably caused three-year-old Becky to categorize herself in a role after she had attended nursery school for only a few days. She was talking with her mother about what she would be when she grew up. First she said she would be a doctor, but then suddenly she clapped her hands over her mouth in an embarrassed way and said, "No, I forgot, I'm a girl. I will have to be a nurse." This idea had become established in her mind even though her mother is a doctor of veterinary medicine.

Girls Can Be Anything by Norma Klein is a good story about career possibilities for girls. In it a small girl argues with her young friend, Adam, about woman's place in society. Reinforced by information she gets from her parents, she announces to Adam that girls can, too, be doctors, pilots, and even presidents. Adam has told her, "That's not the way it goes," but she proves him wrong.

Eve Merriam's Boys and Girls, Girls and Boys is a light-hearted little story about several couples, in each case a boy and a girl, who never assume a traditional male or female role. Instead they are happy children with the same interests, activities, and ambitions.

On the other hand, authors of some books overreact. In their books every person in an important administrative position is a woman; everyone seen doing a menial job is a man. This, again, is dishonest.

Books that show children as children, not typed in any special role are to be desired. We have some books that show small boys in natural situations. One of the best of these is Ira Sleeps Over by Bernard Waber. Ira is spending his first night away from home, and is greatly troubled as to whether he should take his teddy bear. The problem is compounded by his older sister who is enjoying the situation. The solution comes when Ira finds that his friend must also have a teddy bear to sleep with and comes to realize that he need not be ashamed of his desire for his "security blanket." The illustrations in this book are an interesting break from the stereotype of the traditional family. In one the father is shown helping to cook dinner. In another he is playing his cello while the mother is reading the newspaper.

William's Doll by Charlotte Zolotow tells of a very normal, active little boy who wants a doll. Everyone tries to dissuade him until a wise grandmother sees the need and buys the doll.

I Don't Care by Marjorie W. Sharmat is a story of Jonathan, who has a beautiful blue balloon that he loves, but the string by which he is holding it slips out of his hand and the balloon sails away. All day Jonathan tries to pretend that he doesn't really care, but that evening he faces the fact that his balloon is gone. He has a really good cry. Afterward he tells his understanding parents, "I'm done." Everyone feels better and they go to dinner together.

In Miriam Schlein's book The Girl Who Would Rather Climb Trees, Melissa is a happy, active girl who enjoys doing many things, but she is perplexed when her grand-

mother and her mother's best friend bring her a large doll
and baby carriage.   The gifts don't seem the least bit interesting to Melissa, but she is able to free herself from the
role of the doll's mother that she was expected to assume
without upsetting anyone.   Then it is back to climbing trees!

Religion and Values

The sturdy structure of the family's value system is of
great importance to the healthy psychological development of
children.   Values of parents are reflected in children's attitudes, in their perspective of themselves and of their world.
Evelyn Pickarts and Jean Fargo say, "Parents who know
what they believe in and who maintain a consistency between
responses to daily interaction provide both guidelines for the
child's early growth and something solid against which the
maturing child can assess his own experiences."[26]   Parents
should not want children to accept all of their thinking.
However, children should have as their birthright a background in which life has meaning and value, and a framework of guidelines by which they can eventually assess what
is best for them and for others.   They need a system of
values from their family in order to appraise their own experiences.

In discussing characteristics of four-and-a-half- to five-
year-old children, Ames and Ilg say that they are now becoming aware of "good" things and "bad" things, and that
"prayers, especially spontaneous ones, are welcome at this
age and often allay children's bedtime fears.   The thought
of God the Father, and the thought that He is everywhere,
can be comforting to some."[27]   These children have what
to them is a real concept of God.

If you would like to give your child a book of prayers,
you will find some that are especially appropriate for small
children.   Lee Bennett Hopkins has selected an outstanding
group of "prayers, lullabies and dream-poems" for the book
And God Bless Me.   He has included some of the best writings we have to express the wonder and beauty of a child's
world.   Patricia Henderson Lincoln's illustrations for this
book are beautifully done without the sweet nostalgia that
sometimes characterizes books of this kind.

Bernice Hogan has gone beyond prayers of request or
thanksgiving in her book Now I Lay Me Down to Wonder....
Her poems are more like conversations with God initiated

by a naive child who wants to share the glories of his or her world.

Song of the Sun: From the Canticle of the Sun was written by Francesco d'Assisi. Elizabeth Orton Jones has illustrated a version of this writing and produced a beautiful book that lifts the spirit with its praise and awareness. A Prayer for Little Things by Eleanor Farjeon shows a sensitivity to the world around us and speaks of thanksgiving for animals, children, and things in the circle of a child's world.

You will find many books that are collections of Bible stories, others that give a single story. Several artists have illustrated Noah's Ark. Peter Spier's meticulously detailed illustrations won the Caldecott Award. His book is one for a child to study closely because the entire story is told through pictures with tiny details to expand the imagination. The text, a translation of "The Flood" by Jacobus Revius, is placed at the beginning of the book. After that the story is given in pictures of such detail that children often spend hours studying them. A Basket in the Reeds by Raphael Saporta elaborates in a poetic text the story of finding the baby Moses and also shows children unusual illustrations done in an Egyptian style.

Some of the poetry from the Bible that can be enjoyed by small children has been put into picture books. Tony Palazzo uses lovely scenes to illustrate The Lord Is My Shepherd, A Time for All Things, and Wings of the Morning. Bible verses for Wings of the Morning were selected by Robin Palmer. Tasha Tudor created beautiful pictures to illustrate the tiny book of The Lord Is My Shepherd: The Twenty-Third Psalm.

Of course we cannot expect a four- to-five-year-old to comprehend the language of the Bible in any depth; however, the stately cadence of its language should be experienced early and will gradually be understood. Charlotte Huck says, "Whatever our religious persuasion or non-persuasion, children should not be denied their right to knowledge of the traditional literature of the Bible. For other literature cannot be fully understood unless children are familiar with the outstanding characters, incidents, poems, proverbs, and the parables of this literature of the Western world of thought."[28]

Dorothy White gives an interesting account of her daughter Carol's love of The Christ Child by Maud and Miska Peter-

sham. Carol's responses give a very realistic picture of
what we can expect of a small child's interpretation of Bib-
lical stories. She was especially attracted to the book and
asked many questions when her mother read it to her. She
showed love for Mary, but insisted that the shepherds were
girls because they wore dresses. She seemed to realize in-
stinctively that her mother was glossing over the brutal parts
of the story about King Herod. Her final reaction to the
book was, "I'm going to keep this book forever and ever.
And now we'll have The Man in the Moon." Such comments
illustrate a not-quite-five-year-old child's quick reactions to
stories that stretch comprehension and yet have a very basic
appeal. 29

There are many lovely presentations of the Christmas
story in picture-book form. Christmas in the Stable by
Astrid Lindgren gives the story the proper dignity and even
a feeling of awe, yet relates closely with a small child's
experiences and actually does not mention the Divinity. This
book has fascinating, luminous illustrations. The setting is
contemporary, with people wearing modern clothing, yet there
is a prevailing peace and simplicity about this book that can
bring children into the real beauty of Christmas. The Friendly Beasts by Laura Nelson Baker, illustrated by Nicholas
Sidjakov, is a lovely Christmas story developed around the
old English carol of the same name. The music of the
carol is included.

When you share The Little Drummer Boy, words and music by Katherine Davis and illustrations by Ezra Jack Keats,
with children, you feel almost compelled to sing your way
through its exhilarating pictures that cannot help but add to
the joy of the holiday season. The pages fairly vibrate with
striking colors and the beat of "pa-rum-pum-pum-pum, Me
and my drum."

Twelve Days of Christmas is a funny portrayal of the old
English folk song. Jack Kent's cartoon art adds to the confusion and excitement of all the gifts. The music is included.

A wealth of Christmas stories, ones to fit almost any
mood, will be on display at libraries and add real joy to
the holiday season. However, amid all the excitement of
the time, your children should hear and have the opportunity to learn to love the beautiful nativity story. College
students often tell of their family custom of reading the

story together as part of the Christmas festivities. Such experiences seem to make up some of their fondest childhood memories.

Roots and Wings

Remember the old saying, "There are only two lasting bequests we can give our children--one is roots, the other wings." In this exciting preschool period, the developmental stage at which environmental influences have more effect on intellectual growth than they will at any other time, you as a parent have a wonderful opportunity to contribute to your child's future academic success. Since your youngster's infancy you have no doubt been helping him or her to develop reading readiness skills--roots of reading. Now you respond with enthusiasm and sometimes near-amazement as you watch rapid progress in the area of language learning. Through conversations, games, and books you are helping develop your child's verbal skills. Through fun with word games you are promoting enjoyment of language and the first understanding of phonics. You are helping your child improve visual discrimination as you study sizes and shapes in picture books and perhaps discuss letter and word forms.

Because you are taking time to discuss details and share storytelling qualities of illustrations in picture books, your little boy or girl is learning to interpret pictures, an art that is necessary to deal with the first reading books that will be encountered in school. With concept books you provide information that will help later on in reading comprehension. As you and your son or daughter read fine storybooks together, you are instilling in him or her a positive attitude toward literature, the feeling that reading is fun. Poetry is helping your child respond to the beauty of the language and move toward word analysis, an understanding of phonics, and an interest in sounds of words. In all these ways you are assisting with the development of the reading readiness skills that send necessary roots down into the fascinating world of books and knowledge.

Just when the magical moment will come when your little boy or girl will start to recognize words and eventually comprehend the meaning of a printed page is a moot question. Personal, individualized experiences in the security of the home are giving him or her the fine background from which to draw when that developmental stage is reached. Some educators say that children are ready to read when they have developed a real desire to read. Probably the greatest contribution you are making toward your child's future academic success is in inspiring him or her to truly want to read, thus providing the "wings" that will carry the youngster through the hard work that is necessary to acquire the skills of reading.

Children must see themselves as capable of meeting challenges. A child's first and very lasting self-image comes through experiences in the family. Tinker says, "What goes on between parent and child is the introduction to all human relationships."[30] Parents are working with sensitive human potential. If they think and act as if their children are bright and capable, their youngsters usually live up to their expectations. Parents provide the framework for a positive self-image that will give wings for successful school experiences.

In working with your child you may find that you may not receive immediate gratification for your efforts. Your son or daughter may be one who needs time to build up a rich background. If you are willing to enjoy the process with the youngster, encouraging successes without expecting performances that go beyond his or her present developmental level, your child will attain the self-assurance to move out into the academic world motivated to learn and confident of his or her ability to do so. These are the wings that we want a preschooler to have.

Throughout the course of your youngster's early childhood you give your little boy or girl a wonderful gift by sharing the best of books for young children and in this way introducing our great literary heritage. As you read together, you and your child are enjoying the beauty of the language. You are stimulating curiosity and often bringing relaxation that comes with humor. You are letting your child taste of the satisfaction that comes with learning and enjoy the security of knowing that he or she is capable of learning from the printed page.

Walter de la Mare once said, "Only the rarest kind of best in anything can be good enough for the young." It will be a satisfaction to you to know that you are sharing some of the "rarest kind of best" with your child during this very impressionable period.

Arbuthnot says, "The best of these books will train their

eyes to appreciate various art media, their ears to enjoy the
cadence and meaning of words, and their minds to respond
to something of the richness of life, real and imagined."[31]
The fine experiences with literature that you and your child
are enjoying together will supply wings to explore creatively
the wonderful wealth of books in the reading that he or she
will soon be encountering.

Notes

[1]A. A. Milne, "Sneezles," in Now We Are Six, illus.
by Ernest H. Shepard (New York: E. P. Dutton, 1927),
pp. 15-16.

[2]Martin Haberman, "The Meaning of Reading Readiness for Young Children," Childhood Education, 55 (April-
May 1979), p. 288D.

[3]Nancy Larrick, A Parent's Guide to Children's Reading, 4th ed. (Garden City, NY: Doubleday and Company,
1975), p. 53.

[4]"Handbook for Tutors of 'Right to Read' Program,"
quoted in Butte Vocational-Technical Center, Handbook for
Tutors of Project Prepare Guide, Butte Vocational-Technical
Center (Washington, D.C.: Office of Education) (ERIC ED
109 492), p. 26.

[5]Dolores Durkin, Children Who Read Early: Two
Longitudinal Studies (New York: Teachers College Press,
1966), pp. 133-138.

[6]Susanna Whitney Pflaum, The Development of Language and Reading in the Young Child (Columbus, OH:
Charles E. Merrill Publishing Co., 1974), p. 177.

[7]Ruth Lowes, "Do We Teach Reading in Kindergarten?" Young Children, 30 (1974-75), p. 328.

[8]James A. Smith and Dorothy M. Park, Word Music
and Word Magic (Boston: Allyn & Bacon, Inc., 1977),
p. 134.

[9]Eric Carle, I See a Song (New York: Thomas Y.
Crowell, 1973), n. p.

[10]Mary Ann Spencer Pulaski, Understanding Piaget:
An Introduction to Children's Cognitive Development (New
York: Harper & Row, 1972), pp. 49-52.

[11]Ed Emberley, The Wing on a Flea: A Book About
Shapes (Boston: Little, Brown, 1961), p. 6.

[12]John Steptoe, Stevie (New York: Harper & Row,
1969), n. p.

[13]Judith Viorst, The Tenth Good Thing About Barney, illus. by Erik Blegvad (New York: Atheneum Publishers, 1971), p. 24.

[14]Dorothy Butler, Babies Need Books (New York: Atheneum Publishers, 1980), p. 131.

[15]Kornei Chukovsky, From Two to Five, trans. and edited by Miriam Morton (Berkeley: University of California Press, 1966), p. 125.

[16]Nicholas Tucker, "Books That Frighten," in Children and Literature: Views and Reviews, ed. Virginia Haviland (New York: Lothrop, Lee & Shepard, 1973), p. 109.

[17]Ibid. p. 105.

[18]Bruno Bettelheim, The Uses of Enchantment: The Meaning and Importance of Fairy Tales (New York: Alfred A. Knopf, 1976), pp. 3-11.

[19]Maud Petersham and Miska Petersham, The Rooster Crows: A Book of American Rhymes and Jingles (New York: Macmillan Company, 1945), n.p.

[20]Munroe and Francis, The Only Three Mother Goose Melodies (New York: Reproduced by Dover Publications, Inc., 1970), n.p.

[21]Abram Bunn Ross, "Two in a Bed," in Time for Poetry, comp. May Hill Arbuthnot, illus. by Arthur Paul (Glenview, IL: Scott, Foresman and Co., 1961), p. 5.

[22]Myra Cohn Livingston, "Sliding," in Whispers and Other Poems, illus. by Jacqueline Chwast (New York: Harcourt, Brace, 1958), p. 20.

[23]Dorothy White, Books Before Five, illus. by Joan Smith (New York: Oxford University Press, 1954), pp. 142-143.

[24]Annis Duff, "Bequest of Wings": A Family's Pleasures with Books (New York: The Viking Press, 1944), pp. 95-101.

[25]Leonore J. Weitzman et al., "Sex-Role Socialization in Picture Books for Preschool Children," American Journal of Sociology, 77 (May 1972), p. 1128.

[26]Evelyn Pickarts and Jean Fargo, Parent Education: Toward Parental Competence (New York: Appleton-Century-Crofts, 1971), p. 20.

[27]Louise Bates Ames and Frances L. Ilg, Your Four Year Old: Wild and Wonderful (New York: Dell Publishing Co., 1976), pp. 10-12.

[28]Charlotte Huck, Children's Literature in the Elementary Schools, 3rd ed. (New York: Holt, Rinehart & Winston, 1976), p. 230.

[29]White, pp. 152-154.

[30]Miles A. Tinker, Preparing Your Child for Reading (New York: Holt, Rinehart & Winston, 1971), p. 4.

[31]May Hill Arbuthnot, Children's Reading in the Home (Glenview, IL: Scott, Foresman and Co., 1969), p. 73.

Books Discussed in This Chapter

Agree, Rose, comp. How to Eat a Poem and Other Morsels. Illus. by Peggy Wilson. New York: Pantheon, 1967.
Aldis, Dorothy. All Together: A Child's Treasury of Verse. Illus. by Helen D. Jameson. New York: G. P. Putnam's Sons, 1952.
Alexander, Martha. And My Mean Old Mother Will Be Sorry, Blackboard Bear. New York: Dial Press, 1972. (Paperback. 1977.)
_____. Blackboard Bear. New York: Dial Press, 1969. (Paperback. 1977.)
_____. I Sure Am Glad to See You, Blackboard Bear. New York: Dial Press, 1976. (Paperback. 1979.)
_____. We're in Big Trouble, Blackboard Bear. New York: Dial Press, 1980.
Andersen, Hans Christian. The Little Mermaid. Illus. by Dorothy Lathrop. New York: Macmillan Company, 1939.
Andersen, Karen Born. What's the Matter, Sylvie, Can't You Ride? New York: Dial Press, 1981.
Anno, Mitsumasa. Anno's Alphabet: An Adventure in Imagination. New York: Harper & Row, 1975.
_____. Anno's Animals. New York: William Collins, 1979.
_____. Topsy-Turvies: Pictures to Stretch the Imagination. Philadelphia, PA: Weatherhill, 1970.
Arbuthnot, May Hill, comp. Time for Poetry. Illus. by Arthur Paul. Glenview, IL: Scott, Foresman and Co., 1952.
Aruego, Jose. Look What I Can Do. New York: Charles Scribner's Sons, 1971.
Association for Childhood Education International, comp. Sung Under the Silver Umbrella. Illus. by Dorothy P. Lathrop. New York: Macmillan Company, 1972.
Azarian, Mary. A Farmer's Alphabet. Boston: David R. Godine Publishing, 1981.
Baker, Laura Nelson. The Friendly Beasts. Illus. by Nicholas Sidjakov. Oakland, CA: Parnassus, 1957.
Bannerman, Helen. The Story of Little Black Sambo. Philadelphia, PA: J. B. Lippincott, 1951.
Bate, Lucy. Little Rabbit's Loose Tooth. Illus. by Diane

DeGroat. New York: Crown Publishers, 1975.
(Paperback. New York: Scholastic Book Services,
1978.)

Batterberry, Ariane Ruskin. The Pantheon Story of Art for
Young People. Rev. ed. New York: Pantheon, 1975.

Bayley, Nicola. One Old Oxford Ox. New York: Atheneum
Publishers, 1977.

Baylor, Byrd. Guess Who My Favorite Person Is. Illus.
by Robert Andrew Parker. New York: Charles
Scribner's Sons, 1977.

Behn, Harry, comp. The Little Hill. New York: Harcourt, Brace, 1949.
_____, comp. Windy Morning. New York: Harcourt,
Brace, 1953.
_____, comp. Wizard in the Well. New York: Har-
court, Brace, 1956.

Behrens, June. Looking at Beasties. Vol 3 of Adventures
in Art Series. Pictures by Bernard Shapiro. Chi-
cago: Childrens Press, 1978.
_____. Looking at Children. Vol. 2 of Adventures in
Art Series. Pictures by Bernard Shapiro. Chicago:
Childrens Press, 1977.
_____. Looking at Horses. Vol. 1 of Adventures in Art
Series. Pictures by Bernard Shapiro. Chicago:
Childrens Press, 1976.

Berenstain, Stan, and Jan Berenstain. The Berenstain
Bears' Counting Book. New York: Random House,
1976.

Beskow, Elsa. Pelle's New Suit. Trans. Marion Letcher
Woodburn. New York: Harper, 1929. (Paperback.
New York: Scholastic Book Services, 1974.)

Brooke, Leslie L. Johnny Crow's Garden. New York:
Frederick Warne & Co., 1935.

Brown, Marcia. Dick Whittington and His Cat. New York:
Charles Scribner's Sons, 1950.

Brown, Margaret Wise. The Dead Bird. Illus. by Remy
Charlip. Reading, MA: Addison-Wesley, 1958.

Bruno, Janet, and Peggy Dakan. Cooking in the Classroom.
Belmont, CA: Fearon Publishers, 1974.

Burningham, John. Come Away from the Water, Shirley.
New York: Harper & Row, 1977.
_____. Time to Get Out of the Bath, Shirley. New
York: Harper & Row, 1978.

Burroughs, Margaret, comp. Did You Feed My Cow?
Rev. ed. Illus. by Joe E. de Velasco. Chicago:
Follett Publishing Co., 1969.

Burton, Virginia L. Mike Mulligan and His Steam Shovel.
Boston: Houghton Mifflin, 1939. (Paperback. 1979.)

Caines, Jeannette Franklin. Abby. Illus. by Steven Kellogg.
New York: Harper & Row, 1973.
_____. Daddy. Illus. by Ronald Himler. New York:
Harper & Row, 1977.
Campbell, Ann. Let's Find Out About Color. Illus. by
Boche Kaplan and Roz Abisch. New York: Franklin
Watts, Inc., 1975.
Cauley, Lorinda Bryan. Pease Porridge Hot: A Mother
Goose Cookbook. New York: P. G. Putnam's Sons,
1977.
Chase, Alice Elizabeth. Famous Artists of the Past. New
York: Platt & Munk, 1964.
Chase, Alice. Famous Paintings: An Introduction to Art
for Young People. Rev. ed. New York: Platt &
Munk, 1962.
Ciardi, John. I Met a Man. Illus. by Robert Osborn.
Boston: Houghton Mifflin, 1961. (Paperback. 1973.)
_____. The Man Who Sang the Sillies. Illus. by Edward
Gorey. New York: Harper & Row, 1961.
_____. You Read to Me, I'll Read to You. Illus. by
Edward Gorey. New York: Harper & Row, 1961.
Clifton, Lucille. The Boy Who Didn't Believe in Spring.
Illus. by Brinton Turkle. New York: E. P. Dutton,
1978.
Cole, William, comp. I Went to the Animal Fair. Cleve-
land: Collins-World, 1958.
_____, ed. Oh, What Nonsense. Illus. by Tomi Unger-
er. New York: The Viking Press, 1966.
Craig, Jean M. The Dragon in the Clockbox. Illus. by
Kelly Oechsli. New York: W. W. Norton & Co.,
1962.
Craven, Thomas. A Treasury of Art Masterpieces. New
York: Simon & Schuster, 1952.
Crews, Donald. Ten Black Dots. New York: Charles
Scribner's Sons, 1968.
D'Assisi, Francesco. Song of the Sun: From the Canticle
of the Sun. Illus. by Elizabeth Orton Jones. New
York: Macmillan Company, 1952.
De Brunhoff, Jean. The Story of Babar the Little Elephant.
Trans. Merle S. Haas. New York: Random House,
1937.
De Forest, Charlotte B. The Prancing Pony: Nursery
Rhymes From Japan. Illus. by Keiko Aida. Phila-
delphia, PA: Weatherhill, 1968.
De La Mare, Walter. Come Hither. 3rd ed. Illus. by
Warren Chappell. New York: Alfred A. Knopf, 1957.
_____. Peacock Pie: A Book of Rhymes. Illus. by W.
Heath Robinson. New York: Henry Holt & Co., 1925.

Delton, Judy. My Mom Hates Me in January. Illus. by John Faulkner. Chicago: Albert Whitman & Co., 1977.

De Paola, Tomie. Watch Out for the Chicken Feet in Your Soup. Englewood Cliffs, NJ: Prentice-Hall, 1974.

De Regniers, Beatrice Schenk, and Irene Haas. Something Special. Illus. by Irene Haas. New York: Atheneum Publishers, 1964.

Dobrin, Arnold. Peter Rabbit's Natural Foods Cookbook. Illus. by Beatrix Potter. New York: Frederick Warne & Co., 1977.

Dragonwagon, Crescent. When Light Turns into Night. Illus. by Robert Andrew Parker. New York: Harper & Row, 1975.

_____. Will It Be Okay? Illus. by Ben Shecter. New York: Harper & Row, 1977.

Duvoisin, Roger. The House of Four Seasons. New York: Lothrop, Lee & Shepard, 1956.

Elkin, Benjamin. Gillespie and the Guards. Illus. by James Daugherty. New York: The Viking Press, 1956.

Ellison, Virginia H. The Pooh Cook Book. New York: E. P. Dutton, 1969. (Paperback. New York: Dell Publishing Co., 1975.)

Emberley, Ed. Green Says Go. Boston: Little, Brown, 1968.

Ets, Marie Hall. Gilberto and the Wind. New York: The Viking Press, 1963.

Farjeon, Eleanor. A Prayer for Little Things. Illus. by Elizabeth Orton Jones. Boston: Houghton Mifflin, 1945.

_____. Then There Were Three. Philadelphia, PA: J. B. Lippincott, 1965.

Felt, Sue. Rosa-Too-Little. Garden City, NY: Doubleday and Company, 1950.

Fisher, Aileen. Going Barefoot. Illus. by Adrienne Adams. New York: Harper & Row, 1960.

_____. My Mother and I. Illus. by Kazue Mizumura. New York: Thomas Y. Crowell, 1967.

_____. Once We Went on a Picnic. Illus. by Tony Chen. New York: Harper & Row, 1975.

Fowke, Edith. How Many Strawberries Grow in the Sea? A Songbook of Mother Goose Rhymes. Music by Earl Bichel. Illus. by George Saycoka. Chicago: Follett Publishing Co., 1969.

_____. Sally Go Round the Sun: Three Hundred Children's Songs, Rhymes, and Games. Illus. by Carlos

Marchiori. Garden City, NY: Doubleday and Company, 1971.

Frasconi, Antonio. The House that Jack Built: A Picture Book in Two Languages. New York: Harcourt, Brace, 1958.

Glazer, Tom, comp. Eye Winker, Tom Tinker, Chin Chopper. Illus. by Ron Himler. Garden City, NY: Doubleday and Company, 1973.

Goff, Beth. Where Is Daddy? The Story of a Divorce. Illus. by Susan Perl. Boston: Beacon Press, 1969.

Goodall, John S. The Adventures of Paddy Pork. New York: Harcourt Brace Jovanovich, 1968.

_____. An Edwardian Christmas. New York: Atheneum Publishers, 1978.

_____. An Edwardian Summer. New York: Atheneum Publishers, 1976.

_____. Jacko. New York: Harcourt, Brace & World, 1972.

_____. Naughty Nancy. New York: Atheneum Publishers, 1975.

_____. Paddy's Evening Out. New York: Atheneum Publishers, 1973.

Gramatky, Hardie. Little Toot. New York: G. P. Putnam's Sons, 1939. (Paperback. 1978.)

Greenberg, Barbara. The Bravest Babysitter. Illus. by Diane Paterson. New York: Dial Press, 1977.

Grimm Brothers. Three Grimm's Fairy Tales: The Fox and the Geese, the Magic Porridge Pot, the Silver Pennies. Illus. by Bernadette Watts. Boston: Little, Brown, 1981.

Guilfoile, Elizabeth. Nobody Listens to Andrew. Illus. by Mary Stevens. Chicago: Follett Publishing Co., 1957. (Paperback. New York: Scholastic Book Services, 1973.)

Haas, Irene. The Maggie B. New York: Atheneum Publishers, 1975.

Haley, Gail E., retold by. A Story, a Story. New York: Atheneum Publishers, 1970. (Paperback. 1976.)

Hall, Donald. Ox-Cart Man. Illus. by Barbara Cooney. New York: The Viking Press, 1979.

Haskins, Ilma. Color Seems. New York: The Vanguard Press, 1974.

Hazen, Barbara Shook. Why Couldn't I Be an Only Kid Like You, Wigger. Illus. by Leigh Grant. New York: Atheneum Publishers, 1975. (Paperback. 1979.)

Hirsh, Marilyn. How the World Got Its Color. New York: Crown Publishers, 1972.

Hoban, Russell. A Baby Sister for Frances. Illus. by Lillian Hoban. New York: Harper & Row, 1964. (Paperback. 1976.)
_____. Bedtime for Frances. Illus. by Garth Williams. New York: Harper & Row, 1960. (Paperback. New York: Harper & Row, 1976.)
_____. Bread and Jam for Frances. Illus. by Lillian Hoban. New York: Harper & Row, 1964. (Paperback. New York: Scholastic Book Services, 1969.)
Hoban, Tana. Look Again! New York: Macmillan Company, 1971.
Hogan, Bernice. Now I Lay Me Down to Wonder.... Illus. by Susan Perl. Nashville: Abingdon Press, 1961.
Hopkins, Lee Bennett. And God Bless Me: Prayers, Lullabies and Dream Poems. Illus. by Patricia Henderson Lincoln. New York: Alfred A. Knopf, 1982.
Ipcar, Dahlov. Brown Cow Farm. Garden City, NY: Doubleday and Company, 1959.
Iverson, Genie. I Want to Be Big. Illus. by David McPhail. New York: E. P. Dutton, 1979.
Jackson, Louise A. Grandpa Had a Windmill, Grandma Had a Churn. Illus. by George Ancona. New York: Scholastic Book Services, 1977.
Jeffers, Susan. Three Jovial Huntsmen: A Mother Goose Rhyme. Scarsdale, NY: Bradbury Press, 1973. (Paperback. New York: Penguin, 1977.)
Joslin, Sesyle. What Do You Do, Dear? Illus. by Maurice Sendak. Reading, MA: Addison-Wesley, 1961.
_____. What Do You Say, Dear? Illus. by Maurice Sendak. Reading, MA: Addison-Wesley, 1958. (Paperback. New York: Scholastic Book Services, 1980.)
Kantrowitz, Mildred. When Violet Died. Illus. by Emily A. McCully. New York: Parents' Magazine Press, 1973.
Kapp, Paul. A Cat Came Fiddling and Other Rhymes of Childhood. Illus. by Irene Haas. New York: Harcourt, Brace, 1956.
Keats, Ezra Jack. The Little Drummer Boy. New York: Macmillan Company, 1968. (Paperback. 1972.)
Kellogg, Steven. Can I Keep Him? New York: Dial Press, 1971. (Paperback. 1976.)
_____. Much Bigger Than Martin. New York: Dial Press, 1976. (Paperback. 1978.)
_____. Pinkerton, Behave! New York: Dial Press, 1979.
Kent, Jack. Twelve Days of Christmas. New York: Parents' Magazine Press, 1973.

Kessler, Ethel, and Leonard Kessler. Two, Four, Six, Eight: A Book About Legs. New York: Dodd, Mead & Co., 1980.

Klein, Norma. Girls Can Be Anything. Illus. by Roy Doty. New York: E. P. Dutton, 1975.

Krasilovsky, Phyllis. The Man Who Didn't Wash His Dishes. Illus. by Barbara Cooney. Garden City, NY: Doubleday and Company, 1950.

Kuskin, Karla. Herbert Hated Being SMALL. Boston: Houghton Mifflin, 1979.

_____. Roar and More. New York: Harper & Row, 1956. (Paperback. 1977.)

Leaf, Munro. The Story of Ferdinand. Illus. by Robert Lawson. New York: The Viking Press, 1936. (Paperback. New York: Penguin, 1977.)

Lear, Edward. Nonsense Books. Boston: Little, Brown, 1943.

Lexau, Joan. Me Day. Illus. by Robert Weaver. New York: Dial Press, 1971.

Leydenfrost, Robert. Ten Little Elephants. Garden City, NY: Doubleday and Company, 1975.

Lindgren, Astrid. Christmas in the Stable. Illus. by H. Wiberg. New York: Coward-McCann, 1962. (Paperback. 1979.)

Little, Lessie Jones, and Eloise Greenfield. I Can Do It By Myself. Illus. by Carole Byard. New York: Harper & Row, 1978.

Livingston, Myra Cohn. Happy Birthday! Illus. by Erik Blegvad. New York: Harcourt, Brace, 1964.

_____. The Moon and a Star and Other Poems. Illus. by Judith Shahn. New York: Harcourt, Brace, 1965.

_____. Wide Awake and Other Poems. Illus. by Jacqueline Chwast. New York: Harcourt, Brace, 1959.

Lobel, Arnold. Frog and Toad Are Friends. New York: Harper & Row, 1970. (Paperback. 1979.)

_____. Frog and Toad Together. New York: Harper & Row, 1972. (Paperback. 1979.)

_____. On Market Street. Illus. by Anita Lobel. New York: Greenwillow, 1981.

Mac Agy, Douglas, and Elizabeth Mac Agy. Going for a walk with a line: A Step into the World of Modern Art. Garden City, NY: Doubleday and Company, 1959.

Maestro, Betsy, and Giulio Maestro. Harriet Reads Signs and More Signs. New York: Crown Publishers, 1980.

Mayer, Mercer. A Boy, a Dog, and a Frog. New York: Dial Press, 1967. (Paperback. 1979.)

_____. Frog Goes to Dinner. New York: Dial Press, 1974. (Paperback. 1977.)

_____. Frog On His Own. New York: Dial Press, 1973. (Paperback. 1980.)

_____. What Do You Do With a Kangaroo? New York: Four Winds Press, 1974. (Paperback. New York: Scholastic Book Services, 1975.)

McCloskey, Robert. One Morning in Maine. New York: The Viking Press, 1952. (Paperback. New York: Penguin, 1976.)

_____. Time of Wonder. New York: The Viking Press, 1957.

McGinley, Phyllis. All Around the Town. Illus. by Helen Stone. Philadelphia, PA: J. B. Lippincott, 1948.

Merriam, Eve. Boys and Girls, Girls and Boys. Illus. by Harriet Sherman. New York: Holt, Rinehart & Winston, 1972.

_____. Catch a Little Rhyme. Illus. by Imero Gobbato. New York: Atheneum Publishers, 1966.

_____. There Is No Rhyme for Silver. Illus. by Joseph Schindelman. New York: Atheneum Publishers, 1962.

Miles, Miska. Apricot ABC. Illus. by Peter Parnall. Boston: Little, Brown, 1969.

Mosel, Arlene. Tikki Tikki Tembo. Illus. by Blair Lent. New York: Holt, Rinehart & Winston, 1968. (Paperback. New York: Scholastic Book Services, 1972.)

Munari, Bruno. Bruno Munari's ABC. Cleveland, OH: Collins-World, 1979.

Ness, Evaline. Old Mother Hubbard and Her Dog. New York: Holt, Rinehart & Winston, 1972.

Oxenbury, Helen. Pig Tale. New York: William Morrow, 1973.

Palazzo, Tony. The Lord is My Shepherd. New York: Henry Z. Walck, 1965.

_____. A Time for All Things. New York: Henry Z. Walck, 1966.

Palmer, Robin, comp. Wings of the Morning, Verses from the Bible. Illus. by Tony Palazzo. New York: Henry Z. Walck, 1968.

Paul, Aileen, and Arthur Hawkins. Kids Cooking. Garden City, NY: Doubleday and Company, 1970.

Peppé, Rodney. Rodney Peppé's Puzzle Book. New York: The Viking Press, 1977.

Peter, Adeline, and Ernest Raboff. Art for Children Series. 15 vols. Garden City, NY: Doubleday and Company, 1968-74.

Petersham, Maud, and Miska Petersham. The Christ Child.

Garden City, NY: Doubleday and Company, 1931.
(Paperback. 1980.)

Piper, Watty. The Little Engine That Could. Illus. by
George Hauman and Doris Hauman. New York:
Platt & Munk, 1976. (Paperback. New York:
Scholastic Book Services, 1979.)

Poems. Illus. by Patricia Henderson Lincoln. New York:
Alfred A. Knopf, 1982.

Preston, Edna Mitchell. The Temper Tantrum Book. Illus.
by Rainey Bennett. New York: The Viking Press,
1969. (Paperback. New York: Penguin, 1976.)

Provensen, Alice, and Martin Provensen. Peaceable Kingdom: The Shaker Abecedarius. New York: The Viking Press, 1978.

_____. Play on Words. New York: Random House,
1972.

Purdy, Susan. Books for You to Make. New York: Harper
& Row, 1973.

_____. Christmas Cookbook. New York: Franklin
Watts, Inc., 1976.

_____. Halloween Cookbook. New York: Franklin
Watts, Inc., 1977.

_____. If You Have a Yellow Lion. Philadelphia, PA:
J. B. Lippincott, 1966.

Raskin, Ellen. Nothing Ever Happens on My Block. New
York: Atheneum Publishers, 1966. (Paperback.
New York: Scholastic Book Services, 1977.)

_____. Spectacles. New York: Atheneum Publishers,
1968. (Paperback. 1972.)

Rey, H. A., and Margaret Rey. Curious George Goes to the
Hospital. Boston: Houghton Mifflin, 1966.

Reyher, Becky, retold by. My Mother is the Most Beautiful
Woman in the World: A Russian Folktale. Illus. by
Ruth Gannett. New York: Lothrop, Lee & Shepard,
1945.

Rice, Eve. Sam Who Never Forgets. New York: Greenwillow, 1977. (Paperback. New York: Penguin,
1980.)

Rodgers, Frederick A., and Katherine A. Larson. Let's
Do Some Cooking. Illus. by Randy Titus. Champaign, IL: Continuing Education Publication Co.,
1977.

Ruffins, Reynold. My Brother Never Feeds the Cat. New
York: Charles Scribner's Sons, 1979.

Saporta, Raphael. A Basket in the Reeds. Illus. by H.
Hechtkopf. Minneapolis, MN: Lerner Publishing
Co., 1965.

Sauer, Julia L. Mike's House. Illus. by Don Freeman.
New York: The Viking Press, 1954.

Scheer, Julian. Rain Makes Applesauce. Illus. by Marvin
Bileck. New York: Holiday House, 1964.

Schlein, Miriam. The Girl Who Would Rather Climb Trees.
Illus. by Judith Gwyn Brown. New York: Harcourt
Brace Jovanovich, 1975.

Schwartz, Alvin. A Twister of Twists, a Tangler of Tongues.
Illus. by Glen Rounds. New York: Harper & Row,
1972. (Paperback. New York: Bantam, 1977.)

Selsam, Millicent E. Is This a Baby Dinosaur? And Other
Science Picture Puzzles. New York: Harper & Row,
1972.

Sendak, Maurice. Alligators All Around (An Alphabet). New
York: Harper & Row, 1962.
_____. One Was Johnny. New York: Harper & Row,
1962.

Seuss, Dr. The 500 Hats of Bartholomew Cubbins. New
York: The Vanguard Press, 1938.
_____. Horton Hatches the Egg. New York: Random
House, 1940.

Sharmat, Marjorie W. I Don't Care. Illus. by Lillian
Hoban. New York: Macmillan Company, 1977.

Siewert, Margaret, and Kathleen Savage. Bear Hunt. Illus.
by Leonard Shortall. Englewood Cliffs, NJ: Prentice-
Hall, 1976.

Simon, Nord. Nobody's Perfect, Not Even My Mother.
Illus. by Dora Leder. Chicago: Albert Whitman &
Co., 1981.

Sivulich, Sandra Stoner. I'm Going on a Bear Hunt. Illus.
by Glen Rounds. New York: E. P. Dutton, 1973.

Smith, William Jay. Laughing Time: Nonsense Poems.
Illus. by Fernando Krahn. New York: Delacorte
Press, 1980.

Sonneborn, Ruth A. Friday Night Is Papa Night. Illus. by
Emily A. McCully. New York: The Viking Press,
1970.

Spier, Peter. Noah's Ark. Garden City, NY: Doubleday
and Company, 1977. (Paperback. 1981.)

Steig, William. Sylvester and the Magic Pebble. New
York: Simon & Schuster, 1969.

Stevenson, Robert Louis. A Child's Garden of Verses.
Illus. by Brian Wildsmith. New York: Franklin
Watts, Inc., 1966.

Thompson, Blanche Jennings, comp. All the Silver Pennies.
Illus. by Ursula Arndts. New York: Macmillan
Company, 1967.

Titus, Eve, retold by. The Two Stonecutters. Illus. by
Yoko Mitsuhashi. Garden City, NY: Doubleday and
Company, 1967.
Tripp, Wallace, retold by. The Tale of a Pig. New York:
McGraw-Hill, 1968.
Tudor, Tasha. The Lord Is My Shepherd: The Twenty-
Third Psalm. Cleveland: Collins-World, 1980.
Udry, Janice May. The Moon Jumpers. Illus. by Maurice
Sendak. New York: Harper, 1959.
_____. What Mary Jo Shared. Illus. by Eleanor Mill.
Chicago: Albert Whitman & Co., 1966. (Paperback.
New York: Scholastic Book Services, 1970.)
Ueno, Noriko. Elephant Buttons. New York: Harper &
Row, 1973.
Ungerer, Tomi. Snail, Where Are You? New York: Har-
per & Row, 1962.
Vigna, Judith. She's Not My Real Mother. Chicago: Al-
bert Whitman & Co., 1980.
Viorst, Judith. Alexander and the Terrible, Horrible, No
Good, Very Bad Day. Illus. by Ray Cruz. New
York: Atheneum Publishers, 1976.
_____. I'll Fix Anthony. Illus. by Arnold Lobel. New
York: Harper & Row, 1969.
Waber, Bernard. Ira Sleeps Over. Boston: Houghton Miff-
lin, 1972. (Paperback. 1975.)
Walker, Barbara M. The Little House Cookbook. Illus. by
Garth Williams. New York: Harper & Row, 1979.
Wallace, Daisy, ed. Monster Poems. Illus. by Kay Chorao.
New York: Holiday House, 1976.
Weiss, Harvey. How to Make Your Own Books. New York:
Harper & Row, 1974.
Wildsmith, Brian. What the Moon Saw. New York: Oxford
University Press, 1978.
Wood, Ray. The American Mother Goose. Illus. by Ed
Hargis. Philadelphia, PA: J. B. Lippincott, 1939.
Wyndham, Robert. Chinese Mother Goose Rhymes. Illus.
by Ed Young. Cleveland: Collins-World, 1968.
Yashima, Taro. Umbrella. New York: The Viking Press,
1958. (Paperback. New York: Penguin, 1977.)
Zemach, Harve, retold by. Duffy and the Devil. Illus. by
Margot Zemach. New York: Farrar, Straus and
Giroux, 1973.
_____. Salt: A Russian Tale. Illus. by Margot Zemach.
New York: Farrar, Straus and Giroux, 1977.
Zolotow, Charlotte. A Father Like That. Illus. by Ben
Shecter. New York: Harper & Row, 1971.
_____. If You Listen. Illus. by Marc Simont. New
York: Harper & Row, 1980.

_____. *Mr. Rabbit and the Lovely Present*. Illus. by
Maurice Sendak. New York: Harper & Row, 1962.
(Paperback. 1977.)
_____. *William's Doll*. Illus. by William Pené Du Bois.
New York: Harper & Row, 1972.

Additional Wordless Books

Alexander, Martha. *Out! Out! Out!* New York: Dial
Press, 1968.
_____. *We Never Get to Do Anything*. New York: Dial
Press, 1970.
Ardizzone, Edward. *The Wrong Side of the Bed*. Garden
City, NY: Doubleday and Company, 1970.
Arnosky, Jim. *Mud Time and More Nathaniel Stories*.
Reading, MA: Addison-Wesley, 1979.
Aruego, Jose. *Look What I Can Do*. New York: Charles
Scribner's Sons, 1971.
Bang, Molly. *Grey Lady and the Strawberry Snatcher*.
New York: Scholastic Book Services, 1980.
Briggs, Raymond. *The Snowman*. New York: Random
House, 1978.
Burningham, John. *Seasons*. Indianapolis, IN: Bobbs-
Merrill Co., 1970.
Goodall, John S. *The Ballooning Adventures of Paddy Pork*.
New York: Harcourt, Brace and World, 1969.
_____. *The Midnight Adventures of Kelly, Dot and Es-
meralda*. New York: Atheneum Publishers, 1973.
_____. *Shrewbettina's Birthday*. New York: Harcourt,
Brace and World, 1971.
Hoban, Tana. *Big Ones, Little Ones*. New York: Green-
willow, 1976.
Hogrogian, Nonny. *Apples*. New York: Macmillan Com-
pany, 1972.
Keats, Ezra J. *Skates*. New York: Franklin Watts, Inc.,
1973.
Krahn, Fernando. *A Flying Saucer Full of Spaghetti*. New
York: E. P. Dutton, 1970.
_____. *How Santa Claus Had a Long and Difficult Jour-
ney Delivering His Presents*. New York: Delacorte
Press, 1970. (Paperback. 1977.)
_____. *The Self-Made Snowman*. Philadelphia, PA: J.
B. Lippincott, 1974.
Mari, Iela, and Enzo Mari. *The Apple and the Moth*. Illus.
by Iela Mari. New York: Pantheon, 1970.

_____. The Chicken and the Egg. Illus. by Iela Mari. New York: Pantheon, 1970.

Mayer, Mercer. Ah-Choo. New York: Delacorte Press, 1976.

_____. A Boy, a Dog, a Frog, and a Friend. Illus. by Mercer Mayer. New York: Dial Press, 1971.

_____. Frog Goes to Dinner. New York: Dial Press, 1974.

_____. Frog On His Own. New York: Dial Press, 1973.

_____. Oops. New York: Dial Press, 1977.

_____, and Marianna Mayer. One Frog Too Many. New York: Dial Press, 1975.

Meyer, Renate. Hide-and-Seek. Scarsdale, NY: Bradbury Press, 1972.

Seeger, Pete, and Charles Seeger. The Foolish Frog. New York: Macmillan Company, 1973.

Turkle, Brinton. Deep in the Forest. New York: E. P. Dutton, 1976.

Ungerer, Tomi. One, Two, Where's My Shoe? New York: Harper & Row, 1964.

_____. Snail, Where Are You? New York: Harper & Row, 1962.

Wezel, Peter. Good Bird. New York: Harper & Row, 1966.

Winter, Paula. The Bear and the Fly. New York: Crown Publishers, 1976.

Some Books to Encourage Beginning Reading

Benchley, Nathaniel. The Deep Dives of Stanley Whale. Illus. by Mischa Richter. New York: Harper & Row, 1973.

_____. Oscar Otter. Illus. by Arnold Lobel. New York: Harper & Row, 1966.

Bonsall, Crosby N. And I Mean It, Stanley. New York: Harper & Row, 1974.

_____. The Case of the Cat's Meow. New York: Harper, 1965.

_____. The Case of the Scaredy Cats. New York: Harper & Row, 1971.

_____. The Day I Had To Play with My Sister. New York: Harper & Row, 1972.

_____. Piggle. New York: Harper & Row, 1973.

Charlip, Remy. Fortunately. New York: Parents' Magazine Press, 1964.

Cohen, Miriam. When Will I Read? Illus. by Lillian Hoban.
New York: Greenwillow, 1977.
Delton, Judy. Two Good Friends. Illus. by Giulio Maestro.
New York: Crown Publishers, 1974.
Eastman, Philip D. Are You My Mother? New York:
Random House, 1960.
_____. Go, Dog, Go! New York: Random House, 1961.
Freshet, Bernice. Moose Baby. Illus. by Jim Arnosky.
New York: G. P. Putnam's Sons, 1979.
Gackenback, Dick. Hattie Be Quiet, Hattie Be Good. New
York: Harper & Row, 1977.
Gage, Wilson. Squash Pie. Illus. by Glen Rounds. New
York: Greenwillow, 1976. (Paperback. New York:
Dell, 1980.)
Garelick, May. Just Suppose. Illus. by Brinton Turkle.
New York: Scholastic Book Services, 1969.
Heilbroner, Joan. This Is the House Where Jack Lives.
Illus. by Aliki. New York: Harper & Row, 1962.
Himler, Ronald. Wake Up, Jeremiah. New York: Harper
& Row, 1979.
Hoban, Lillian. Arthur's Honey Bear. New York: Harper
& Row, 1974.
Hoff, Syd. Danny and the Dinosaur. New York: Harper,
1958. (Paperback. New York: Harper & Row,
1978.)
_____. The Horse in Harry's Room. New York: Har-
per & Row, 1970.
Holland, Marion. A Big Ball of String. New York: Ran-
dom House, 1958.
Hurd, Edith Thatcher. Last One Home Is a Green Pig.
Illus. by Clement Hurd. New York: Harper, 1959.
Hutchins, Pat. Titch. New York: Macmillan Company,
1971.
Johnson, Crockett. Harold and the Purple Crayon. New
York: Harper, 1958.
Keats, Ezra Jack. Jennie's Hat. New York: Harper &
Row, 1966.
Le Sieg, Theo. Ten Apples Up on Top. New York: Ran-
dom House, 1961.
Lexau, Joan M. The Homework Caper. Illus. by Syd Hoff.
New York: Harper & Row, 1966.
Lobel, Arnold. Frog and Toad All Year. New York: Har-
per & Row, 1976.
_____. Frog and Toad Together. New York: Harper &
Row, 1972.
_____. How the Rooster Saved the Day. Illus. by Anita
Lobel. New York: Greenwillow, 1977. (Paperback.
New York: Penguin, 1979.)

_____. Owl at Home. New York: Harper & Row, 1975.

_____. Small Pig. New York: Harper & Row, 1969.

Low, Joseph. Benny Rabbit and the Owl. New York: Greenwillow, 1978.

McLeod, Emilie Warren. The Bear's Bicycle. Illus. by David McPhail. Boston: Little, Brown, 1975.

Miles, Miska. Chicken Forgets. Boston: Little, Brown, 1976.

Minarik, Else Holmelund. Cat and Dog. Illus. by Fritz Siebel. New York: Harper & Row, 1960.

_____. Father Bear Comes Home. Illus. by Maurice Sendak. New York: Harper, 1959.

_____. A Kiss for Little Bear. Illus. by Maurice Sendak. New York: Harper & Row, 1968.

_____. Little Bear. Illus. by Maurice Sendak. New York: Harper & Row, 1978.

_____. Little Bear's Friend. Illus. by Maurice Sendak. New York: Harper & Row, 1960.

_____. No Fighting, No Biting! Illus. by Maurice Sendak. New York: Harper, 1958.

Moore, Lilian, and Gioia Fiammenghi. Little Raccoon and the Thing in the Pool. Illus. by Gioia Fiammenghi. New York: McGraw-Hill, 1963.

Myers, Bernice. Come Out, Shadow, Wherever You Are! New York: Scholastic Book Services, 1970.

Nodset, Joan L. Come Here, Cat. New York: Harper & Row, 1973.

Perkins, Al. The Ear Book. Illus. by William O'Brien. New York: Random House, 1968.

Rice, Eve. Papa's Lemonade and Other Stories. New York: Greenwillow, 1976.

_____. Sam Who Never Forgets. New York: Greenwillow, 1977.

Rockwell, Anne. The Toolbox. Illus. by Harlow Rockwell. New York: Macmillan Company, 1974.

Rockwell, Harlow. I Did It. New York: Macmillan Company, 1974.

Ross, Pat. Hi, Fly. Illus. by John Wallner. New York: Crown Publishers, 1974.

Seuss, Dr. The Cat in the Hat. New York: Random House, 1957.

_____. The Cat in the Hat Comes Back. New York: Random House, 1958.

_____. Hop on Pop. New York: Random House, 1963.

Shaw, Evelyn. Alligator. Illus. by Frances Zweifel. New York: Harper & Row, 1972.

Stevens, Carla. Pig and the Blue Flag. Illus. by Rainey Bennett. Boston: Houghton Mifflin, 1977.

Stolz, Mary. Emmett's Pig. Illus. by Garth Williams.
New York: Harper, 1959.
Tether, Graham. Skunk and Possum. Illus. by Lucinda
McQueen. Boston: Houghton Mifflin, 1979.
Wiseman, Bernard. Morris and Boris: Three Stories.
New York: Dodd, Mead & Co., 1974.
Zion, Gene. Harry and the Lady Next Door. Illus. by
Margaret B. Graham. New York: Harper & Row,
1960.

Other Book Suggestions for This Age Level

Aardema, Verna. Half-a-Ball-of-Kenki. Illus. by Diane
Stanley Zuromskis. New York: Frederick Warne &
Co., 1979.
_____, retold by. Why Mosquitoes Buzz in People's
Ears: A West African Tale. Illus. by Leo Dillon
and Diane Dillon. New York: Dial Press, 1975.
Adoff, Arnold. Black Is Brown Is Tan. Illus. by Emily
McCully. New York: Harper & Row, 1973.
Aliki. The Two of Them. New York: Greenwillow, 1979.
Allard, Harry. Miss Nelson Is Missing! Illus. by James
Marshall. Boston: Houghton Mifflin, 1977.
Ancona, George. I Feel: A Picture Book of Emotions.
New York: E. P. Dutton, 1977.
Andersen, Hans Christian. The Emperor's New Clothes.
Illus. and trans. by Erik Blegvad. New York: Har-
court, Brace & World, 1959.
_____. Woman with the Eggs. Adapted by Jan Wahl.
Illus. by Ray Cruz. New York: Crown Publishers,
1974.
Anderson, Lonzo, and Adrienne Adams. Two Hundred Rab-
bits. Illus. by Adrienne Adams. New York: The
Viking Press, 1968.
Anno, Mitsumasa. Anno's Counting Book. New York:
Thomas Y. Crowell, 1977.
_____. The King's Flower. Cleveland: Collins-World,
1979.
Babbitt, Natalie. The Something. New York: Farrar,
Straus and Giroux, 1970.
Bartoli, Jennifer. In a Meadow, Two Hares Hide. Illus.
by Ashida Takeo. Chicago: Albert Whitman & Co.,
1978.
Bayley, Nicola. Nicola Bayley's Book of Nursery Rhymes.
New York: Alfred A. Knopf, 1977.

Beim, Jerrold. Andy and the School Bus. Illus. by Leonard Shortall. New York: William Morrow, 1947.
_____. The Smallest Boy in Class. Illus. by Meg Wohlberg. New York: William Morrow, 1949.
Benarde, Anita. The Pumpkin Smasher. New York: Walker and Company, 1972.
Bishop, Claire Huchet. The Man Who Lost His Head. Illus. by Robert McCloskey. New York: The Viking Press, 1942.
Black, Irma Simonton. The Little Old Man Who Could Not Read. Illus. by Seymour Fleishman. Chicago: Albert Whitman & Co., 1968.
Blaine, Marge. The Terrible Thing that Happened at Our House. Illus. by John Wallner. New York: Parents' Magazine Press, 1975.
Bodecker, N. M. "It's Raining," Said John Twaining: Danish Nursery Rhymes. New York: Atheneum Publishers, 1973. (Paperback. 1977.)
_____. Let's Marry Said the Cherry, and Other Nonsense Rhymes. New York: Atheneum Publishers, 1974.
Bourne, Miriam Anne. Raccoons Are for Loving. Illus. by Marion Morton. New York: Random House, 1968.
Brandenburg, Franz. No School Today. Illus. by Aliki. New York: Macmillan Company, 1975. (Paperback. New York: Scholastic Book Services, 1978.)
Briggs, Raymond. Father Christmas. New York: Coward-McCann & Geoghegan, 1973.
Bright, Robert. Georgie. Garden City, NY: Doubleday and Company, 1959.
Brown, Marcia. The Little Carousel. New York: Charles Scribner's Sons, 1946.
_____. Peter Piper's Alphabet. New York: Charles Scribner's Sons, 1959.
Brown, Margaret Wise. Christmas in the Barn. Illus. by Barbara Cooney. New York: Thomas Y. Crowell, 1949.
_____. The Little Island. Illus. by Leonard Weisgard. Garden City, NY: Doubleday and Company, 1946.
_____. Sleepy ABC. Illus. by Esphyr Slobodkina. New York: Lothrop, Lee & Shepard, 1953.
Brown, Myra Berry. First Night Away from Home. Illus. by Dorothy Bronson Marino. New York: Franklin Watts, Inc., 1960.
Brown, Ruth. A Dark Dark Tale. New York: Dial Press, 1981.
Buck, Pearl Sydenstricker. Welcome Child. Illus. by Alan D. Haas. New York: Harper & Row, 1963.

Budbill, David. Christmas Tree Farm. Illus. by Donald
  Carrick. New York: Macmillan Company, 1974.
Bunin, Catherine, and Sherry Bunin. Is That Your Sister?
  A True Story of Adoption. New York: Pantheon,
  1976.
Burton, Virginia Lee. Katy and the Big Snow. Boston:
  Houghton Mifflin, 1943.
_____. Mike Mulligan and his Steam Shovel. Boston:
  Houghton Mifflin, 1939. (Paperback. 1979.)
Caldecott, Randolph. Sing a Song of Sixpence. New York:
  Frederick Warne & Co., 1880.
Calhoun, Mary. Wobble the Witch Cat. Illus. by Roger
  Duvoisin. New York: William Morrow, 1958.
Cameron, Polly. The Green Machine. Illus. by Consuelo
  Joerns. New York: Coward-McCann, 1969.
Carle, Eric. The Grouchy Ladybug. New York: Thomas
  Y. Crowell, 1977.
_____. The Tiny Seed. New York: Thomas Y. Crowell,
  1970.
Caudill, Rebecca, and James S. Ayars. Contrary Jenkins.
  Illus. by Glen Rounds. New York: Holt, Rinehart &
  Winston, 1969.
Charlip, Remy, and Burton Supree. Harlequin and the Gift
  of Many Colors. Illus. by Remy Charlip. New York:
  Parents' Magazine Press, 1973.
Chaucer, Geoffrey. Chanticleer and the Fox. Illus. by
  Barbara Cooney. New York: Thomas Y. Crowell,
  1958.
Clifton, Lucille. Don't You Remember? Illus. by Evaline
  Ness. New York: E. P. Dutton, 1973.
_____. Everett Anderson's Nine Month Long. Illus. by
  Ann Grifalconi. New York: Holt, Rinehart & Win-
  ston, 1978.
Coatsworth, Elizabeth. The Fox Friend. Illus. by John
  Hamberger. New York: Macmillan Company, 1966.
Cohen, Miriam. The New Teacher. Illus. by Lillian Hoban.
  New York: Macmillan Company, 1972.
_____. When Will I Read? Illus. by Lillian Hoban.
  New York: Greenwillow, 1977.
Cole, William. I Went to the Animal Fair. Illus. by
  Colette Roselli. New York: Philomel, 1958.
_____. What's Good for a Four-Year-Old? Illus. by
  Tomi Ungerer. New York: Holt, Rinehart &
  Winston, 1967.
Cretan, Gladys Yessayan. Me, Myself, and I. Illus. by
  Don Bolognese. New York: William Morrow, 1969.
Cutler, Ivor. The Animal House. Illus. by Helen Oxenbury.
  New York: William Morrow, 1977.

Dalgliesh, Alice. The Thanksgiving Story. Illus. by Helen
Moore Sewell. New York: Charles Scribner's Sons,
1954.

Daugherty, James Henry. Andy and the Lion. New York:
The Viking Press, 1938. (Paperback. New York:
Penguin, 1970.)

Dayrell, Elphenstone. Why the Sun and the Moon Live in
the Sky. Illus. by Blair Lent. Boston: Houghton
Mifflin, 1968. (Paperback. Boston: Houghton Mifflin, 1977.)

De Groat, Diane. Alligator's Toothache. New York:
Crown Publishers, 1977.

Delton, Judy. On a Picnic. Illus. by Mamoru Funai.
Garden City, NY: Doubleday and Company, 1979.

Doane, Pelagie. A Small Child's Book of Verse. New
York: Henry Z. Walck, 1948.

Duvoisin, Roger. Petunia. New York: Alfred A. Knopf,
1950.

_____. Petunia's Christmas. New York: Alfred A.
Knopf, 1952.

_____. Veronica. New York: Alfred A. Knopf, 1961.

Ehrlich, Amy. Zeek Silver Moon. Illus. by Robert Andrew
Parker. New York: Dial Press, 1972.

Elkin, Benjamin. The Loudest Noise in the World. Illus.
by James Daugherty. New York: The Viking Press,
1954.

Emberley, Ed. Ed Emberley's Amazing Look Through Book.
Boston: Little, Brown, 1979.

Ets, Marie Hall. Mr. T. W. Anthony Woo. New York:
The Viking Press, 1951.

_____ and Aurora Labastida. Nine Days to Christmas.
Illus. by Marie Hall Ets. New York: The Viking
Press, 1959.

Evans, Katherine. The Boy Who Cried Wolf. Chicago:
Albert Whitman & Co., 1960.

Farber, Norma. As I Was Crossing Boston Common.
Illus. by Arnold Lobel. New York: E. P. Dutton,
1975.

Fassler, Joan. Howie Helps Himself. Illus. by Joe Lasker.
Chicago: Albert Whitman & Co., 1975.

Feelings, Muriel. Jambo Means Hello: Swahili Alphabet
Book. Illus. by Tom Feelings. New York: Dial
Press, 1974.

_____. Moja Means One: Swahili Counting Book. Illus.
by Tom Feelings. New York: Dial Press, 1971.

Fife, Dale. Adam's ABC. Illus. by Don Robertson. New
York: Coward-McCann & Geoghegan, 1971.

Fitch, Florence Mary. A Book About God. Illus. by

Leonard Weisgard. New York: Lothrop, Lee & Shepard, 1953.

Flora, James. The Day the Cow Sneezed. New York: Harcourt, Brace, 1957.

Freeman, Don. Mop Top. New York: The Viking Press, 1955.

_____. Norman the Doorman. New York: The Viking Press, 1959.

Freschet, Bernice. Grizzly Bear. Illus. by Donald Carrick. New York: Charles Scribner's Sons, 1975.

Gackenbach, Dick. Harry and the Terrible Whatzit. New York: Seabury Press, 1977.

Gág, Wanda. Gone Is Gone. New York: Coward-McCann, 1935.

_____, trans. Tales from Grimm. New York: Coward-McCann, 1936.

Galdone, Paul. The Monkey and the Crocodile. New York: Seabury Press, 1969.

_____, retold by. The Three Sillies. New York: Clarion Books, 1981.

Gardner, Beau. The Turn About, Think About, Look About Book. New York: Lothrop, Lee & Shepard, 1980.

Garelick, May. About Owls. Illus. by Tony Chen. New York: Four Winds Press, 1975.

_____. Down to the Beach. Illus. by Barbara Cooney. New York: Four Winds Press, 1973.

_____. Look at the Moon. Illus. by Leonard Weisgard. New York: Young Scott Books, 1969.

_____. Where Does the Butterfly Go When It Rains. Illus. by Leonard Weisgard. Reading, MA: Addison-Wesley, 1961.

Garrison, Christian. Little Pieces of the West Wind. Illus. by Diane Goode. Scarsdale, NY: Bradbury Press, 1975.

Goodall, John S. The Midnight Adventures of Kelly, Dot and Esmeralda. New York: Atheneum Publishers, 1972.

Goudey, Alice E. Houses from the Sea. Illus. by Adrienne Adams. New York: Charles Scribner's Sons, 1959.

Hader, Berta, and Elmer Hader. The Big Snow. New York: Macmillan Company, 1948.

Hanlon, Emily. What If a Lion Eats Me and I Fall into a Hippopotamus' Mud Hole? Illus. by Leigh Grant. New York: Delacorte Press, 1975.

Hefter, Richard, and Martin Stephen Moskof. Everything: An Alphabet, Number, Reading, Counting, and Color Identification Book. Illus. by Richard Hefter. New York: Parents' Magazine Press, 1971.

Heine, Helme. The Pig's Wedding. New York: Atheneum
    Publishers, 1979.
Heyward, Du Bose. The Country Bunny and the Little Gold
    Shoes. Illus. by Marjorie Flack. Boston: Houghton
    Mifflin, 1939.
Hickman, Martha Whitmore. My Friend William Moved
    Away. Illus. by Bill Myers. Nashville: Abingdon
    Press, 1979.
Hirsh, Marilyn Joyce. Could Anything Be Worse? New
    York: Holiday House, 1974.
_____. Hanukkah Story. New York: Bonim, 1977.
Hoban, Russell C. A Birthday for Frances. Illus. by Lil-
    lian Hoban. New York: Harper & Row, 1968.
_____. Emmet Otter's Jug-Band Christmas. Illus. by
    Lillian Hoban. New York: Parents' Magazine Press,
    1971.
_____. Ten What? A Mystery Counting Book. Illus. by
    Sylvia Selig. New York: Charles Scribner's Sons,
    1974.
Hoff, Sydney. Oliver. New York: Harper & Row, 1960.
Hogrogian, Nonny. Carrot Cake. New York: Greenwillow,
    1977.
Horwitz, Elinor. When the Sky Is Like Lace. Illus. by
    Barbara Cooney. Philadelphia, PA: J. B. Lippin-
    cott, 1975.
Hughes, Shirley. Up and Up. Englewood Cliffs, NJ:
    Prentice-Hall, 1979.
Hutchins, Pat. Don't Forget the Bacon. New York: Green-
    willow, 1976.
_____. The Surprise Party. New York: Macmillan
    Company, 1969.
Ipcar, Dahlov. A Flood of Creatures. New York: Holiday
    House, 1973.
Iwasaki, Chihiro. Will You Be My Friend? New York:
    McGraw-Hill, 1970.
Kahl, Virginia. The Duchess Bakes a Cake. New York:
    Charles Scribner's Sons, 1955.
Keats, Ezra Jack. Goggles. New York: Macmillan Com-
    pany, 1969.
_____. Regards to the Man in the Moon. New York:
    Four Winds Press, 1981.
Kellogg, Steven. The Mystery of the Missing Red Mitten.
    New York: Dial Press, 1974.
_____. Won't Somebody Play With Me? New York:
    Dial Press, 1972. (Paperback. 1976.)
Kent, Jack. Fat Cat. New York: Parents' Magazine
    Press, 1971. (Paperback. New York: Scholastic
    Book Services, 1972.)

_____. There's No Such Thing as a Dragon. Racine, WI: Western Publishing Co., 1975.

Kessler, Ethel, and Leonard Kessler. All Aboard the Train. Garden City, NY: Doubleday and Company, 1964.

Krahn, Fernando. Who's Seen the Scissors? New York: E. P. Dutton, 1975.

Krasilovsky, Phyllis. The Cow Who Fell in the Canal. Illus. by Peter Spier. Garden City, NY: Doubleday and Company, 1972.

Krauss, Ruth. I'll Be You and You Be Me. Illus. by Maurice Sendak. New York: Harper & Row, 1954.

Kroll, Steven. Is Milton Missing? Illus. by Dick Gackenbach. New York: Holiday House, 1975.

Kumin, Maxine. What Color is Caesar? Illus. by Evaline Ness. New York: McGraw-Hill, 1978.

Kuskin, Karla. In the Middle of the Trees. New York: Harper & Row, 1958.

_____. James and the Rain. New York: Harper & Row, 1957.

_____. A Space Story. Illus. by Marc Simont. New York: Harper & Row, 1978.

Langstaff, John. Hi! Ho! The Rattlin' Bog, and Other Folk Songs for Group Singing. Illus. by Robin Jacques. New York: Harcourt, Brace & World, 1969.

_____. Over In the Meadow. Illus. by Feodor Rojankovsky. New York: Harcourt, Brace & World, 1967. (Paperback. 1973.)

Langstaff, John, and Feodor Rojankovsky. Frog Went a Courtin'. Illus. by Feodor Rojankovsky. New York: Harcourt, Brace & World, 1955. (Paperback. 1972.)

Lapp, Eleanor J. In the Morning Mist. Illus. by David Cunningham. Chicago: Albert Whitman & Co., 1978.

Lathrop, Dorothy P. Who Goes There? New York: Macmillan Company, 1963.

Leaf, Munro. The Story of Ferdinand. Illus. by Robert Lawson. New York: The Viking Press, 1938.

Le Sieg, Theo. Wacky Wednesdays. Illus. by George Booth. New York: Random House, 1974.

Le-Tan, Pierre. Happy Birthday Oliver! New York: Random House, 1979.

Lewis, Richard, ed. In a Spring Garden. Illus. by Ezra Jack Keats. New York: Dial Press, 1965.

Lexau, Joan M. Benjie. Illus. by Don Bolognese. New York: Dial Press, 1964.

Lindgren, Astrid. The Tomten. Illus. by Harold Wiberg. New York: Coward-McCann, 1961.

Lionni, Leo. The Biggest House in the World. New York:
  Pantheon, 1968.
  _____. In the Rabbitgarden. New York: Pantheon, 1975.
Livingston, Myra Cohn, ed. Listen, Children, Listen.
  Illus. by Trina S. Hyman. New York: Harcourt,
  Brace & World, 1972.
Lobel, Arnold. Gregory Griggs and Other Nursery Rhyme
  People. New York: Greenwillow, 1978.
  _____. Zoo for Mister Muster. New York: Harper &
  Row, 1962.
Loss, Joan. What Is It? A Book of Photographic Puzzles.
  Garden City, NY: Doubleday and Company, 1974.
Lund, Doris Herold. The Paint-Box Sea. Illus. by Symeon
  Shimin. New York: McGraw-Hill, 1973.
Lynch, Marietta, and Patricia Perry. Mommy and Daddy
  Are Divorced. New York: Dial Press, 1978.
Maestro, Betsy. Harriet Goes to the Circus. Illus. by
  Giulio Maestro. New York: Crown Publishers, 1977.
Mahy, Margaret. The Boy Who Was Followed Home. Illus.
  by Steven Kellogg. New York: Franklin Watts, Inc.,
  1975.
Marshall, James. What's the Matter with Carruthers? A
  Bedtime Story. Boston: Houghton Mifflin, 1972.
Martin, Patricia Miles. The Rice Bowl Pet. Illus. by
  Ezra Jack Keats. New York: Thomas Y. Crowell,
  1962.
Mayer, Mercer. Frog, Where Are You? New York: Dial
  Press, 1969.
  _____. There's a Nightmare in My Closet. New York:
  Dial Press, 1968. (Paperback. 1976.)
McCloskey, Robert. Burt Dow, Deep-Water Man. New
  York: The Viking Press, 1963.
  _____. Lentil. New York: The Viking Press, 1940.
  (Paperback. New York: Penguin, 1978.)
McGovern, Ann. Feeling Mad, Feeling Sad, Feeling Bad,
  Feeling Glad. Illus. by Hope Wurmfeld. New York:
  Walker and Company, 1977.
  _____. Zoo, Where Are You? Illus. by Ezra Jack
  Keats. New York: Harper & Row, 1964.
McLeod, Emilie W. The Bear's Bicycle. Illus. by David
  McPhail. Boston: Little, Brown, 1975.
Miller, Barry. Alphabet World. New York: Macmillan
  Company, 1971.
Miller, Edna. Mousekin's ABC. Englewood Cliffs, NJ:
  Prentice-Hall, 1972.
Milne, A. A. Pooh's Alphabet Book. Illus. Ernest H.
  Shepard. New York: E. P. Dutton, 1975.

_____. The Pooh Song Book. Music by H. Fraser-Simson. Illus. by Ernest H. Shepard. New York: E. P. Dutton, 1961.

_____. The World of Christopher Robin. New York: E. P. Dutton, 1958.

Moss, Jeffrey, et al. The Sesame Street ABC Storybook. Illus. by Peter Cross and others. New York: Random House, 1974.

Ness, Evaline. Sam, Bangs & Moonshine. New York: Holt, Rinehart & Winston, 1966.

Newberry, Clare Turlay. Marshmallow. New York: Harper, 1942.

_____. Mittens. New York: Harper & Brothers, 1936.

Niland, Deborah. ABC of Monsters. New York: McGraw-Hill, 1978.

Oakley, Graham. The Church Mouse. New York: Atheneum Publishers, 1972.

Opie, Iona Archibald, and Peter Opie, comps. The Puffin Book of Nursery Rhymes. Illus. by Pauline Baynes. New York: Penguin, 1964. (Paperback.)

Oppenheim, Joanne. On the Other Side of the River. Illus. by Aliki. New York: Franklin Watts, Inc., 1972.

Ormondroyd, Edward. Broderick. Illus. by John Larrecq. Oakland, CA: Parnassus, 1969.

Palazzo, Tony. Magic Crayon. New York: Lion Press, 1967.

Peet, Bill. The Caboose Who Got Loose. Boston: Houghton Mifflin, 1971.

_____. The Wump World. Boston: Houghton Mifflin, 1970.

Peppe, Rodney. Odd One Out. New York: The Viking Press, 1974. (Paperback. New York: Penguin, 1975.)

Perrault, Charles. Puss in Boots. Illus. by Hans Fischer. New York: Harcourt, Brace, 1959.

Peterson, Jeanne Whitehouse. I Have a Sister: My Sister Is Deaf. Illus. by Deborah Ray. New York: Harper & Row, 1977.

Piatti, Celestino. The Happy Owls. New York: Atheneum Publishers, 1964. (Paperback. 1978.)

Plante, Patricia, and David Bergman. The Turtle and the Two Ducks: Animal Fables Retold from LaFontaine. Illus. by Anne Rockwell. New York: Harper & Row, 1981.

Politi, Leo. The Butterflies Come. New York: Charles Scribner's Sons, 1957.

_____. Moy Moy. New York: Charles Scribner's Sons, 1960.

Potter, Beatrix. The Pie and the Patty-Pan. New York:
Frederick Warne & Co., 1905. (Paperback. New
York: Dover Publications, Inc., 1976.)
_____. The Tale of Benjamin Bunny. New York: Fred-
erick Warne & Co., 1904. (Paperback. 1974.)
_____. The Tale of Jemima Puddle-Duck. New York:
Frederick Warne & Co., 1908.
_____. The Tale of Squirrel Nutkin. New York: Fred-
erick Warne & Co., 1903. (Paperback. New York:
Dover Publications, Inc., 1972.)
_____. The Tale of Two Bad Mice. New York: Fred-
erick Warne & Co., 1904. (Paperback. New York:
Dover Publications, Inc., 1974.)
Power, Barbara. I Wish Laura's Mommy Was My Mommy.
Illus. by Marylin Hafner. New York: Harper &
Row, 1979.
Prelutsky, Jack. The Queen of Eene. Illus. by Victoria
Chess. New York: Greenwillow, 1978.
Preston, Edna M. One Dark Night. Illus. by Kurt Werth.
New York: The Viking Press, 1969.
Provensen, Alice, and Martin Provensen. The Year at
Maple Hill Farm. New York: Atheneum Publishers,
1978.
Ransome, Arthur, retold by. The Fool of the World and
the Flying Ship. Illus. by Uri Shulevitz. New York:
Farrar, Straus and Giroux, 1968.
Rey, Margret Elisabeth Waldstein. Curious George Flies a
Kite. Illus. by Hans A. Rey. Boston: Houghton
Mifflin, 1958.
Robbins, Ruth. The Harlequin and Mother Goose; Or, The
Magic Stick. Illus. by Nicolas Sidjakov. Oakland,
CA: Parnassus, 1965.
Robinson, Tom. Buttons. Illus. by Peggy Bacon. New
York: Penguin, 1976.
Rockwell, Anne. Games (and How to Play Them). New
York: Thomas Y. Crowell, 1973.
Rockwell, Anne F., and Harlow Rockwell. Machines. Illus.
by Harlow Rockwell. New York: Macmillan Company,
1972.
Rossetti, Christina. What Is Pink? Illus. by Jose Aruego.
New York: Macmillan Company, 1971.
Roy, Ronald. A Thousand Pails of Water. Illus. by Vo
Dinh Mai. New York: Alfred A. Knopf, 1978.
Ryan, Cheli D. Hildilid's Night. Illus. by Arnold Lobel.
New York: Macmillan Company, 1971. (Paperback.
1974.)
Scarry, Richard. Richard Scarry's What Do People Do All
Day? New York: Random House, 1968.

Schlein, Miriam. Fast is Not a Ladybug: A Book About
Fast and Slow Things. Illus. by Leonard Kessler.
Reading, MA: Addison-Wesley, 1953.
_____. Shapes. Illus. by Sam Berman. Reading, MA:
Addison-Wesley, 1952.
Segal, Lore. Tell Me a Mitzi. Illus. by Harriet Pincus.
New York: Farrar, Straus and Giroux, 1970. (Pa-
perback. New York: Scholastic Book Services,
1978.)
Sendak, Maurice. Hector Protector, and As I Went Over
the Water. New York: Harper & Row, 1965.
_____. Seven Little Monsters. New York: Harper &
Row, 1977.
Seuss, Dr. (Geisel, Theodor Seuss). How the Grinch Stole
Christmas. New York: Random House, 1957.
_____. If I Ran the Zoo. New York: Random House,
1950.
_____. The Sneetches and Other Stories. New York:
Random House, 1961.
Sewall, Marcia. Master of All Masters. Boston: Little,
Brown, 1972.
Sharmat, Marjorie. A Big Fat Enormous Lie. Illus. by
David McPhail. New York: E. P. Dutton, 1978.
_____. I Want Mama. Illus. by Emily Arnold McCully.
New York: Harper & Row, 1974.
_____. The Trolls of 12th Street. Illus. by Ben
Shecter. New York: Coward-McCann & Geoghegan,
1979.
Shimin, Symeon. A Special Birthday. New York: McGraw-
Hill, 1976.
Shulevitz, Uri. Dawn. New York: Farrar, Straus and
Giroux, 1974.
_____. The Treasure. New York: Farrar, Straus and
Giroux, 1979.
Simon, Norma. I'm Busy Too. Illus. by Dora Leder.
Chicago: Albert Whitman & Co., 1980.
Singer, Marilyn. The Dog Who Insisted He Wasn't. Illus.
by Kelly Oechsli. New York: E. P. Dutton, 1976.
_____. Will You Take Me to Town on Strawberry Day?
Illus. by Trinka Hakes Noble. New York: Harper &
Row, 1981.
Skorpen, Liesel Moak. Outside My Window. Illus. by Mer-
cer Mayer. New York: Harper & Row, 1968.
Slobodkin, Louis. Magic Michael. New York: Macmillan
Company, 1944. (Paperback. 1973.)
Sobol, Harriet L. Jeff's Hospital Book. Illus. by Patricia
Agre. New York: Henry Z. Walck, 1975.

Spier, Peter. Hurrah, We're Outward Bound! Garden City, NY: Doubleday and Company, 1968.

Steig, William. Farmer Palmer's Wagon Ride. New York: Farrar, Straus and Giroux, 1974. (Paperback. New York: Penguin, 1978.)

_____. Tiffky Doofky. New York: Farrar, Straus and Giroux, 1978.

Stein, Sara Bonnett. About Handicaps. Illus. by Dick Frank. New York: Walker and Company, 1974.

_____. The Adopted One. Illus. by Erika Stone. New York: Walker and Company, 1979.

_____. On Divorce. Illus. by Erika Stone. New York: Walker and Company, 1979.

Stevenson, James. Could Be Worse! New York: Greenwillow, 1977. (Paperback. New York: Penguin, 1979.)

Storm, Theodor. Little John. Illus. by Anita Lobel. New York: Farrar, Straus and Giroux, 1972.

Taylor, Mark. Henry Explores the Jungle. Illus. by Graham Booth. New York: Atheneum Publishers, 1968.

_____. Henry the Explorer. Illus. by Graham Booth. New York: Atheneum Publishers, 1966. (Paperback. 1976.)

Titus, Eve. Anatole and the Cat. Illus. by Paul Galdone. New York: McGraw-Hill, 1957.

Tobias, Tobi. A Day Off. Illus. by Ray Cruz. New York: G. P. Putnam's Sons, 1973.

Tolstoy, Leo. Little Stories. Illus. by Erica Klein. Nashville: Aurora Publishers, 1971.

Tompert, Ann. Little Fox Goes to the End of the World. Illus. by John Wallner. New York: Crown Publishers, 1976.

Tresselt, Alvin R. The Frog and the Well. Illus. by Roger Duvoisin. New York: Lothrop, Lee & Shepard, 1958.

_____. White Snow, Bright Snow. Illus. by Roger Antoine Duvoisin. New York: Lothrop, Lee & Shepard, 1947.

Tripp, Wallace. Grafa Grig Had a Pig, and Other Rhymes without Reason from Mother Goose. Boston: Little, Brown, 1976.

_____. A Great Big Ugly Man Came Up and Tied His Horse To Me: A Book of Nonsense Verse. Boston: Little, Brown, 1973.

Turkle, Brinton. The Adventures of Obadiah. New York: The Viking Press, 1972. (Paperback. 1974.)

_____. Rachel and Obadiah. New York: E. P. Dutton, 1978.

_____. Thy Friend Obadiah. New York: The Viking Press, 1969.

Udry, Janice May. "Oh, no, Cat!" Illus. by Mary Chalmers. New York: Coward-McCann & Geoghegan, 1976.

Ungerer, Tomi. Ask Me a Question. New York: Harper & Row, 1968.

_____. The Three Robbers. New York: Atheneum Publishers, 1962. (Paperback. 1975.)

Van Allsburg, Chris. The Garden of Abdul Grasazi. Boston: Houghton Mifflin, 1979.

Waber, Bernard. An Anteater Named Arthur. Boston: Houghton Mifflin, 1967.

_____. The House on East 88th Street. Boston: Houghton Mifflin, 1962. (Paperback. 1975.)

_____. You're a Little Kid With a Big Heart. Boston: Houghton Mifflin, 1980.

Ward, Lynd Kendall. The Biggest Bear. Boston: Houghton Mifflin, 1952.

Watson, Clyde. Father Fox's Penny Rhymes. Illus. by Wendy Watson. New York: Thomas Y. Crowell, 1971. (Paperback. New York: Scholastic Book Services, 1975.)

Watts, Bernadette. Little Red Riding Hood. Cleveland: Collins-World, 1969.

Welber, Robert. The Train. Illus. by Deborah Ray. New York: Pantheon, 1972.

Wildsmith, Brian. The Little Wood Duck. New York: Franklin Watts, Inc., 1973.

Williams, Jay. Everyone Knows What a Dragon Looks Like. Illus. by Mercer Mayer. New York: Four Winds Press, 1976.

Worth, Valerie. More Small Poems. Illus. by Natalie Babbitt. New York: Farrar, Straus and Giroux, 1976.

Yashima, Taro. Crow Boy. New York: The Viking Press, 1955.

Yolen, Jane. An Invitation to the Butterfly Ball. Illus. by Jane Breskin Zalben. New York: Parents' Magazine Press, 1976.

Young, Miriam. If I Drove a Car. Illus. by Robert Quackenbush. New York: Lothrop, Lee & Shepard, 1971.

_____. If I Rode a Dinosaur. Illus. by Robert Quackenbush. New York: Lothrop, Lee & Shepard, 1974.

Zemach, Harve. The Judge: An Untrue Tale. Illus. by Margot Zemach. New York: Farrar, Straus and Giroux, 1969.

Zolotow, Charlotte. Do You Know What I'll Do? Illus. by
      Garth Williams. New York: Harper & Row, 1958.
            . If It Weren't for You. Illus. by Ben Shecter.
      New York: Harper & Row, 1966.
            . The New Friend. Illus. by Arvis L. Stewart.
      New York: Abelard-Schuman, Ltd., 1968.
            . The Storm Book. Illus. by Margaret Bloy
      Graham. New York: Harper & Row, 1952.
            . When I Have a Little Girl. Illus. by Hilary
      Knight. New York: Harper & Row, 1965.

INDEX OF AUTHORS

INDEX OF SUBJECTS

About the Authors

Leah Wilcox and Ellen Mahoney are a mother-daughter team who share a real interest in children's literature. They each concentrated on literature for early childhood in their graduate and postgraduate studies.

For the past twelve years Wilcox has been a member of the English department at Illinois State University, where she teaches children's literature, storytelling, and literature for preschool children.

Mahoney has taught children's literature at various universities. She is presently a children's librarian for the San Francisco Public Library, where she offers regular programming in infant/toddler "lap-sits" and storytelling for older preschool children.